THE INVARIABLE EVOLUTION

POLICE USE OF FORCE IN AMERICA

DO NOT CROSS   POLICE LINE DO NOT CROS

POLICE   POLICE   POLICE

Kendall Hunt
publishing company

second edition

JEFFREY SCHWARTZ

MICHAEL VIRGA

M000308320

Cover image © Shutterstock.com

www.kendallhunt.com
Send all inquiries to:
4050 Westmark Drive
Dubuque, IA 52004-1840

Published in the United States of America

*To my daughters, Lauren and Brittany, no matter what life brings always know
I love you!*

—Jeffrey

For my daughters, Lena and Lucy, I'll love you, always.

*For my wife, Emily, with you I know what it means to truly love, showering our
girls with tenderness becomes effortless.*

—Michael

CONTENTS

PREFACE

In 1966, Jerome Skolnick shaped ***danger and authority*** as defining traits assigned to the police "working personality" and its inverse effect on police-citizen relationships. These two features of policing and their influence are at the heart of the issues surrounding police use of force. The recognition of danger by the police, fearing for the protection of the public and their own lives, drives local police policy and legal precedence in United States courts. Authority, born from legal sources as well, points to the maintenance of order and the rule of law. These elements exist and mandate the police to address complete chaos (danger) and departure from societal norms by employing data-driven initiatives and general deterrence measures to enforce laws (authority). Blend them together. Challenges against the authority bestowed upon the police to maintain order, accompanied with police perception of danger in the form of serious injury or death, create the forum for potential volatile confrontations with citizens and police. Policing is not only the duty of the officer; however, for its civic success, it must secure a covenant between the police and public to work concurrently for the same goal: providing a haven of a free society, so people can go about their lives and not concern themselves with constant ***danger*** or having to burden themselves with the responsibility of ***authority***.

Patrol officers on the "street" are the principal providers of law enforcement service; and conversely, they are the officers "rubbing shoulders," or comingling with the public at large. Police officers, through personal experience and solidarity with others in the workforce, develop an enhanced awareness or "suspicion" of the general resident, which can alienate them from everyday citizens. While the police community gels from the dangerousness of their work, they can withdraw from the common populace; creating a severance of communication with the public they are obliged to serve. Conversely, the public can undervalue the tasks they ask their law enforcement officers to complete in service and to maintain peace, so they can go about their lives with limited worry. These gaps must be bridged.

Painted nationally, in examined instances of police use of force, this text will show that general use of force in policing is directly the result of the need for the police and the public to bind an understanding to one another. Mostly, police use of force encounters are relatively minor displays of authority to enforce the law (i.e. compliance holds & other limited physical force) for the completion of a lawful objective. However, as many have viewed in news reports and social media posts, incidents of deadly force captured on video exacerbate police relationships with everyone, specifically portions of the population that have traditionally troublesome relationships with the police. Recently, the police and the public have been ensconced in several violent encounters garnering national notoriety. The following recent clashes in American municipalities underscore this theme and are briefly stated, purposely devoid of detail:

- **August 9, 2014—Ferguson, Missouri**
  Michael Brown, 18, unarmed, was shot and killed by the police, the officer was not indicted for criminal charges.
- **October 20, 2014—Chicago, Illinois**
  Laquan McDonanld, 17, in possession of a knife, was shot and killed by the police, the officer was indicted for murder charges and official misconduct.
- **November 12, 2014—Cleveland, Ohio**
  Tamir Rice, 12, carrying a fake firearm, shot and killed by police at close range, the officer was not indicted for criminal charges.
- **April 4, 2015—North Charleston, South Carolina**
  Walter L. Scott, 50, was shot in the back and killed while fleeing police, the officer was fired and indicted with murder charges.
- **April 12, 2015—Baltimore, Maryland**
  Freddie Gray, 25, his spine was injured while in police custody, died approximately one week later. Six police officers were indicted on charges ranging from murder to manslaughter. All have since been found not guilty or charges dismissed.
- **July 19, 2015—University of Cincinnati—Campus**
  Samuel Dubose, 43, shot and killed during a motor vehicle stop, the incident was captured on the officer's body-warn camera. The officer has been charged with murder.
- **July 5, 2016—Baton Rouge, Louisianna**
  Alton Sterling, 37, apprehended by two officers, was shot and killed while on the ground. The officers have to date not been charged by prosecutors.
- **July 6, 2016—Falcon Heights, Minnesota**
  Philando Castile, 32, died while being shot by police during a motor vehicle stop. The officer has not been indicted for charges resulting from the encounter.

All of these police officer involved shootings have earned national media scrutiny. Shortly after the police-involved shootings in Louisiana and Minnesota, five Dallas Police officers were murdered while providing security for a peaceful protest in downtown Dallas. Officers Lorne Ahrens, Michael Krohl, Michael Smith, Brent Thompson, and Patrick Zamarripa were killed in the planned ambush, specifically for retaliatory violence in response to the recent killings of African Americans at the hands of the police. (Fernandez, Perez, Pena, & Bromwhich, July 9, 2016) NYT.

The details of these encounters are not present because we, as citizens, are not privy to on-going criminal investigations, which often last months or even years in serious cases involving deaths and serious injuries. At this point the American legal system is activated, which at times can slow to a crawl in observance of due process and personal civil rights. It is careless to hurdle to conclusions prematurely in criminal investigations, even in situations where the defendant may be an employed officer of the law.

Additionally, with the onset of outrage from certain segments of the population and political groups, theories and concepts asserting a so-called "Ferguson effect" surfaced. The *Ferguson Effect* is an idea formed describing the cause and effect on general policing or *de-policing*, due to the intense scrutiny on police officers following the case involving the death of Michael Brown in Ferguson, Missouri and the resulting protests and riots that followed. The result, hypothesized, is that crime will soar due do less police interference in criminal activity, allowing criminals to prosper and crime to flourish. Undoubtedly, this is not what is intended for our communities and serving law enforcement officials

Clearly, there is a need for crystalizing the goals of the public and the police. In the 19th Century, Sir Robert Peel gave us, *"the police are the public and the public are the police."* Students of policing must recognize this key linchpin to understand legal police procedure and the public's willingness to support the police in those methods. Is the public challenging the police during the moment of enforcing the law, thus creating violence, or are police officers hasty to resort to force in unpredictable encounters. And how to we evaluate these confrontations as citizens? This text aims to attempt to explain the intricacies of policing a free society through the lens of "Use of Force."

Chapter Elements

The chapters of this text are divided to examine the "Use of Force" concept from a variety of angles. The chapters include **Key Terms** to hone the reader into definitions, which must be mastered for a clear understanding of the material presented.

Next, the authors provide **Learning Objectives** to guide readers to the critical points and issues they must absorb to grasp a true understanding of the concepts.

The text flows and incorporates various historical issues in policing regarding the use of force, along with the legal framework supporting law enforcement and additionally providing remedies for citizens when governmental officials suppress civil rights of citizens.

Lastly, we provided **Discussion Points** to plant seeds for thought and ultimately engage dialogue with the reader. Ultimately, honest conversations in these issues are the key to "bridging the gap."

Chapter Overview

Chapter One visits the history of policing in America. It highlights Peelian Principles and the constant review of police procedures as examined by police commissions. This chapter addresses moments of civil unrest stemming from police-citizen relationships and their imprint on police policy. Chapters Two tunnels into the legality of police action, specifically by determining lawfulness of police action from the initial encounter and everything leading up to the seizures and the use of force, and even to deadly force, the most severe seizure. Legal precedence is explained in Chapter Three, emphasizing the role of the United States Supreme Court while relating landmark cases in scenarios for student-instructor discussion.

Chapter Four focuses on the use of force in correction facilities by exploring pivotal case law and the principles of the 8th Amendment of the United States Constitution. Additionally, it brings civil actions and remedies to the discussion, which sets up Chapter 5. Chapter 5 reveals civil rights violations under federal and state laws. It applies the *Graham v. Connor* decision as it connects to instances where the use of force by law enforcement is examined in allegations of civil rights violations.

Chapter 6 addresses open public records and access to certain publicly recorded data. Additionally, the *Use of Force Report* is deconstructed, stripped down by variable and explained in detail. Data is also presented from public records from a U.S. Mid-Atlantic county over a three-year period concerning municipal use of force reports. Use of force policies are also introduced in this chapter.

Chapter 7 explores the 1994 Violent Crime Control & Law Enforcement Act and the Justice Department's Civil Rights Unit. Consent decrees and police reform are discussed, specifically in areas of improved use of force policies, supervision, and the introduction of body-warn cameras. Chapter 8 reveals a summary of use of force findings, additional data, and some concluding thoughts.

Throughout the chapters, this book delivers the theme of the "use of force" in policing across a variety of issues (history, legality, procedure, public opinion, etc.) Police-citizen encounters that turn violent are challenging. Challenging for police decision-making, challenging for legal analysis, and challenging for the general public to fully understand. This book aims to bridge the gaps of understanding in these events and provide a sound foundation for evaluating whether the use of force is legitimate or not.

—Jeff Schwartz and Michael Virga

ABOUT THE AUTHORS

Michael Virga is an active police officer with the Township of Hamilton Police Department, in Mays Landing, NJ. He has worked as a patrolman and a police detective, and now works as a front-line supervisor in the role of a patrol sergeant. He is also a professor at Rowan University in the Law and Justice Studies Department in Glassboro, NJ. He received his PhD in Criminal Justice from Nova Southeastern University, in Fort Lauderdale, FL. His dissertation focused on the perceptions of stress by law enforcement officers. He is interested in research affecting policing and other current criminal justice issues. He is extensively trained in criminal investigations, such as interview and interrogation, child forensic interviews, and fingerprint classification and comparison. He served as a detective for a significant portion of his police career, leading and participating in many criminal investigations throughout southern New Jersey. In addition to lecturing at Rowan University, he is a member of the instructional staff for the New Jersey State Association of Chiefs of Police Command and Leadership Academy, where students in police command and supervisory positions learn to hone their skills to affectively lead and manage police personnel using select leadership theories and best practices.

Jeffrey L. Schwartz is an Assistant Professor of Rowan University Law and Justice Studies Department. Professor Schwartz, besides possessing advanced educational degrees, has numerous certifications and ongoing practical experience in the law enforcement field. He is a retired police officer, a former manager of a guard force for the Department of Defense, an approved trainer with the Federal Protective Service, the General Services Administration, the Department of Defense, the National Rifle Association (both as a civilian training counselor and as a law enforcement division instructor), and the Federal Law Enforcement Training Center and has been certified by the New Jersey Police Training Commission as an instructor since 1989. A certified lethal weapons instructor (including baton, handcuffing, defensive tactics, and firearms) for Pennsylvania State Police and an instructor for the Delaware State Police (baton, handcuffing, pepper spray, firearms). Professor Schwartz is a recognized firearms instructor for the Retired Police Officer program for the New Jersey State Police (NJSP).

Professor Schwartz is a subject matter expert in the area of terrorism, use of force, supervision, and tactical training. Professor Schwartz is an instructor trainer in pepper spray, handcuffing, baton, defensive tactics, and firearms. He is a certified SORA instructor, Delaware security instructor, and a Pennsylvania 235 instructor. He has instructed at various police academies, security training academies, consulted with public and private schools, as well as, consulted with numerous private businesses. Professor Schwartz founded and continues to be the academic advisor to the Criminal Justice Preparation Club at Rowan University. Professor Schwartz assists numerous students interested in the field of law enforcement. He has published articles, contributed to text books, authored a text book on internships and victimology.

Student Name _____ Date _____

Course Section _____ Chapter _____

Discuss the overall expectation of the public regarding police in use of force situations, the implications of due process, equal protection of the law, and generally the guidelines as you understand that govern the use of force by police.

_____

_____

_____

_____

_____

_____

_____

_____

_____

_____

_____

_____

_____

_____

_____

Student Name _____ Date _____

Course Section _____

PRE-TEST

1. When can police use force? Are there different rules between using lethal and non-lethal force?

   _____

   _____

2. Most police shootings are the result of bias; do you agree or disagree? Why?

   _____

   _____

3. As a citizen of the United States, you have the right to resist arrest; do you agree or disagree? Why?

   _____

   _____

4. What level of proof (if any) must the police have to make an arrest? How about to lawfully stop a motorist or a pedestrian?

   _____

   _____

5. Police across the United States receive the same amount and type of training regarding the use of force; do you agree or disagree? Why?

   _____

   _____

6. More African American males are shot and killed by the police in the United States than White males; do you agree or disagree? Why?

_____

_____

7. There is little oversight on police use of force; do you agree or disagree? Why?

_____

_____

8. It is difficult to win a civil rights lawsuit against the government; do you agree or disagree? Why?

_____

_____

9. The police can indiscriminately shoot down anyone they want and there are no consequences if lethal force is improperly used; do you agree or disagree? Why?

_____

_____

10. The use of force in Corrections differs from the rules on use of force in policing; do you agree or disagree? Why?

_____

_____

This form must be completed and turned in for credit. No copies or other format will be accepted.

Student Name _____ Date _____

Course Section _____

Reaction essay/paper to be submitted on this form only:

Police abuse their power. Police officers can use force at any time and never must worry about justifying their actions. Police are racist and base their actions on bias rather than facts/circumstances. There is a fundamental issue in policing on the street and innocent people are being indiscriminately killed.

With the above in mind, respond and provide your own reasoning to your answers:

_____

_____

_____

_____

_____

_____

_____

_____

_____

_____

_____

_____

_____

CHAPTER 1

POLICING HISTORY AND USE OF FORCE

The primary object of an efficient police is the prevention of crime: the next that of detection and punishment of offenders if crime is committed. To these ends all the efforts of police must be directed. The protection of life and property, the preservation of public tranquility, and the absence of crime, will alone prove whether those efforts have been successful and whether the objects for which the police were appointed have been attained.

—Sir Richard Mayne, 1829

Key Terms

4th Amendment, Seizure, Due Process, Peelian Principles, Police Legitimacy, Group Norms, Watches, Progressivism, Rioting, and Police Commissions

Learning Objectives

After exploring Chapter 1, the student will be able to:

1. Explain the importance of the 4th and 14th Amendment of the U.S. Constitution as they apply to policing in America.
2. Describe the contemporary relevance of Peel's Principles of Policing.
3. Explain "due process" in the context of the use of force by police officers.
4. Describe "police legitimacy" and its significance to the police-citizen encounter.
5. Explain "Progressivism" and its importance to early American police reform.
6. Describe the separate police commissions in American history and their fundamental role in police procedures.
7. List three moments of civil unrest in American police history that were sparked by a police-citizen encounter.

INTRODUCTION

When the police resort to using force, it's nasty. When is violence ever pretty? Attempting to control someone who struggles, resists, and even challenges an officer is not simple and it doesn't appear decent to anyone upon first glance. Police officers are empowered to apprehend or capture offenders of the law with the purpose of providing a free environment; so everyone can enjoy their own liberties. Additionally, the police must uphold the precious, vital freedoms and civil liberties guaranteed to all citizens. That is, police must arrest, seize, and detain free citizens with only enough force to accomplish legitimate law enforcement goals. The question remains in every circumstance, nationwide in commonplace and highly broadcasted instances: what led up to the decision to use force and why was that level of force used? Also, is challenging the officer or police authority at this moment the right forum to contest the application of the law?

Police officers make use of force decisions daily, often in "split-second" judgments. Whether it's putting hands on someone, handcuffing, or using a firearm in deadly force scenarios; a police officer's mission is to balance the rights of every citizen (arrestee, suspect, victim, witness, other officers, etc.) and then act. The decision to use force is typically not prepared and usually erupts in brief, succinct moments. Police officers are instructed and function under the notion of "the objective reasonableness" standard set by the U.S. Supreme Court in 1989 under Graham. But let us not get ahead of ourselves, we will dig deep into the case law that steers policy and acceptable police action.

Billion Photos/Shutterstock.com

Many may think of the use of force by police as defined by the high-profile police shootings observed on cable news networks, which feed on the sensationalism of the event, reporting speculation prior to the revelation of fact, or respecting the due process of the accused in typical "yellow journalism" fashion. These instances come under high scrutiny, as they should; however, overall they are very rare (Milton, Halleck, Lardner, & Albrecht, 1977). Most use of force incidents usually do not rise to a level much above exerting some sort of physical control (complaince holds) or even constructive authority. With that being said, police use force daily all over the nation, mostly it is minor actions which do not welcome much scrutiny. However, when the police do use force on the street, they are acting under the color of law on behalf of the United States government. So, the real focus of police-involved use of force on free citizens is interwoven with the 4th Amendment of the U.S. Constitution and the legality of a "seizure."

The 4th Amendment Reads

[t]he right of the people to be secure in their persons, houses, papers, and effects, against unreasonable searches and seizures, shall not be violated, and no Warrants shall issue, but upon probable cause, supported by Oath or affirmation, and particularly describing the place to be searched, and the persons or things to be seized.

To have governmental force used against a citizen constitutes as "seizure." If you are detained by police—you are seized, if you are stopped in your motor vehicle—you are seized, if you are arrested by police—you are seized, if you are killed by police—you are seized (the greatest, extreme seizure of them all). The use of force by police is currently regulated and measured by the 4th Amendment of the United States Constitution. People perhaps connect the 4th Amendment with issues concerning search, written and verbal consent, and expectations of privacy. However, the use of force presents an area of governmental authority, which at times, has been controversial in U.S. history. Periodic case law outlines current procedure on many grounds concerning police activity, but in terms of the use of force, *Graham v. Connor* (1989) freshly addresses police behavior and the "reasonableness" or "unreasonableness" noted in the 4th Amendment in post-analysis of use of force incidents. The "calculus of reasonableness," in a "rapidly evolving environment" cornerstones oversight in police use of force determinations (*Graham v. Connor*, 1989).

Prior to examining use of force under the lens of the 4th Amendment, the Supreme Court of the United States observed these types of incident with the 14th Amendment in mind (*Rochin v. California*, 1952). The 14th

Casimiro PT/Shutterstock.com

Amendment provides equal protection under the law, emphasizing "due process." Due process ensures fair and equal treatment for all citizens as they move through the justice system. Essentially, these accusations investigated by the courts measured if detainees were robbed of their liberties and exposed to punishment without due process and equal protection under the 14th Amendment, establishing the "shocks the conscience" tests for use of force (Karsch, 1989).

This will be featured in depth later in this text as the primary concept for understanding the "why" and "how" police officers use force. What makes the use of force lawful? What conditions must be met in order for police to use force? In fact, to what extent can force be used and when? These concepts will be addressed in the next few chapters.

Nonetheless, to grasp the concept of the use of force in policing, we must revert to the origins of policing in America. Why do the police exist? Why do we need or want them and what is their purpose? These inquiries will be explored in the first chapter, as the United States of America steals an idea from their former rulers across the Atlantic in the United Kingdom.

zefart/Shutterstock.com

THE HISTORY OF POLICING AND THE USE OF FORCE IN AMERICA

Exploring American policing is a study of evolution. Our past casts the conversion from antiquated "watch systems" into the professional crime suppression organizations commonly observed today in national, state, and local police agencies. Additionally, the progression illustrates the fundamental roots of policing, specifically, its effect on the public trust of the police, which fluctuates by time, circumstance, and space. The wavering of public opinion of the police forms uncertainty and discord among groups; however, legal framework, case law, and precedence guide police procedure, administratively and practically in the field.

The foundation of American policing shadows the creation of a specialized police force previously surfacing in the urban city of London, England. Prior to professional police, an essential "watch" system was established to deter people from impinging on others personal freedoms and property. "Watches" were the coordination of volunteers for local security, functioning as the only crime containment tool available to communities. The precipitous urbanization of western society, specifically in the sprawl of London's metropolis, the demand for a constant, licensed, certified "watch" was required to offset the personal indulgences of a burgeoning population. The London Metropolitan Police Act eventually supplanted the "watch" method. The "watch system" proved inadequate to the transforming environment as an outdated method for maintaining order in a large, crowded population.

In 1829, Sir Robert Peel championed the idea of professional policing. Thus, the first model of deliberate, specialized policing with The London Metropolitan Police Service was envisioned and put into practice. This service was significantly organized and credited to Sir Robert Peel and his dual commissioners, Charles Rowan and Richard Mayne. The syndicate of the police service transformed local security, placing "citizens in uniform" originating with nine general police instructions (Peelian principles), serving as precepts of policing from the past, present, and future (Lentz & Chaires, 2007). These Peelian principles were, in fact, the first policies and procedures for modern police and hold true in present day. One must only take the time to read the Peelian Principles and they will understand that they are timeless.

Sir Robert Peel's Principles of Law Enforcement 1829

1. The basic mission for which police exist is to prevent crime and disorder as an alternative to the repression of crime and disorder by military force and severity of legal punishment.
2. The ability of the police to perform their duties is dependent upon public approval of police existence, actions, behavior, and the ability of the police to secure and maintain public respect.
3. The police must secure the willing cooperation of the public in voluntary observance of the law to be able to secure and maintain public respect.
4. The degree of cooperation of the public that can be secured diminishes, proportionately, to the necessity for the use of physical force and compulsion in achieving police objectives.
5. The police seek and preserve public favor, not by catering to public opinion, but by constantly demonstrating absolutely impartial service to the law, in complete independence of policy, and without regard to the justice or injustice of the

substance of individual laws; by ready offering of individual service and friendship to all members of society without regard to their race or social standing, by ready exercise of courtesy and friendly good humor; and by ready offering of individual sacrifice in protecting and preserving life.

6. The police should use physical force to the extent necessary to secure observance of the law or to restore order only when the exercise of persuasion, advice and warning is found to be insufficient to achieve police objectives; and police should use only the minimum degree of physical force which is necessary on any particular occasion for achieving a police objective.

7. The police at all times should maintain a relationship with the public that gives reality to the historic tradition that the police are the public and the public are the police; the police are the only members of the public who are paid to give full-time attention to duties which are incumbent on every citizen in the intent of the community welfare.

8. The police should always direct their actions toward their functions and never appear to usurp the powers of the judiciary by avenging individuals or the state, or authoritatively judging guilt or punishing the guilty.

9. The test of police efficiency is the absence of crime and disorder, not the visible evidence of police action in dealing with them.

(https://www.durham.police.uk/About-Us/Documents/Peels_Principles_Of_Law_Enforcement.pdf)

This new form of policing from the London Metropolitan Police Act is based upon the public trust. The method operates on the "common consent" of the people at large. This idea was revolutionary, because it does not impose power by fear; rather it gains its authority and command from the favor and approval of the community. The

original idea of this police service operates on legitimacy, or the right and acceptance of authority, as is does in its present form in the United States of America, the people must accept the police as their guardians. Without legitimacy, the police are an occupying force employed against the will of the people being governed. This concept is crucial for us to understand the application of force upon citizens in free societies. The notion of legitimacy is prevalent throughout the

Ron Ellis/Shutterstock.com

history of policing in America, and as you will see, perceptions of police legitimacy ebb and flow with public perception and high-profile events within the history of policing in the United States.

With the generation of London's new police service, customs and traditions grew. For instance, badge numbers were prominently displayed for identification purposes and the selection processes of officers were established. The modern uniforms and group norms were being established early, refined and reformed as police departments operated in their specific environments. Group norms are sets of informal rules that direct individual conduct in group settings.

These policing philosophies are sweeping into the United States in the late 19th century, when professional policing is about to shape itself in urban areas, desperately in need for an answer to secure personal liberties and property as crime rates were surpassing population growth. Watches were established in major U.S. cities in the 17th century. They were not very efficient, often not taken seriously or used as a form of punishment for male residents. The first police departments in the United States began to emerge in Philadelphia, Boston, and New York City in the mid-19th century.

As reported, the urban locales of Boston, New York, and Philadelphia had already enacted the familiar "watches" in the mid- to late-17th centuries, as was operating across the Atlantic Ocean in England. The "watches" presented an effort to suppress crime and provide early law enforcement service; however, the effort proved ineffective as time moved through the new era of the industrial revolution (Gaines, Kappler, & Vaughn, 1999). The Industrial Revolution created many jobs in urban centers, swelling their populations, and creating a need for social order. The traditional "watch" system began to collapse. Its implementation and effectiveness rapidly declined and faded away in American cities. As a result, with eyes across the Atlantic, U.S. cities began do enact "around the clock" professional forces, known as police departments.

stockelements/Shutterstock.com

PROGRESSIVISM

The transformation to professional police forces is widely attributed to the Progressivism movement to the late 19th century to the beginning of the 20th century. The adjustment in thinking bred out of the numerous social and economical essentials required for the public good surfacing from swift industrialization. These ideas were advanced in political arenas, most notably advocated by the 26th President of the United States, Theodore Roosevelt, in 1901.

As the Progressive movement took shape and police departments began to form, regulation of the police became an important subject to politicians and citizens. Throughout the inception of policing in America, guideposts have been planted directing new forms of procedure. They uncovered police misconduct throughout the years, correcting the practice, and eventually setting new policy to ensure past harms are remedied. Committees and exploratory commissions memorialize these timestamps, which rectify prior practice and outline new policy and procedure for policing, locally and at large. There have been many of these sort of commissions or inquiries of the years that explored police conduct. In this text we explore the Lexow, Wickersham, and Kerner commissions respectively.

Principally, in the 19th century in America, the use of force was a precarious topic because many laws were circulated outlawing general conduct that was accepted as routine in the past. In the era, popular opinion considered police physical interference into any personal business (public drunkenness, disorderly conduct) as a norm to restore order, regardless of the methods to accomplish the objective. Essentially, in early American policing, excessive force was accepted as a measure to calm burgeoning cities with their sprawling populaces. As a result of police conduct or, in fact, misconduct, going unrestrained into certain areas of the country for many years, the public began to call for a "policing" of the police. The move to the professional police department created agencies that were detached from the public and insulated from the people they were sworn to protect. This was a product of new technology (the radio patrol car) and public perceptions of the police as displayed in the media. As time moves on and in different spaces in the U.S., tensions and fissures begin to emerge between the police and the public.

THE LEXOW COMMISSION

During the time of technological and social advancement amid the Industrial Revolution and eclipse to the 20th century, police departments were often used as an instrument to intimidate and regulate opposing politics, along with supporting associates for positive partisan gain. Customarily, influential political magnates accomplished this by using the police to look the other way when enforcing laws on friends, or exercising police authority to suppress political opposition (Gaines & Kappeler, 1999).

One of the earliest commissions of note in the United States convened in the city of New York in 1894, headed by New York State Senator and Chairman of the committee, Clarence Lexow. The New York State Committee on the Police Department of the City of New York, 1894, uncovered police involvement in counterfeiting, bribery, graft, tampering with public elections, and extortion. A separate committee formed in 1899. It spawned from the original inquiry into police corruption established by sitting Governor of New York, Theodore Roosevelt. Governor Roosevelt would eventually sign legislation streamlining police authority with a police commissioner rather than a board or chief, which presently stands as the top of the chain of command in policing in New York City. Some of these assertions of wrong doing against the New York City Police Department (NYPD) include: improper use of physical force to accomplish the goals of imposing fear to extort, bribe, and to steal (actual robbery of citizens by police). This commission is an early American example of oversight into government providing oversight to the operation of a police agency.

Commissions are ordered for appointees to convene and to discuss reform with the purpose to develop a path for the future. As early policing in America was wrought with corruption and inefficiency, in 1929, President Herbert Hoover assigned members to assemble for the National Commission on Law Observance and Law Enforcement. This pioneering police commission became known as the Wickersham Commission (Gaines & Kappeler, 1999).

hxdbzxy/Shutterstock.com

THE WICKERSHAM COMMISSION

The Wickersham Commission was named after the chairman of the commission, former Attorney General George Wickersham. The commission was a huge undertaking, as it sought to include all facets of crime and law enforcement policy in the United States.

The Wickersham Commission produced 14 volumes, one of which was labeled *Lawlessness in Law Enforcement.* This section explained the common use of police misconduct in regard to civil rights, notably the misuse of force to coerce witnesses and to mistreat criminal suspects for the purpose of completing law enforcement objectives. The Commission's work had a profound effect on the future of American policing; it was the stimulus for police reform in terms of policy and the administration/execution of the law (http://www.lexisnexis.com/documents/academic/upa_ cis/1965_WickershamCommPt1.pdf).

As shown by the Wickersham Commission, police commissions serve as yardsticks. Through the passage of time in the United States, police commissions were comprised of politically appointed bodies to investigate complications with police behavior and procedure. Now, from history to more modern day, these federations exist and produce proposals for police reform.

Most notably and distinguishable, in terms of the modern police use of force, the Christopher Commission in 1991 served to investigate the alleged excessive use of force by the Los Angeles Police Department (LAPD). This particular commission was chosen in the aftermath of the arrest of Rodney King, where his apprehension became broadcasted across the world with a citizen's personal video camera. At this moment, the recording of police-citizen encounters mainstreams into popular culture in America and begins the trend toward recordation of these events, by both citizens and government. We examine the Rodney King case, among others, later in this chapter.

RIOTS AND CIVIL UNREST

The police commissions often operate as guideposts propagated by civil unrest and rioting. Many riots have occurred in U.S. history. This book features rioting resulting from police-citizen contacts as realized in the Harlem, New York Riots of 1935, the Watts, California Riots in 1965, the Newark, New Jersey Riots in 1967, and the zenith of the summer of 1967 in Detroit, Michigan. It is important to note that these events were prompted by the culmination of police behavior and the response from sections of the public. Many times these disturbances,

M-SUR/Shutterstock.com

right or wrong, are inspired by an emotional response to a police use of force scenario. Recently, there have been uprisings in Ferguson, Missouri and Baltimore, Maryland. Both were the result of perceptions and analysis of incidents involving police use of force. Here's a snapshot of what occurred to spark the some of the most significant civil disturbances in U.S. history.

125th Street, Harlem, New York: March 19, 1935

The first Harlem Riot occurred in March 1935, and is commonly perceived as one of the earliest significant riots in 20th century New York City resulting from police conduct. The public's trust is the nucleus of police legitimacy; this particular unrest erupted from sustained, perceived behavior of the police and its interaction with certain groups. The low socioeconomic status of the community created an environment of unease and conflict. This, paired with the regular opinion of police brutality in these communities initiated the events following an otherwise mundane shoplifting incident.

On March 19, 16-year old Lino Rivera stole a penknife at the Kress Five & Ten Store located on 125th Street in Harlem. The penknife was priced at 10 cents. During the shoplifting, Rivera was spotted and caught in the act by the storeowner and assistant manager. In Rivera's capture, a minor scuffle developed from Rivera's attempt to flee the store.

In the aftermath when the dust settled, store management called the NYPD, who dutifully responded to the scene. While the officer gathered statements and inspected, a crowd began to collect outside the store showing interest in the police activity.

Meanwhile, the storeowner came to the decision to not formally charge Rivera with the theft offense; however, he only wanted the property returned and the juvenile removed. In an effort to circumvent the crowd, which was starting to become rowdy, the police officer took Rivera to the rear entrance to release him. As the crowd observed, Rivera being taken to the rear of the building, an onlooker assumed the officer was going to take him away to mishandle him. This was the first of several assumptions of police misconduct at this moment; each one taking its turn to ignite the crowd into a frenzy.

Furthermore, the second event provoking turmoil was the arrival of an ambulance. To onlookers, the presence of ambulance personnel implied that Mr. Rivera was beaten gravely enough to merit medical care. Unbeknownst to the crowd, the ambulance was summoned to treat the storeowner and assistant manager, who experienced minor injuries while attempting to stop Rivera during the shoplifting incident. Without facts and concrete information, the gathering assumed the worst-case scenario.

Fueling the masses once more, a hearse pulled up nearby and parked on 125th Street in an unrelated matter. Again, the now raucous group theorized the hearse was present to remove the body of a dead Lino Rivera. Many police officers appeared at the scene to quell the disturbance outside the store, which lead to the closing of the street after 3 hr. The crown insisted on seeing an unharmed Rivera, but was denied by police.

The buzz scattered through Harlem swiftly, broadcasting the police brutalized a young boy on 125th Street. The reaction was tumultuous, with thousands gathering to protest. Eventually, items began to be thrown at the store and other buildings as police attempted to diffuse the crowd to no avail. The rioting began to move to other sections of Harlem. When the sun fell, the looting commenced, leaving what is estimated as millions of dollars in property loss and damage. Six people were killed and 70 others were injured during the unrest. The rioting lasted until the next day (Greenberg, 1992).

a katz/Shutterstock.com

Many examples of rioting and civil unrest mark America's history in response to police use of force issues. Protests, peaceful assemblies, and rioting differ in substance and nature. A peaceful protest is dissimilar to its rioting counterpart. Peaceful assemblies are nonviolent resistances, displaying discontentment with the purpose of making a statement for

Bokic Bojan/Shutterstock.com

change. The riot, conversely, is violent, causes destruction of property, and involves mass destructive behavior. Often, the riot incites responses to engage police in untraditional use of force scenarios with large crowds to illicit predetermined responses. This can be observed when rocks and debris are thrown at police who are just standing in a line, trying to maintain order. No other time in U.S. history were circumstances harmonized for these events, peaceful and violent, than the era of the 1960s.

116th Street and Avalon Boulevard, Los Angeles, California: August 11, 1965

On August 11, 1965, Officer Lee Minikus of the California Highway Patrol (CHP) searched for an erratic driver that was called in by a citizen in the Watts district of Los Angeles. CA. In response to the call, Officer Minikus located and stopped Marquette Frye, 21, at 116th Street and Avalon Boulevard. Officer Minikus administered field sobriety tests to Frye, which he failed, providing probable cause for his arrest. While Minikus was investigating, crowds swarmed the area to seize a view.

According to accounts, Officer Minikus and Marquette Frye were friendly and non-confrontational, as could be during an arrest situation, until Frye's family paraded to the traffic stop. Frye's mother and stepbrother came to claim the car, which would be otherwise impounded. Frye's mother scolded him for driving drunk, and he became frantic.

With the scrutiny of the mounting crowd, officers positioned to handcuff Frye and he challenged the arrest, physically resisting. Frye was struck with a police baton, and his mother jumped onto the back of an arresting officer. The crowd expanded to hundreds, believing the police provoked violence and mistreated Frye and family (Queally, 2015).

Riots enflamed, fueled by the festering strain among the police and Los Angeles' black populace. Rocks and all types of objects were flung at police cars and businesses were plundered. Buildings burned and firefighters were attacked. South Los Angeles was on fire, literally and symbolically. There was eventually over 30 dead and 1,000 more injured during the disturbances that stretched over seven days.

California National Guardsmen poured into the city to assist over 2,000 local police as South Los Angeles burned. Curfews were installed and the violence began to steadily decline and by August 15, the riots were pacified enough for government officials to arise and measure damages. Estimates differed, however it is believed the riots produced over 40 million in damages through South Los Angeles. This riot is known as the Watts riot and was the first of its kind with more in the horizon in the tumultuous decade of the 1960s (Queally, 2015).

15th Avenue, Newark, New Jersey: July 12, 1967

On July 12, 1967, in Newark, New Jersey, an African American cab driver, John Smith, passed a police cruiser on 15th Avenue. The original reasoning for the motor vehicle stop was improper passing of a motor vehicle, a common traffic offense to our New Jersey readers. The details of the primary encounter are unclear; however, Smith was charged with multitude of traffic violations, along with resisting arrest. Smith sustained injuries from the two police officers that arrested him during the motor vehicle stop, which took place near the William B. Hayes housing project in the Central Ward of Newark, New Jersey. Speculation circulated throughout the city of Smith's arrest and alleged brutality, even to the extent he was killed while in the custody of the Newark Police Department. Smith was transported to the fourth precinct, where he was processed for the charges placed against him. Smith was eventually transferred to a hospital to receive treatment for the injuries he sustained during the arrest on the traffic stop (Siegal, 2006).

Crowds began to form and the rioting began shortly thereafter. As people mustered into groups, they became increasingly incensed. The destruction of property commenced and crowds attacked police, producing injuries to both rioters and officers. The riots lasted from July 12 to July 15 and left several people dead (including a police officer and firefighter killed by sniper fire) and hundreds more wounded (Bigart, 1967). At one point, the National Guard descended on the city during the most intense and violent time of the rioting. This riot was the most devastating since the Watts, Los Angeles, California riot in 1965, which also was preceded by the events occurring on a motor vehicle stop by police, as previously discussed.

a katz/Shutterstock.com

12th Street and Clairmount Avenue, Detroit, Michigan: July 22, 1967

Just as the fires were extinguished and property owners were assessing their damages in Newark, New Jersey; across the country in Detroit, Michigan, anger was smoldering in a similar community about to flash into the largest urban disturbance in modern U.S. history (Grimshaw, 1970; Herman, 2002).

On the night of July 22, 1967, Detroit Police detectives sprung into an unlicensed bar and arrested many African Americans who were commemorating the homecoming of two local servicemen returning from the Vietnam War. The police arrested everyone on scene. While having many people in custody, the police officers needed to make preparations to haul all of their prisoners to a precinct. Meanwhile, throngs of people assembled on 12th Street and Clairmount Avenue and began to taunt the police; there were suspicions of harsh treatment of the arrestees (Herman, 2002). Eventually, bottles started to fly at police. The rousing mass began to disperse and the looting launched. The National Guard was again summoned to assist local law enforcement with restoring order. Along with the looting and property damage, policemen, firemen, and Army Guardsmen were fired upon by rioters. Forty-three people were killed in the disturbance, including one Detroit police officer, two Detroit firefighters and one Michigan National Guardsman (Bergesen, 1982).

The City of Detroit experienced widespread damages to thousands of private businesses and displaced over 380 families from their homes. The monetary losses from the looting and fire damages were estimated to be in excess of $40 million dollars (National Advisory Commission on Civil Disorders, 1968).

The Newark and the Detroit riots of 1967, along with others, hatched the need to examine this turbulent urban phenomenon: rioting. As seen previously via the Lexow and Wickersham Commission, governing bodies seek remedies to solve problems through committees with purpose of proving recommendations for improvement in policy and procedure.

The common theme was surely, the lack of public trust displayed by a history of abuse or (at least) unfair treatment of residents, particularly minorities. The lack of community policing efforts, the lack of transparency and poor tactics; can all contribute to a powder keg for a community to erupt.

KERNER COMMISSION

During the violence and disorder in the summer of 1967, President Lyndon B. Johnson appointed the National Advisory Commission on Civil Disorders, famously branded as the Kerner Commission. President Johnson solicited this committee to explore exactly what happened during these riots, why they happened, and what preventive measures can be employed so similar events will not occur in the future. In the report, among the "why" these events occurred, investigators concluded that the African American population has a "widespread belief in the existence of police brutality," coupled with a "double-standard in the criminal justice system" among white and black America (National Advisor

a katz/Shutterstock.com

Commission on Civil Disorders, 1968). Ultimately, the Kerner Commission branded impoverishment and racial bias as the origin of rioting in the 1960s.

71st Street and Normandie Avenue, Los Angeles, California: April 29, 1992

On March 3, 1991, Rodney King was arrested after a high-speed chase (speeds exceeding 115 mph) with officers from the California Highway Patrol (CHP). Eventually, five Los Angeles Police Department (LAPD) officers on scene arrested Rodney King. King was subdued by LAPD officers with the use of a Taser, police batons, and kicks; he was struck numerous times while lying on the ground. The arrest was recorded by a nearby citizen on videotape and broadcasted for the world to see. To most, this case was the epitome of excessive use of force. Four police officers were charged with the assault of Rodney King stemming from the excessive use of force. The media coverage of this event was extensive and the video clip of the arrest was played continually.

On April 29, 1992, all four accused LAPD officers were acquitted of all charges placed against them by the Los Angeles District Attorney. Juveniles smashed into a liquor store and items were stolen near Normandie Avenue. As officers responded to the scene, a crowd began to gather at 71st Street and Normandie Avenue (Bergesen & Herman, 1998). Officers approached the crowd but retreated believing they were ill equipped to stifle the masses. Several businesses began to be looted and citizens were attacked, no other more famous than the attack of Reginald Denny; memorialized by video footage from a news helicopter. Irate protesters gather near the Parker Center (LAPD Police Headquarters) in their attempt to show discontent for the decision regarding the police use of force. Fires were ablaze, police and firemen were attacked, curfews were installed and general mayhem followed. As the situation in Los Angeles began to rapidly deteriorate, National Guard units were deployed to assist local police (Delk, 1995).

Over 50 people dead, hundreds of businesses were scorched and damages exceeded over one billion dollars. The costs were above cruel and harsh in poverty-stricken, lower income areas. This was the largest urban uprising since the preceding riots discussed in the summer of 1967 (Bergesen & Herman, 1998).

We examined the case, trial, and outcomes for the police officers criminally charged in the Rodney King case. During

mikeledray/Shutterstock.com

the prosecution's case, intent was allowed to be called into question. Further, this case was one of the first to use civil rights violations, the so-called Section 1983 Law Suit, against the police. In fact, two of the officers served 30-month prison sentences from the civil law suit (the only civil statute to allow an incarceration penalty). Important to note, jail time based upon preponderance of the evidence, rather than proof beyond a reasonable doubt. To continue, convictions that may have been political in nature to quell the public outcry. Were these officers truly guilty of the civil rights violations? We look at this later.

We discuss State violation of civil rights, Federal violations, and the several other protections and remedies available to citizens who might be the victims of deprivation of their civil rights.

9101 West Flourisant Ave. & Canfield Drive, Ferguson, Missouri-: August 9, 2014

A description of a suspect is broadcasted to Ferguson police officers after a subject committed assault and robbery at Ferguson Market and Liquor. Officer Darren Wilson responds to the area and locates a subject matching the description of the person portrayed by the victim and relayed to police dispatchers. It was Michael Brown, who was

© Katherine Welles/Shutterstock.com

established as the person in security surveillance as the person who committed the crimes at the convenience store.

When Officer Wilson locates Brown on a roadway, he reports that when he tried to engage the suspect he was attacked and Brown attempting to gain possession of his loaded service weapon. Wilson indicated that Brown almost accomplished removing his firearm from him and during the altercation a round was discharged, striking Brown. At this point Brown begins to flee and Wilson began to chase him on foot. Wilson stated that after a short time Brown turns to confront him and charges at him. When this occurs, Wilson fatally shoots Brown with multiple rounds (Robles & Bosman, 2014).

The police release of information and response to the shooting was greatly condemned by the community and later in the evening people began to assemble for a memorial to Michael Brown. As the evening proceeded, some rioting and unrest began to spark.

Police officers began to arrive in riot gear as private businesses began to be looted and burned, personal property vandalized, along with violent confrontations with police. Thirty arrests were made on the first night and two police officers reported injuries (Barker, 2014).

The riots continued and the police resorted to using less than lethal ammunition (bean bag rounds) and tear gas to subdue the crowds and quell the rioting. The rioting continued for approximately two weeks. During the unrest, curfews were implemented and a state of emergency was declared by Missouri Governor Jay Nixon. Reuters reported that more than 400 protesters were arrested during the unrest. In addition to the arrests, an estimated 5.7 million dollars in damages were estimated for the first month of the rioting.

Mount Street and North Avenue, Baltimore, Maryland: April 12, 2015

On April 12, 2015, Freddie Gray Jr. was arrested by the Baltimore Police Department for possession of an illegal knife. Gray ran from police originally and was apprehended on the 1700 block of Presbury Street and reported to be "without force or incident." Gray is transported by a police van to be taken to district headquarters for processing. During the transport, Gray becomes unconscious and is taken to a local hospital for treatment. Gray dies on April 19, 2015, his death is credited to injuires he sustained to his spinal cord (Graham, 2015).

After an preliminary internal investigation by the Baltimore Police Department, six officers involved with Freddie Gray's arrest and transport are suspended with pay awaiting a full inquiry into the events that occurred in the transport van.

On April 25, 2015, large protests and riots erupted in downtown Baltimore roducing widespread violence. Looting, arson, and general civil disorder ruled for several nights. Maryland Governor Larry Hogan declared a state of emergency for the area. The National Gaurd was organized along with many other law enforcment agencies from the mid-Atlantic area. Curfews were installed until the disorder dissolved and the city began to recover from the damages. More than 200 people were arrested and over 150 fires were startedwithin the the city limits of Baltimore that were directly related to the rioting. Reports indicated the damages for the unrest were estimated to exceed 20 million dollars.

© duckeesue/Shutterstock.com

On May 1, 2015, prosecutors filed charges for second degree murder against the six officers and on the 21st of May, a local grand jury indicted the officers on the original charges. At the duration of the legal issues surrounding the officers, none of them were found guilty of any charges.

In the aftermath of the Ferguson rioting and civil unrest, U.S. President Barack Obama commisioned the *President's Task Force on 21st Century Policing Implementation Guide: Moving from Recommendations to Action*. The following is the Executive Summary of this undetraking:

Executive Summary of the Six Pillars by Topics

Pillar One: Building Trust & Legitimacy

- Changing the culture of policing—guardian versus warrior culture of policing
- Role of policing in past injustices
- Culture of transparency and accountability
- Procedural justice: internal legitimacy
- Positive nonenforcement activities

- Research crime-fighting strategies that undermine or build public trust
- Community surveys
- Workforce diversity
- Decouple federal immigration enforcement from local policing

Pillar Two: Policy & Oversight

- Community input and involvement
- Use of force
- Nonpunitive peer review of critical incidents
- Scientifically supported identification procedures
- Demographic data on all detentions
- Mass demonstration policies
- Local civilian oversight
- No quotas for tickets for revenue
- Consent and informed search and seizure
- Officer identification and reason for stops
- Prohibit profiling and discrimination, in particular as it relates to LGBT and gender nonconforming populations
- Encourage shared services between jurisdictions
- National Register of Decertified Officers

Pillar Three: Technology & Social Media

- New technology standards for compatibility and interoperability
- Address human rights and privacy concerns
- Technology designed considering local needs and people with special needs
- Body-worn cameras and other emerging technologies
- Public records laws—update to keep up with emerging technologies
- Transparency and accessibility for the community through technology
- Develop new less than lethal technology

Pillar Four: Community Policing & Crime Reduction

- Community engagement in managing public safety
- Infuse community policing throughout law enforcement organizations

- Use multidisciplinary teams
- Protect the dignity of all
- Neighborhood problem solving
- Reduce aggressive law enforcement that stigmatizes youth
- Address the school-to-prison pipeline
- Youth engagement

Pillar Five: Training & Education

- High quality training and training innovation hubs
- Engage community members in trainings
- Leadership training for all officers
- National postgraduate program of policing for senior executives
- Incorporate the following in basic recruit and in-service trainings:
    - Policing in a democratic society
    - Implicit bias and cultural responsiveness
    - Social interaction skills and tactical skills
    - Disease of addiction
    - Crisis intervention teams (mental health)
    - Reinforce policies on sexual misconduct and sexual harassment
    - How to work with LGBT and gender nonconforming populations
- Higher education for law enforcement officers
- Use of technology to improve access to and quality of training
- Improve field training officer programs

Pillar Six: Officer Wellness & Safety

- Multifaceted officer safety and wellness initiative
- Promote officer wellness and safety at every level
- Scientifically supported shift lengths
- Tactical first aid kit and training
- Anti-ballistic vests for every officer
- Collect information on injuries and near misses as well as officer deaths
- Require officers to wear seat belts and bulletproof vests
- Pass peer review error management legislation
- Smart car technology to reduce accidents

Ultimately, the project urged the community, local government, and law enforcement (the stakeholders to do the following to implement the recommendations):

Five Ways Stakeholder Groups Can Implement the Task Force's Recommendations

Local government

1. Create listening opportunities with the community.
2. Allocate government resources to implementation.
3. Conduct community surveys on attitudes toward policing, and publish the results.
4. Define the terms of civilian oversight to meet the community's needs.
5. Recognize and address holistically the root causes of crime.

Law enforcement

1. Review and update policies, training, and data collection on use of force, and engage community members and police labor unions in the process.
2. Increase transparency of data, policies, and procedures.
3. Call on the POST Commission to implement all levels of training.
4. Examine hiring practices and ways to involve the community in recruiting.
5. Ensure officers have access to the tools they need to keep them safe.

Communities

1. Engage with local law enforcement; participate in meetings, surveys, and other activities.
2. Participate in problem-solving efforts to reduce crime and improve quality of life.
3. Work with local law enforcement to ensure crime-reducing resources and tactics are being deployed that mitigate unintended consequences.
4. Call on state legislators to ensure that the legal framework does not impede accountability for law enforcement.
5. Review school policies and practices, and advocate for early intervention strategies that minimize involvement of youth in the criminal justice system.

CONCLUSION

If anything, it's crucial to understand the use of force by police is a serious issue demanding attention from the public, scholars, and students. Understanding why the police use force, when they use force, and to what extent can cultivate a thoughtful discussion about current procedure and future issues in policing a free society. The United States of America is an institution of transparency, as you can see, the nation constantly reevaluates operations through oversight commissions, pushing forward for ways to improve. The evolution of police practice, specifically in the area of use of force, is perpetual and inevitable. As the political and environmental landscape changes, so will the criminal justice system (police, courts, corrections, etc.).

As this is being written, the aftermath of the riots in Ferguson, Missouri, in 2014 and Baltimore, Maryland, 2015 are shaping policy in America, challenging past practices, and offering new methods to effectively deliver police service. Are they just a response to a current trend of politics, or is there a need for serious police reform in terms of use of force?

When employed with an impartial and fitting reaction to the specific law enforcement objective, the use of force by police is an indispensable method to ensure safe communities (Kuhns & Knuttson, 2010). Although this is a necessary component to enforcing the law, American history illustrates when police engage in the misuse of force, it can disintegrate the faith and trust of the governed population. This book's pursuit and purpose explores the blending of police behavior, law enforcement's objective of providing safe environments for the community, with respecting fundamental civil rights—all viewed through eyes of the use of force debate. This quest goes on for lawmakers, legal practitioners, and law enforcement policy makers. So, let's take a look at the fundamentals of police use of force in America from the ground level.

David Fowler/Shutterstock.com

Discussion points

1. Peelian principle number 4 states "The degree of cooperation of the public that can be secured diminishes, proportionately, to the necessity for the use of physical force and compulsion in achieving police objectives."
   - Keeping in mind the Peelian principles are from 1829, how can we use the basic concept Sir Robert Peele envisioned prior to social media and the Internet to improve relationships between the community and the police?
   - In terms of police use of force, describe how public opinion is swayed (no matter the reason) when an incident is broadcast and race/racism appears to be the impetus of the confrontation.
2. In looking at some of the examples that led to civil unrest in the early to mid-20th century, are there parallels to the riots/protests of late?
   - Does the relationship a police agency has with the community play a larger role in the effects of a celebrated use of force case and potential for civil unrest?
   - Does the initial police response to the beginning of civil unrest, even the beginning of a protest, set the stage for violence/looting/mayhem?

References

Barker, T. (August 11, 2014) 'Ferguson-area businesses cope with aftermath of weekend riot." *St. Louis Post-Dispatch*. Retrieved from https://www.stltoday.com/news/local/ferguson-area-businesses-cope-with-aftermath-of-weekend-riot/article_4a310ec-94de-57dd-95f7-4e350f6a6fa2.html

Bergesen, A. (1982). Race riots of 1967: An analysis of police violence in Detroit and Newark. *Journal of Black Studies, 12*(3), 261–274.

Bergesen, A., & Herman, M. (1998). Immigration, race, and riot: The 1992 Los Angeles uprising. *American Sociological Review, 63*(1), 39–54.

Bigart, H. (1967, July 16). Newark Riot Deaths at 21 as Negro Sniping Widens; Hughes May Seek U.S. Aid. *The New York Times*. Retrieved from https://partners.nytimes.com/library/national/ race/071667race-ra.html

Delk, J. D. (1995). *Fires & furies: The LA riots, what really happened*. Palm Springs, CA: ETC Publications.

Gaines, L., Kappeler, V., & Vaughn, J. (1999) *Policing in America* (3rd ed.). Cincinnati, OH: Anderson Publishing Company.

Graham, D. (2015, April 22). "The Mysterious Death of Freddie Gray." *The Atlantic*. Retrieved from https://www.theatlantic.com/politics/archive/2015/04/the-mysterious-death-of-freddire-gray/391119.

Greenberg, C. (1992). The politics of disorder reexamining Harlem's Riots of 1935 and 1943. *Journal of Urban History*, 18(4), 395–441.

Grimshaw, A. D. (1970). Interpreting collective violence: An argument for the importance of social structure. *The ANNALS of the American Academy of Political and Social Science*, 391(1), 9–20.

Herman, M. (2002). *Ethnic succession and urban unrest in Newark and Detroit during the summer of 1967*. Newark, NJ: Cornwall Center for Metropolitan Studies.

Karsch, M. W. (1989). Excessive force and the Fourth Amendment: When does seizure end. *Fordham Law Review, 58*, 823.

Kuhns, J., & Knutsson, J. (Eds.). (2010). *Police use of force: A global perspective*. Santa Barbara, CA: Praeger Publishers.

Lentz, S. A., & Chaires, R. H. (2007). The invention of Peel's principles: A study of policing "textbook" history. *Journal of Criminal Justice, 35*(1), 69–79. doi:10.1016/j.jcrimjus.2006.11.016

Milton, C., Halleck, J., Lardner, J., & Albrecht, G. (1977). *Police use of deadly force*. Washington, DC: Police Foundation.

National Advisory Commission on Civil Disorders. (1968). *Report of the national advisory commission on civil disorders*. New York, NY: Bantam Books.

Queally, J. (2015, July 29). Watts Riots: Traffic stop was the spark that ignited the days of destruction in L.A. *The Los Angeles Times*. Retrieved from http://www.latimes.com/local/lanow/a-me-ln-watts-riots-explainer-20150715-htmlstory.html

Robles, F. & Bosman, J. (August 17, 2014). "Autopsy Shows Michael Brown Was Struck at Least 6 Times." *The New York Times*. http:www.nytimes.com/2014/08/18/us/michael-brown-autopsy-shows-he-was-shot-at-least-6-times.html?smid=tw-share

Siegal, K. (2006). Silent no longer: voices of the 1967 Newark race riots. *CUREJ-College Undergraduate Research Electronic Journal, 31*, 3–6.

Student Name _____ Date _____

Course Section _____ Chapter _____

Describe your understanding of when and to what extent should the police use force, include your perceptions of "levels of force", the tools at the police officer's disposal, the prevailing case law applicable. Basically, an overall view of when and how the police use force and should there be more accountability. Further, is there "too much" accountability already? How would you change things if you could?

_____

_____

_____

_____

_____

_____

_____

_____

_____

_____

_____

_____

_____

CHAPTER 2

FOUNDATIONS OF FEDERAL AND STATE LAW

If men were angels, no government would be necessary. If angels were to govern men, neither external nor internal controls on government would be necessary. In framing a government which is to be administered by men over men, the great difficulty lies in this: you must first enable the government to control the governed; and in the next place, oblige to control itself.

—James Madison in the Federalist Papers (Federalist No. 51)

Key Terms

Force Continuum, Jurisdiction, Justification, Articulation, Pedestrian Stop, Probable Cause, Investigative Detention, Pat Down, Frisk, Use of Force, Warrantless Search, Warrantless Seizure, *Graham v. Connor*, *Terry v. Ohio*, *Tennessee v. Garner*, *Delaware v. Prouse*, Title 18 Section 241.

Learning Objectives

After exploring Chapter 2, the student will be able to:

1. Define use of force
2. Explain jurisdiction, justification, and articulation
3. Describe use-of-force continuum
4. Define probable cause
5. Describe when a pat down or frisk is lawful
6. List exceptions to the requirement of a warrant

In order to understand what constitutes force and (subsequently) excessive force, one must view the progression of case law and understand key terms.

According to the landmark Supreme Court of the United States (SCOTUS) case of *Graham v. Connor*, 490 U.S. 386 (1989);

> *The Fourth Amendment "reasonableness" inquiry is whether the officers' actions are "objectively reasonable" in light of the facts and circumstances confronting them, without regard to their underlying intent or motivation. The "reasonableness" of a particular use of force must be judged from the perspective of a reasonable officer on the scene, and its calculus must embody an allowance for the fact that police officers are often forced to make split-second decisions about the amount of force necessary in a particular situation (pp. 490 U.S. 396–397).*

Historically, from 1952 to 1985, the Supreme Court applied a 14th Amendment substantive due process analysis to excessive force claims against police (*Rochin v. California*, 342 U.S. 165, 172 (1952); *Tennessee v. Garner*, 471 U.S. 1, 7 (1985)).

It was not until 1972 when the Second Circuit Court of Appeals provided a four-part test and a definitive statement to further define the shocks-the-conscience standard, ". . . force that is brutal and offensive to human dignity . . ." (*Johnson v. Glick*, 481 F.2d 1028 (1973)). In 1985, the U.S. Supreme Court's landmark case *Tennessee v. Garner* began a slight shift in clearly established law and away from 14th Amendment substantive due process analysis.

The court ruled, "the use of deadly force to apprehend a suspect is a seizure under the 4th Amendment objective reasonableness standard . . ." A police officer may not seize an unarmed, non-dangerous (fleeing felon) suspect by shooting him dead (*Tennessee v. Garner*, 471 U.S. 1, 7 (1985)). The court went on to provide guidance for lower courts conducting judicial analysis of officer's decisions in this particular circumstance.

In 1989, in *Graham v. Connor*, the Court moved the judicial analytical focus from the long used 14th Amendment substantive due process, to the 4th Amendment objective reasonableness standard. The court expanded post incident analysis to include all uses of force.

The years from 1985 to 1989 created a change in clearly established law. *Tennessee v. Garner* and *Graham v. Conner* changed the post use-of-force analysis process for the courts and indirectly provided an opportunity for change for the law enforcement community. Some argue it mandated change via clearly established law.

In the mid-1970s, Prof. Gregory Connor created the first "force continuum" as an instructional aide, designed to assist criminal justice trainers throughout the country. (Gregory Connor, "Understanding and Application of Force Alternatives: Overview," www.use-of-force. com). Los Angeles Police Department (LAPD) developed the "Force Continuum Barometer," which was published

somsak suwanput/Shutterstock.com

in their 1978 training bulletin. In 1980, longtime international trainer, Kevin Parsons, Ph.D., developed the "Confrontational Continuum."

According to Parsons, "The concept of the continuum was to explain to officers 'when' to use force options as opposed to the traditional defensive tactics class which dealt only with 'how' to use force options. Thus, the continuum was designed to be a training tool" (John G. Peters and Michael A. Brave, "Force Continuums: Are They Still Needed?" *Police and Security News* 22, no. 1 (Jan./Feb. 2006)). John C. Desmedt of Protective Safety Systems, Inc. developed a "Use of Force Model" concept in 1981.

Through the years, continuums increased in complexity it seems for no other reason than to reinvent the wheel producing several differing standards to explain to a jury. So why have varying use-of-force continuums been accepted by law enforcement trainers and the legal community without debate for so many years?

The general concept of use of force is, "A law enforcement officer may use that amount of force upon a person that the law allows. A law enforcement officer may not use more force upon a person than the law allows" (Michael Brave, "TASER Electronic Control Devices (ECDs): Legal Update" (December 19, 2010)).

As the Tenth Circuit Court of Appeals stated, "Clearly established law dictates training, not the other way around" (*Weigle v. Broad*, 544 F.3d 1143 (10th Cir. 2008)).

Thus, an understanding of clearly established law is imperative for understanding the use-of-force principals. Clearly established Federal law is defined as "the governing legal principle or principles set forth by the Supreme Court at the time the state court renders its decision" (*McClish v. Evans*, 2009 U.S. Dist. Lexis 80666 (E.D. Cal. August 21, 2009)).

The U.S. Supreme Court provided directive guidance in the *Tennessee v. Garner* case, providing factors to aid in describing the totality of the circumstances. Along with these factors new guidance was given to fact finders (courts) analyzing uses of force:

1. "Proper application requires careful attention to the facts and circumstances of each particular case.

2. Must be judged from the perspective of a reasonable officer on scene not 20/20 hindsight.

3. Must embody allowance for split-second decisions in tense, uncertain, and rapidly evolving situations.

4. An officer's evil intentions will not make a 4th Amendment

somsak suwanput/Shutterstock.com

violation out of an objectively reasonable use of force; nor will an officer's good intentions make an objectively unreasonable use of force constitutional." (*Graham v. Connor*, 490 U.S. 386, 394 (1989)).

In 1985, the Supreme Court established rigid preconditions for using deadly force (shooting with a firearm) in the context of preventing the escape of a violent fleeing felon. In 2007, the Supreme Court further stated in *Scott v. Harris*, "Garner did not establish a magical on/off switch that triggers rigid preconditions whenever an officer's actions constitute deadly force."

Garner was simply an application of the 4th Amendment's "reasonableness" test, Graham to "the use of a particular type of force in a particular situation." (*Scott v. Harris*, 433 F.3d 807 (2007)).

In the Tenth circuit, as recent as 2010, lower courts continue to use the *Tennessee v. Garner* standard to judge officer's use of deadly force (shooting with a firearm) to prevent escape. (*Brooks v. Gaenzle*, 614 F.3d 1213 (2010)).

Garner provided several factors, the court stated, "if the suspect threatens the officer with a weapon or there is probable cause to believe that he has committed a crime involving the infliction or threatened infliction of serious physical harm, deadly force may be used if necessary to prevent escape, and if, where feasible, some warning has been given" (*Tennessee v. Garner*, 471 U.S. 1, 7 (1985)).

Deadly force may be used if necessary to prevent escape; however, the Garner court did not clearly define what "necessary" means. In 1997, the Ninth Circuit Court of Appeals, further defined necessary, "The necessity inquiry is a factual one "Did a reasonable nondeadly alternative exist for apprehending the suspect?" (*Forrett v. Richardson*, 112 F. 3d 416, citing *Brower v. County of Inyo*, 884 F.2d 1316, 1318 (9th Cir.1989)). If the suspect is fleeing with a gun in hand, tackling the suspect, using OC Spray or a baton to prevent his escape would certainly not be reasonable.

A warning of the imminent use of force, if feasible, must be given. There are two inquiries to be answered by an officer in determining when it is both feasible and appropriate to issue a warning prior to using deadly force to apprehend a fleeing suspect.

1. "An officer first should consider whether the suspect is aware that the police are trying to apprehend him, such that he has knowledge that he should stop."
2. "If an officer reasonably believes, based on the suspect's prior conduct, that such a warning would not cause the suspect to surrender, but rather would provoke the suspect to engage in violent and life-threatening behavior, or to increase his or her efforts to flee, then a warning is not feasible" (*Ridgeway v. City of Woolwich*, 924 F. Supp. 653 (1996)).

The *Graham v. Connor* use-of-force post-analysis factors included, but were not limited to, "the severity of the crime at issue, whether the suspect poses an immediate threat to the safety of the officers or others, and whether he is actively resisting arrest or attempting to evade arrest by flight." (*Graham v. Connor*, 490 U.S. 386, 394 (1989).

However, prior to making any "split second decisions" to use force, deadly or nondeadly force, an officer must first satisfy the following:

Greg Goodman/Shutterstock.com

1. Jurisdiction—was the officer in an area that is permissible by the appropriate governing law/statutes.
2. Justification—did the officer have reasonable suspicion or probable cause to engage in a lawful encounter with the suspect.

3. Articulation—the officer must point to specific facts and circumstances that explain why the encounter was lawful. Then, further explain why force was necessary.

The "encounter" between a police officer and a citizen, when lawful, provides the framework in which an officer may detain, investigate, question, pat down, search, arrest, or use force.

What prevents the police from just approaching anyone, anywhere at any time? The 4th Amendment and the 14th Amendment. So, let us begin:

An officer must first be within their jurisdiction. That is, are they lawfully allowed to be where they are at the time of the encounter. The determination of jurisdiction sounds simple, right? Well, beyond the mere definition of jurisdiction (area of authority; i.e., within the boundaries of the town they are employed), there are numerous factors to consider.

Although an officer might be within the geographical boundaries of the agency for which they are employed, is the officer authorized to be in the exact place and at the exact time for which the encounter occurred?

u3d/Shutterstock.com

Discuss the following scenario:

Officer Smith is within the geographical boundaries of Anytown, USA where the officer is employed. Officer Smith is assigned a foot patrol in a residential area, on Main Street between Maple and Ivy Streets (only in the first two city blocks of Main Street). Officer Smith observes Johnny the Drug Dealer on the third block of Main Street. Since Officer Smith knows Johnny is a drug dealer (from previous arrests Officer Smith made with Johnny possessing and selling drugs), therefore, Officer Smith walks onto the third block of Main Street to get a closer look at what Johnny is doing. Johnny sees Officer Smith approaching and runs. Officer Smith chases Johnny and sees Johnny go into the backyard of a nearby house. Once Johnny reaches the back door of the house, Johnny sits down on the steps. Officer Smith approaches Johnny and asks Johnny what he is doing. Johnny tells Officer Smith he is visiting a friend and realized he was late, so he ran to the house. Officer Smith notices, in plain view, two marijuana plants growing behind an air conditioning unit in the back yard of this house. Officer Smith tells Johnny to get the person in the house Johnny was supposed to meet to verify Johnny's story. Joe the homeowner, comes to the door and verifies Johnny was supposed to meet him. Officer Smith then places Johnny under arrest for running away when Johnny saw Officer Smith approaching. Officer Smith also arrests Joe, the homeowner, for possession of marijuana plants.

Will the arrests be lawful? Was Officer Smith within his jurisdiction?

Answers:

The arrest of Johnny is not lawful. The mere act of running away at the sight of police, in and of itself, is not unlawful. The act of running may provide the police with reasonable suspicion; depending on the totality of circumstances. Be sure to discuss the difference between reasonable suspicion and probable cause, with attention to what factors might change the unlawful scenario arrest to a lawful arrest.

The arrest of Joe the homeowner is lawful. Unlike the fruits of the poisonous tree doctrine, the evidence (in this case the marijuana plants) is not "tainted". Although the officer did not have probable cause to arrest Johnny, the officer was allowed to be in the backyard – there was no fence or other obstacle which prevented the officer from viewing the marijuana plants in the backyard (plain view exception to the warrant requirement).

Officer Smith was in his jurisdiction. Although Officer Smith may have left his designated patrol area, he was still within the boundaries of his jurisdiction.

Jurisdiction continued—

Not only must an officer be within their geographical jurisdiction, the officer must "accomplish a lawful, law enforcement function" when initiating an encounter with a citizen.

The officer must be able to articulate "why" they stopped someone. The concept of accomplishing a lawful, law enforcement function is more complicated than merely enforcing a law or statute. The officer cannot use racial profiling or other unlawful practices as the impetus of a stop. Profiling, in and of itself, is not unlawful (more on that later).

carl ballou/Shutterstock.com

Here, the officer's intent when stopping someone comes under scrutiny. As we see later, an officer's intentions may not have any bearing on a use of force; however, their intentions may very well be the deciding factor if the officer's purpose was to accomplish a valid, law enforcement function.

Discuss the following scenario:

Officer Smith is on vehicle patrol and is assigned a patrol sector. Officer Smith drives in his assigned sector during his shift. When driving down Main Street, Officer Smith observes Tom driving in the opposite direction on Main Street. Officer Smith recently learned that Tom has been having an affair with his wife. Officer Smith turns around and conducts a motor vehicle stop of Tom's car. Officer Smith, orders Tom out of the car and begins to punch and kick Tom. Officer Smith then realizes what just happened and apologizes to Tom. Tom gets back into his vehicle and drives away.

Was the motor vehicle stop lawful? Was Officer Smith accomplishing a lawful, law enforcement objective?

Answers:
The motor vehicle stop was unlawful. Discuss Delaware v. Prouse and the requirement for reasonable suspicion to conduct a motor vehicle stop.

Obviously, Officer Smith was not accomplishing a lawful, law enforcement objective when he stopped Tom. However, if Tom committed a motor vehicle offense, would the initial stop be lawful? Yes, Officer Smith, although wanting to inconvenience or harass Tom by making a motor vehicle stop, would have been lawfully allowed to stop Tom if a motor vehicle offense took place - providing reasonable suspicion for the stop. Here, an officer's intention is not of consequence (pretext stop).

sergign/Shutterstock.com

The 4th Amendment of the Constitution protects citizens from "unreasonable search and seizures." When an officer stops a person on the street or when an officer conducts a motor vehicle stop, the person(s) on the street and the person(s) in the vehicle are now "seized" for the purposes of the 4th Amendment. Therefore, certain thresholds must be met in order for a person(s) to be lawfully seized.

How does an officer lawfully "seize" a person(s)? SCOTUS made it clear in *Delaware v. Prouse*, 440 U.S. 648;

Except where there is at least articulable and reasonable suspicion that a motorist is unlicensed or that an automobile is not registered, or that either the vehicle or an occupant is otherwise subject to seizure for violation of law, stopping an automobile and detaining the driver in order to check his driver's license and the registration of the automobile are unreasonable under the 4th Amendment (pp. 653–663).

(a) Stopping an automobile and detaining its occupants constitute a "seizure" within the meaning of the 4th and 14th Amendments, even though the purpose of the stop is limited and the resulting detention quite brief. The permissibility of a particular law enforcement practice is judged by balancing its intrusion on the individual's 4th Amendment interests against its promotion of legitimate governmental interests (pp. 653–655 [p. 649]).

(b) The State's interest in discretionary spot checks as a means of ensuring the safety of its roadways does not outweigh the resulting intrusion on the privacy and security of the persons detained. Given the physical and psychological intrusion visited upon the occupants of a vehicle by a random stop to check documents, cf. *United States v. Brignoni-Ponce*, 422 U. 3. 873; a person in an automobile does not lose all reasonable expectation of privacy simply because the automobile and its use are subject to government regulation. People are not shorn of all 4th Amendment protection when they step from their homes onto the public sidewalk; nor are they shorn of those interests when they step from the sidewalks into their automobiles (pp. 662–663).

(c) The holding in this case does not preclude Delaware or other States from developing methods for spot checks that involve less intrusion or that do not involve the unconstrained exercise of discretion. Questioning of all oncoming traffic at road-block-type stops is one possible alternative (p. 663).

The Fourth and 14th Amendments are implicated in this case because stopping an automobile and detaining its occupants constitute a "seizure" within the meaning of those amendments, even though the purpose of the stop is limited and the resulting detention quite brief. *United States v. Martinez-Fuerte*, 428 U.S. 543, 556–558 (1976); *United States v. Brignoni-Ponce*, 422 U.S. 873, 878 (1975); cf. *Terry v. Ohio*, 392 U.S. 1, 16 (1968). The essential purpose of the proscriptions in the 4th Amendment is to impose a standard [p. 654] of "reasonableness" upon the exercise of discretion by government officials, including law enforcement agents, in order "'to safeguard the privacy and security of individuals against arbitrary invasions . . .'" *Marshall v. Barlow's*, Inc., 436 U.S. 307, 312 (1978), quoting *Camara v. Municipal Court*, 387 U.S. 523, 528 (1967).

Thus, the permissibility of a particular law enforcement practice is judged by balancing its intrusion on the individual's 4th Amendment interests against its promotion of legitimate governmental interests. Implemented in this manner, the reasonableness standard usually requires, at a minimum, that the facts upon which an intrusion is based be capable of measurement against "an objective standard," whether this be probable cause or a less stringent test. In those situations, in which the balance of interests precludes insistence upon "some quantum [p. 655] of individualized suspicion," other safeguards are generally relied upon to assure that the individual's reasonable expectation of privacy is not "subject to the discretion of the official in the field," *Camara v. Municipal Court*, 387 U.S. at 532. See id. at 534–535; *Marshall v. Barlow's*, Inc., supra at 320–321; *United States v. United States District Court*, 407 U.S. 297, 322–323 (1972) (requiring warrants).

Pedestrian Stops

Terry v. Ohio 392 U.S. 1

Cleveland detective (Martin McFadden), on a downtown beat which he had been patrolling for many years, observed two strangers (petitioner and another man, Chilton) on a street corner. He saw them proceed alternately back and forth along an identical route, pausing to stare in the same store window, which they did for a total of about 24 times. Each completion of the route was followed by a conference between the two on a corner, at one of which they were joined by a third man (Katz) who left swiftly. Suspecting the two men of "casing a job, a stick-up," the officer followed them and saw them rejoin the third man a couple of blocks away in front of a store. The officer approached the three, identified himself as a policeman, and asked their names. The men "mumbled something," whereupon McFadden spun petitioner around, patted down his outside clothing, and found in his overcoat pocket,

ChameleonsEye/Shutterstock.com

but was unable to remove, a pistol. The officer ordered the three into the store. He removed petitioner's overcoat, took out a revolver, and ordered the three to face the wall with their hands raised. He patted down the outer clothing of Chilton and Katz and seized a revolver from Chilton's outside overcoat pocket. He did not put his hands under the outer garments of Katz (since he discovered nothing in his patdown which might have been a weapon), or under petitioner's or Chilton's outer garments until he felt the guns. The three were taken to the police station. Petitioner and Chilton were charged with carrying concealed weapons. The defense moved to suppress the weapons. Though the trial court rejected the prosecution theory that the guns had been seized during a search incident to a lawful arrest, the court denied the motion to suppress and admitted the weapons into evidence on the ground that the officer had cause to believe that petitioner and Chilton were acting suspiciously, that their interrogation was warranted, and that the officer, for his own protection, had the right to pat down their outer clothing hav-

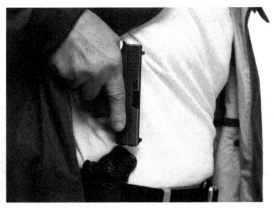

Straight 8 Photography/Shutterstock.com

ing reasonable cause to believe that they might be armed. The court distinguished between an investigatory "stop" and an arrest, and between a "frisk" of the outer clothing for weapons and a full-blown search for evidence of crime. Petitioner and Chilton were found guilty, an intermediate appellate court affirmed, and the State Supreme Court dismissed the appeal on the ground that "no substantial constitutional question" was involved.

Held:

1. The 4th Amendment right against unreasonable searches and seizures, made applicable to the States by the 14th Amendment, "protects people, not places," and therefore applies as much to the citizen on the streets as well as at home or elsewhere (pp. 8–9).
2. The issue in this case is not the abstract propriety of the police conduct, but the admissibility against petitioner of the evidence uncovered by the search and seizure (p. 12).
3. The exclusionary rule cannot properly be invoked to exclude the products of legitimate and restrained police investigative techniques, and this Court's approval of such techniques should not discourage remedies other than the exclusionary rule to curtail police abuses for which that is not an effective sanction (pp. 13–15).
4. The 4th Amendment applies to "stop and frisk" procedures such as those followed here (pp. 16–20).
   a. Whenever a police officer accosts an individual and restrains his freedom to walk away, he has "seized" that person within the meaning of the 4th Amendment

(p. 16). (b) A careful exploration of the outer surfaces of a person's clothing in an attempt to find weapons is a "search" under that amendment (p. 16).

5. Where a reasonably prudent officer is warranted in the circumstances of a given case in believing that his safety or that of others is endangered, he may make a reasonable search for weapons of the person believed by him to be armed and dangerous (p. 3) regardless of whether he has probable cause to arrest that individual for crime or the absolute certainty that the individual is armed (pp. 20–27).

   a. Though the police must, whenever practicable, secure a warrant to make a search and seizure, that procedure cannot be followed where swift action based upon on-the-spot observations of the officer on the beat is required (p. 20).

   b. The reasonableness of any particular search and seizure must be assessed in light of the particular circumstances against the standard of whether a man of reasonable caution is warranted in believing that the action taken was appropriate (pp. 21–22).

   c. The officer here was performing a legitimate function of investigating suspicious conduct when he decided to approach petitioner and his companions (p. 22).

   d. An officer justified in believing that an individual whose suspicious behavior he is investigating at close range is armed may, to neutralize the threat of physical harm, take necessary measures to determine whether that person is carrying a weapon (p. 24).

   e. A search for weapons in the absence of probable cause to arrest must be strictly circumscribed by the exigencies of the situation (pp. 25–26).

   f. An officer may make an intrusion short of arrest where he has reasonable apprehension of danger before being possessed of information justifying arrest (pp. 26–27).

6. The officer's protective seizure of petitioner and his companions and the limited search which he made were reasonable, both at their inception and as conducted (pp. 27–30).

   a. The actions of petitioner and his companions were consistent with the officer's hypothesis that they were contemplating a daylight robbery and were armed (p. 28).

   b. The officer's search was confined to what was minimally necessary to determine whether the men were armed, and the intrusion, which was made for the sole purpose of protecting himself and others nearby, was confined to ascertaining the presence of weapons (pp. 29–30).

7. The revolver seized from petitioner was properly admitted into evidence against him, since the search which led to its seizure was reasonable under the 4th Amendment (pp. 30–31).

And as the right to stop and inquire is to be justified for a cause less conclusive than that which would sustain an arrest, so the right to frisk may be justified as an incident to inquiry upon grounds of elemental safety and precaution which might not initially sustain a search. Ultimately, the validity of the frisk narrows down to whether there is or is not a right by the police to touch the person ques-

Kumpol Chuansakul/Shutterstock.com

tioned. The sense of exterior touch here involved is not very far different from the sense of sight or hearing—senses upon which police customarily act. *People v. Rivera*, 14 N.Y.2d 441, 445, 447, 201 N.E.2d 32, 34, 35, 252 N.Y.S.2d 458, 461, 463 (1964), cert. denied, 379 U.S. 978 (1965).

In this case, for example, the Ohio Court of Appeals stated that we must be careful to distinguish that the "frisk" authorized herein includes only a "frisk" for a dangerous weapon. It by no means authorizes a search for contraband, evidentiary material, or anything else in the absence of reasonable grounds to arrest. Such a search is controlled by the requirements of the 4th Amendment, and probable cause is essential.

> *State v. Terry*, 5 Ohio App.2d 122, 130, 214 N.E.2d 114, 120 (1966). See also, for example, *Ellis v. United States*, 105 U.S.App.D.C. 86, 88, 264 F.2d 372, 374 (1959); Comment, 65 Col.L.Rev. 848, 860, and n. 81 (1965).

In our view, the sounder course is to recognize that the 4th Amendment governs all intrusions by agents of the public upon personal security, and to make the scope of the particular intrusion, in light of all the exigencies of the case, a central element in the analysis of reasonableness. Cf. *Brinegar v. United States*, 338 U.S. 160, 183 (1949) (Mr. Justice Jackson, dissenting). *Compare Camara v. Municipal Court*, 387 U.S. 523, 537 (1967).

This seems preferable to an approach which attributes too much significance to an overly technical definition of "search," and which turns in part upon a judge-made hierarchy of legislative enactments in the criminal sphere. Focusing the inquiry squarely on the dangers and demands of the particular situation also seems more likely to produce rules which are intelligible to the police and the public alike than requiring the officer in the heat of an unfolding encounter on the street to make a judgment as to which laws are "of limited public consequence."

IgorGolovniov/Shutterstock.com

We thus decide nothing today concerning the constitutional propriety of an investigative "seizure" upon less than probable cause for purposes of "detention" and/or interrogation. Obviously, not all personal intercourse between policemen and citizens involves "seizures" of persons. Only when the officer, by means of physical force or show of authority, has in some way restrained the liberty of a citizen may we conclude that a "seizure" has occurred. We cannot tell with any certainty upon this record

Africa Studio/Shutterstock.com

whether any such "seizure" took place here prior to Officer McFadden's initiation of physical contact for purposes of searching Terry for weapons, and we thus may assume that, up to that point, no intrusion upon constitutionally protected rights had occurred.

The importance of the SCOTUS ruling in "stop and frisk" cannot be emphasized enough.

1. Reasonable suspicion to stop a pedestrian.
2. A "stop and frisk" is a limited pat down of a person to protect the officer – looking for weapons only.
3. The officer who conducts a "stop and frisk" must articulate why the pedestrian was stopped and why the officer reasonably believes the pedestrian is armed.

4. The exceptions of plain touch impact the feasibility for obtaining evidence lawfully.
5. The pedestrian stop, if the pedestrian reasonably believes they are not free to leave, implicates the 4th amendment.
6. The use of handcuffs or temporary restraint (i.e., placing the person in the rear of the patrol vehicle) is not equated to an arrest.

PROBABLE CAUSE AND REASONABLE SUSPICION

In order for the police to lawfully stop a person or motor vehicle, the officer must explain the "reasonable suspicion" for such an intrusion on a citizen's right to be free from unreasonable search and seizure.

Reasonable suspicion—more than a hunch, less than probable cause. An exact definition is not known. Perhaps, the following may be used for guidance; "facts and rational inferences that would lead a reasonable officer (with comparable training and experience) to believe criminal activity is afoot."

Probable Cause

The 4th Amendment provides that "no warrants shall issue, but upon probable cause." The Constitution doesn't furnish any definition of "probable cause," leaving that task to the Supreme Court, which has also applied the probable cause standard to certain warrantless activities.

The term "reasonable suspicion" is not of constitutional derivation but was fashioned by the court to describe a level of suspicion lower than probable cause. The court has struggled to provide meaningful definitions of both terms, and law enforcement officers have likewise struggled to understand and apply the court's vague, general pronouncements. In *Ornelas v. U.S.*, the court acknowledged the problem:

> *Articulating precisely what "reasonable suspicion" and "probable cause" mean is not possible. They are commonsense, non-technical conceptions that deal with the factual and practical considerations of everyday life on which reasonable and prudent men, not legal technicians, act. As such, the standards are not readily, or even usefully, reduced to a neat set of legal rules. (Ornelas v. U.S.)*

Though it may not be possible to articulate precisely what "probable cause" means, the court has offered this guidance:

Probable cause does not require the same type of specific evidence of each element of the offense as would be needed to support a conviction. (Adams v. Williams).

Finely-tuned standards, such as proof beyond a reasonable doubt or by a preponderance of the evidence, useful in formal trials, have no place in the probable cause decision. (Maryland v. Pringle).

The rule of probable cause is a practical, nontechnical conception affording the best compromise that has been found for accommodating often opposing interests. (Beck v. Ohio).

The process does not deal with hard certainties, but with probabilities. Long before the law of probabilities was articulated as such, practical people formulated certain commonsense conclusions about human behavior; jurors as fact-finders are permitted to do the same-and so are law enforcement officers. (U.S. v. Cortez).

Gustavo Frazao/Shutterstock.com

We have held that probable cause means a 'fair probability.' (U.S. v. Sokolow).

Whether an arrest is valid depends upon whether, at the moment the arrest was made, the officers had probable cause to make it-whether at that moment the facts and circumstances within their knowledge and of which they had reasonably trustworthy information were sufficient to warrant a prudent man in believing that the person to be arrested had committed or was committing an offense (Beck v. Ohio).

Probable cause - Perhaps, the following may be used for guidance; "facts and rational circumstances that would lead a reasonable officer (with comparable training and experience) to believe a crime has been, is, or will be committed."

It was not until 1968, that the need for a standard lower than probable cause was recognized by the Supreme Court. In *Terry v. Ohio*, the court confronted defense challenges to both the detention of a robbery suspect and the weapons frisk that disclosed the gun he sought to suppress. The court noted that a temporary investigative detention is less of an infringement of a person's liberty than arresting him and taking him into custody. Therefore, said the court, police need not have as much justification for this lower level of restraint as the probable cause that would have been required to make an arrest. The court called this lower justification standard for detentions "reasonable suspicion."

> *This discussion shows why it is a mistake to use the expression "PC for the stop," which mismatches a higher level of justification with a lower level of infringement of individual liberty. "In Terry v. Ohio, we held that the police can stop and briefly detain a person for investigative purposes if the officer has a reasonable suspicion supported by articulable facts that criminal activity is afoot, even if the officer lacks probable cause." U.S. v. Sokolow, 490 U.S. 1 (1989).*

> *As with the concept of "probable cause," the lower standard of "reasonable suspicion" was not easily defined. "The concept of reasonable suspicion, like probable cause, is not readily or even usefully reduced to a neat set of legal rules," but "the level of suspicion required for a Terry stop is obviously less demanding than that for probable cause." U.S. v. Sokolow, 490 U.S. 1 (1989).*

> *"Reasonable suspicion is a less demanding standard than probable cause not only in the sense that reasonable suspicion can be established with information that is different in quantity or content than that required to establish probable cause, but also in the sense that reasonable suspicion can arise from information that is less reliable than that required to show probable cause" Alabama v. White, 496 U.S. 325 (1990).*

NeydtStock/Shutterstock.com

Probable Cause

Over the years, the Supreme Court has tried to describe the level of suspicion that would amount to probable cause, but it has always done so in general wording that leaves it up to courts to apply, case by case. In a 1949 opinion, the court said this about zprobable cause:

> *The rule of probable cause is a practical, nontechnical conception. In dealing with probable cause, we deal with probabilities. These are not technical; they are the factual and practical considerations of everyday life on which reasonable and prudent men, not legal technicians, act. Probable cause exists where the facts and circumstances within the officers' knowledge and of which they have reasonably trustworthy information are sufficient in themselves to warrant a man of reasonable caution in the belief that an offense has been or is being committed. Brinegar v. U.S., 338 U.S. 160 (1949).*

> *Perhaps the central teaching of our decisions bearing on the probable cause standard is that it is a practical, nontechnical conception. The process does not deal with hard certainties, but with probabilities. The evidence must be seen and weighed not in terms of library analysis by scholars, but as understood by those versed in the field of law enforcement. Probable cause is a fluid concept, turning on the assessment of probabilities in particular factual contexts-not readily, or even usefully, reduced to a neat set of legal rules. Illinois v. Gates, 462 U.S. 213, 103 (1983).*

> *The probable-cause standard is incapable of precise definition or quantification into percentages because it deals with probabilities and depends on the totality of the circumstances. The substance of all the definitions of probable cause is a reasonable ground for belief of guilt, and that the belief of guilt must be particularized with respect to the person to be searched or seized. Maryland v. Pringle, 540 U.S. 366 (2003).*

bikeriderlondon/Shutterstock.com

Probable Cause for Arrest

Probable cause for arrest exists when facts and circumstances within the police officer's knowledge would lead a reasonable person to believe that the suspect has committed, is committing, or is about to commit a crime. Probable cause must come from specific facts and circumstances, rather than simply from the officer's hunch or suspicion.

"Detentions" short of arrest do not require probable cause. Such temporary detentions require only "reasonable suspicion." This includes car stops, pedestrian stops, and detention of occupants while officers execute a search warrant. "Reasonable suspicion" means specific facts which would lead a reasonable person to believe criminal activity was at hand and further investigation was required.

Weeks v. United States, 232 U.S. 383 (1914)

Under the 4th Amendment, Federal courts and officers are under such limitations and restraints in the exercise of their power and authority as to forever secure the people, their persons, houses, papers, and effects against all unreasonable searches and seizures under the guise of law.

The 4th Amendment is not directed to individual misconduct of state officers. Its limitations reach the Federal Government and its agencies. *Boyd v. United States*, 116 U.S. 616 (1886).

In *United States v. Cortez*, 449 U.S. 411 (1981), a unanimous Court attempted to capture the "elusive concept" of the basis for permitting a stop. Officers must have "articulable reasons" or "founded suspicions," derived from the totality of the circumstances. "Based upon that whole picture the detaining officer must have a particularized and objective basis for suspecting the particular person stopped of criminal activity." Id. at 417–418. The inquiry is thus quite fact-specific. In the anonymous tip context, the same basic approach requiring some corroboration applies regardless of whether the standard is probable cause or reasonable suspicion; the difference is that less information, or less reliable information, can satisfy the lower standard. *Alabama v. White*, 496 U.S. 325 (1990).

Brown v. Texas, 443 u.s. 47 (1979) (individual's presence in high crime area gave officer no articulable basis to suspect him of crime); *Delaware v. Prouse*, 440 u.s. 648 (1979) (reasonable suspicion of a license or registration violation is necessary to authorize automobile stop; random stops impermissible); *United States v. Brignoni-Ponce*, 422 U.S. 873 (1975) (officers could not justify random automobile stop solely on basis of Mexican appearance of occupants); *Reid v. Georgia*, 448 U.S. 438 (1980) (no reasonable suspicion for airport stop based on appearancethat suspect and another passenger were trying to conceal the fact that they were traveling together). But cf. *United States v. Martinez-Fuerte*, 428 U.S. 543 (1976) (halting vehicles at fixed checkpoints to question occupants as to citizenship and immigration status permissible, even if officers should act on basis of appearance of occupants).

United States v. Mendenhall, 446 U.S. 544, 554 (1980) (opinion of Justice Stewart) ("[A] person has been 'seized' within the meaning of the 4th Amendment only if, in view of all the circumstances surrounding the incident, a reasonable person would have believed that he was not free to leave"). See also *Reid v. Georgia*, 448 U.S. 438 (1980); *United States v. Brignoni-Ponce*, 422 U.S. 873, 878 (1975); *Terry v. Ohio*, 392 U.S. 1, 16–19 (1968); *Kaupp v. Texas*, 538 U.S. 626 (2003). Apprehension by the use of deadly force is a seizure subject to the 4th Amendment's reasonableness requirement. See, for example, *Tennessee v. Garner*, 471 U.S. 1 (1985) (police officer's fatal shooting of a fleeing suspect); *Brower v. County of Inyo*, 489 U.S. 593 (1989) (police roadblock designed to end car chase with fatal crash). *Scott v. Harris*, 550 U.S. 372 (2007) (police officer's ramming fleeing motorist's car from behind in attempt to stop him).

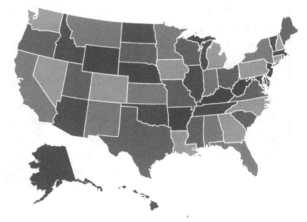

The Terry Court recognized in dictum that "not all personal intercourse between policemen and citizens involves 'seizures' of persons," and suggested that "[o]nly when the officer, by means of physical force or show of authority, has in some way restrained the liberty of a citizen may we conclude that a 'seizure' has occurred."

Vertes Edmond Mihai/Shutterstock.com

KEY CONCEPTS

- **Jurisdiction**—the geographical area in which a law enforcement officer is employed. The extent of the enforcement action available to the officer; that is, federal statutes, state statutes, local, and so on.
- **Justification**—the necessity for the officer to explain why they did whatever they did. Examples: stop a pedestrian, stop a motor vehicle, pat down a person, search a person or vehicle or a place, make an arrest, perform an investigation, question a person.

- **Use of force**—any interaction with a person other than nonresistant handcuffing, guiding someone with touch or other such "normal" activities. Anything above the "norm" is considered a use of force. In some agencies, an officer pointing their firearm at someone is considered a use of force (more on that later).
- **Reasonable Suspicion**— is less than probable cause, the legal standard for arrests and warrants, but more than an "inchoate and unparticularized suspicion or 'hunch'"; *Terry v. Ohio*, 392 U.S. 1, 27 (1968). It must be based on "specific and articulable facts," "taken together with rational inferences from those facts," *Terry v. Ohio*, 392 U.S., at 21(1968) and the suspicion must be associated with the specific individual. *Ybarra v. Illinois*, 444 U.S. 85, 91 (1979). Evaluation is based upon the "reasonable person" or "reasonable officer" standard, *Terry v. Ohio*, 392 U.S., at 21–22 (1968) in which a reasonable officer in the same circumstances could reasonably suspect a person has been, is, or is about to be engaged in criminal activity; it depends upon the totality of circumstances, and can result from a combination of particular facts.
- **Probable Cause**—articulable facts and circumstances that would lead a reasonable person to believe a crime has, is, or will occur. Although the 4th Amendment states that "no warrants shall issue, but upon probable cause," it does not specify what "probable cause" actually means. The Supreme Court has attempted to clarify the meaning of the term on several occasions, while recognizing that probable cause is a concept that is imprecise, fluid, and very dependent on context. In *Illinois v. Gates*, the Court favored a flexible approach, viewing probable cause as a "practical, non-technical" standard that calls upon the "factual and practical considerations of everyday life on which reasonable and prudent men, not legal technicians, act." *Illinois v. Gates*, 462 U.S. 213, 232 (1983).

Fresnel/Shutterstock.com

Investigatory detention

In *United States v. Cortez*, 449 U.S. 411 (1981), a unanimous Court attempted to capture the "elusive concept" of the basis for permitting a stop. Officers must have "articulable reasons" or "founded suspicions," derived from the totality of the circumstances. "Based upon that whole picture the detaining officer must have a particularized and objective basis for suspecting the particular person stopped of criminal activity." *Id.* at 417-18. The inquiry is thus quite fact-specific. In the anonymous tip context, the same basic approach requiring some corroboration applies regardless of whether the standard is probable cause or reasonable suspicion; the difference is that less information, or less reliable information, can satisfy the lower standard. *Alabama v. White,* 496 U.S. 325 (1990).

A Terry search need not be limited to a stop and frisk of the person but may extend as well, to a protective search of the passenger compartment of a car if an officer possesses "a reasonable belief, based on specific and articulable facts . . . that the suspect is dangerous and . . . may gain immediate control of weapons." *Michigan v. Long,* 463 U.S. 1032 (1983). How lengthy a Terry detention may be varying with the circumstances. In approving a 20-minute detention of a driver made necessary by the driver's own evasion of drug agents and a state police decision to hold the driver until the agents could arrive on the scene, the Court indicated that it is "appropriate to examine whether the police diligently pursued a means of investigation that was likely to confirm or dispel their suspicions quickly, during which time it was necessary to detain the defendant." *United States v. Sharpe,* 470 U.S. 675, 686 (1985).

Exceptions to a warrant

There are numerous occasions where circumstances override the need to obtain a warrant for an arrest or a search.

If an officer observes a criminal act, the officer may arrest on sight. Common law dictates if a felony or crime occurs in one's presence, a citizen can make an arrest. Logically, police would have the same right. However, for most misdemeanors and disorderly person offenses, police can act on information and belief, whereas, a citizen cannot act on information and belief.

Barring actually observing a crime in progress, there are some exceptions to the requirement of a warrant. The following circumstances are valid only if the police are lawfully present and accomplishing a valid, law enforcement function.

Gustavo Frazao/Shutterstock.com

1. Plain sight—if the police can see evidence of a crime readily, without manipulation of anything. The use of a flashlight is considered part of plain sight. In most cases, the use of a K-9 sniff is considered plain sight (observing the K-9 "hit" on something).
2. Plain smell—if the police can smell evidence. Example, walking up to a lawfully stopped vehicle the officer smells the odor of burnt marijuana.
3. Plain touch—if the police are lawfully performing a pat-down and can readily identify an object as contraband, in an area where it was lawful to pat-down for weapons.

Eviart/Shutterstock.com

4. Plain hearing—if the police can hear the destruction of evidence, someone in danger, and so on.
5. Exigent circumstances—if the police have an immediate need to preserve life or evidence. Example, police are responding to a 911 call for help and hear a person in the residence reported on the call yelling for help. Remember, some of the exceptions cross each other.
6. Hot pursuit—in some cases the police can continue chasing a person into a structure.
7. Consent—as long as the person is informed they do not have to provide consent, can stop the search at any time, the consent is completely voluntary and the person is free to leave at any time.

DETAILING WARRANTLESS SEARCHES AND SEIZURES

The 4th Amendment of the United States Constitution fortifies the personal privacy of its citizenry. The 4th Amendment is the safeguard, the front-line defender for unreasonable intrusion by the government into personal affairs. The 4th Amendment reads,

The right of the people to be secure in their persons, houses, papers, and effects, against unreasonable searches and seizures, shall not be violated, and no Warrants shall issue, but upon probable cause, supported by Oath or affirmation, and particularly describing the place to be searched, and the persons or things to be seized. (Bill of Rights, 1789)

When the police seize or search without prior judicial approval, the police intrusion is *per se* "unreasonable" and shifts the burden of proof on the State to justify why the search was conducted (*Katz v. United States*, 389 U.S. 347 1967). Under such an examination required by Katz, the State must prove whether the police action was "reasonable" to validate a warrantless search.

Commonly, "The police must, whenever practical, obtain advance judicial approval of searches and seizures through the warrant procedure" (*Terry v. Ohio*, 392 U.S. 1 1968). In reality, most searches and seizures conducted by the police are, in fact, warrantless. How can this be? The 4th Amendment guards against warrantless searches/seizures by requiring police to have a valid search warrant granted by a detached magistrate, right? No, the 4th Amendment guards citizens against "unreasonable" searches and seizures. The burden on the officer, prosecutor, the State, is to prove; in light of the circumstances, the search satisfies the "reasonableness" requirement of the 4th Amendment.

So, if the police can search without a warrant, what are those "reasonable" circumstances? There are allowances or "exceptions" to the warrant requirement, which have been meted out and recognized by the court as valid police procedures that uphold the protections delivered by the 4th Amendment. The exceptions to the warrant requirement are akin to police functioning on the street; lawyers disputing constitutionality, and judges making decisions that form acceptable police practice. The disputes and subsequent rulings are a "gray area" and the point of much contention. The debates shape as personal freedom is balanced against safety, security, and the rule of law. Much case law precedence spawns from warrantless search/seizure encounters. Time and again, warrantless search/seizures are argued in courts across the United States of America in motions to suppress evidence. Here are some of those instances:

PLAIN VIEW

What's more basic than seeing something with your own eyes? Enhance the circumstances of a casual spectator and presume the witness is a trained, professional law enforcement officer. Either way, the onlooker sees criminality in the form of contraband (illegal substance) or criminal behavior. Would it be "reasonable" to search a person, motor vehicle, or dwelling when a police officer observes the unlawful material firsthand and has the ability to recover the evidence immediately?

The Courts have endorsed "plain view" exceptions to the warrant requirement of the 4th Amendment. Plain view guidelines are currently focused on two fundamental requirements.

1. The law enforcement agent must be legitimately in the viewing space and nothing was manipulated by the law enforcement officer to allow such viewing.
2. The law enforcement agent's observation of the article must deliver probable cause to believe the material is related with criminal actions (*Arizona v. Hicks*, 480 U.S. 321, 107 S.Ct. 1149, 94 L. Ed.2d 347 (1987).

PLAIN TOUCH

"Plain touch" seems a little more invasive than "plain view." It should, because it is. Plain touch doctrine spawns off the *Terry v. Ohio* decision to allow a search when contraband is immediately apparent in a pat down (Terry frisk). Plain touch requirements are outlined in *Minnesota v. Dickerson*, 508 U.S. 306 (1993). The requirements supplement the "plain view" doctrine; allowing the officer to move further in the action of a frisk, when the "touch" leads to probable cause of unlawful activity. So, what leads an officer to move further after the "Terry Frisk" and what are the lawful requirements of these searches? It is important to remember a "Terry Frisk" relies on the law enforcement agent's ability to articulate the reasoning for the "stop and frisk." The most generally accepted reasoning for a "stop and frisk" is the search for weapons. The law enforcement officer must explain why, in light of the circumstances, he or she believed the suspect was armed with a weapon.

Kheng Guan Toh/Shutterstock.com

One must have a reasonable belief, based on training and experience (much like Detective Martin McFadden in *Terry v. Ohio*), the suspect being encountered is armed with a weapon. Pat downs or "frisks" are not authorized to search for evidence (unless the evidence is a weapon). Therefore:

1. As previously discussed in the plain view exception, the law enforcement agent must be rightfully in the touching space.
2. The law enforcement agent must be legally in the touching area.
3. When the law enforcement agent touches the object, it must be immediately apparent there is probable cause to connect the material with criminal action.

SEARCH INCIDENT TO ARREST

You're locked up. Let's assume it's a lawful arrest. Are the police going to "run your pockets?" Yes, they are. Search incident to an arrest is an exception to the warrant requirement:

1. In the event of a lawful arrest, the officer is allowed to avert danger by removing any object that may be used to attack the officer.
2. Also, under a lawful arrest, the officer is permitted to search for the purpose of impeding the destruction evidence for which the defendant has been arrested.

Searches incident to arrest are not commonly contentious. Clashes on this exception revolve around the "scope of the search" as it applies to motor vehicles and articles close in proximity to the arrestee. Additionally, the right to arrest must precede the searching of a person. Simply, the courts do not suggest the person must be in physical custody (handcuffed). Meaning, if an officer has probable cause to arrest a person and searches prior to physical detention, the items or contraband recovered as a result of the search would be admissible in court for additional charges; a valid search incident to arrest.

CONSENT SEARCHES

Consent searches are a common form of the warrantless search in the United States. A police officer may ask a citizen for the right to search them or their property. Generally, for a citizen to consent to a search from law enforcement, the permission must be knowingly, voluntarily, and intelligently as highlighted in *Schneckloth v. Bustamonte*, 412 U.S. 218 (1973).

Billion Photos/Shutterstock.com

To be knowing and intelligent, proofs must be provided be the State to support that the person had a choice in the decision. Essentially, the consenting person must understand they had the right to refuse the search and invoke the shelter of the 4th Amendment. In reality, the officer is asking for permission to search for convenience or he or she doesn't have probable cause for the granting of a search warrant.

Federally, law enforcement does not need reasonable suspicion to ask for the consent to search. The same exists in the State of New Jersey for asking to search private homes, businesses, college residences, and so on. (*State v. Domicz*, 188 N.J. 285, 302 2006). However, New Jersey restricts law enforcement officers in the area of consent searches as it applies to motor vehicles. New Jersey courts have ruled that in motor vehicle stops, the circumstances must rise to the legal standard of "reasonable suspicion" for an officer to ask a driver to consent to the search of their vehicle (*State v. Carty*, 170 N.J. 632, 2002). The State Supreme Court of New Jersey injected the reasonable suspicion requirement for consent searches of motor vehicles for what they felt was an abuse of law enforcement, specifically racial profiling on the roadways. Racial-profiling, specifically within New Jersey with the New Jersey State Police, will be discussed in a later chapter. The courts acknowledged in the *Domicz* decision, the apparent problems associated with motor vehicle stops were not insidious during consent searches of persons, dwellings, and so on.

Ultimately, a valid consent search must be free of coercion and the person consenting to the search must be explained they have the right to refuse. Additionally, the person can request the search to be stopped at any time.

EXIGENT CIRCUMSTANCES

What is an "exigent circumstance," and why does it strip away my blanket of protection under the 4th Amendment? Exigent conditions surface when police respond to emergencies and make warrantless access. Police enter and search when they "reasonably" believe a person needs emergent aid or when the police believe a suspect for a crime is still at the location of the search/entry. The home is sacred, and the search of it must be "unreasonable," unless there's *exigency* (Scalia, 1989). Exigent circumstances in the courts have meant:

1. Imminent threat to life
2. Imminent and serious threat to property
3. Imminent escape of a suspect
4. Imminent destruction of evidence

If you understand that "imminent" means (about to happen right now), then the above listed circumstances appear to be reasonable exceptions to the warrant requirement. It's important to grasp this viewpoint; there is no latitude in emergency circumstances. The situation is either exigent or it's not. It's an imminent and emergent situation or it's not. If the police have alternatives, where authentic exigency does not exist, then the police must operate alternatively with other methods. When exigency is lacking, applying for a search warrant or meeting another threshold for an exception would be required.

EMERGENCY AID DOCTRINE

One of the most common of exigent circumstances is known as the "Emergency Aid Doctrine." To excuse warrantless entry for emergency aid, the officer must have a reasonable and objective basis to believe an emergency exists and immediate action is required to protect life and persons from serious injury (*Brigham City v. Stuart*, 547 U.S. 298, 2006).

The officer must not enter or search principally for the aspiration to collect evidence of crime. The gathering of compelling evidence cannot be a factor under the exigent search exception.

Lastly, there must be a "nexus" or link between the areas entered or searched under the "Emergency Aid Doctrine" (*United States v. Goldenstein*, 456 F.2d 1001, 1009, 8th Cir. 1972).

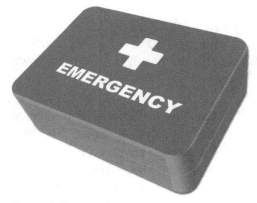

photopixel/Shutterstock.com

It is important to note, that while the entry and search to provide aid is allowed, when the emergency dissolves or is quelled by officer assistance, the legality of warrantless presence also disbands. All police activity from the point when the emergency is under control will not fall under a warrantless search exception.

MOTOR VEHICLE EXCEPTION

When is the United States citizen most exposed from the protections of the 4th Amendment, besides in a public area? A citizen has much less expectation of privacy in a motor vehicle. How is this possible? I own this vehicle; it's my property, just as my home, apartment or backpack. Why do my rights erode while I'm driving my car? Here's what the U.S. Supreme Court thinks about your rights while driving:

In *Carroll v. United States*, 267 U.S. 132 (1925), the motor vehicle exception to the warrant was born. The Carroll Doctrine provides if a police officer has *probable cause* to believe a vehicle has evidence of a crime or contraband located inside of it, a search of the vehicle is permissible without a warrant. The reasoning is built on the vehicle's mobility (it's not a fixed object on a piece of land), allowing it to be removed from the jurisdiction of the officer where the warrant may be obtained. Secondly, the courts believe people have a reduced expectation of privacy in a vehicle.

The motor vehicle exception on the federal level requires two thresholds to be met.

1. The law enforcement officer must have probable cause to believe inside the vehicle contains evidence of a crime or contraband.
2. The vehicle must be capable of ready movement.

Frontpage/Shutterstock.com

The important concept to understand in the motor vehicle exception is the introduction of probable cause into the search scenario; such as previously presented during an arrest setting. The probable cause requirement for search is the same as arrest. Probable cause occurs when facts and circumstances within the police officer's knowledge would lead a reasonable officer to believe that the suspect has committed, is committing, or is about to com-

Andrey_Popov/Shutterstock.com

mit a crime (odor of marijuana emanating from the interior of a vehicle). *United States v. Ross*, 102 S.Ct. 2157 (1982) broadened the *Carroll* decision to include every part of the motor vehicle and its contents (packages, containers, etc.).

Under the exceptions listed earlier and others not visited here, the police are able to enforce the law under the "reasonableness" requirement of the 4th Amendment. Much police works gets done under the warrantless search exceptions, which requires the police to be sharp with their senses and meticulous on detail in report writing. To meet the "reasonableness" requirement, the facts and circumstances must be effectively communicated in report narratives and orally in court.

The idea of Miranda warnings

Do you know the Miranda warnings? Most people believe they do. Why? It was on a television show or a movie, so it must be real. So, when do the police have an obligation to provide Miranda warnings?

Discuss the following scenario:

Officer Smith observes Johnny the drug dealer walking down Main Street. Officer Smith has just confirmed an arrest warrant is active for Johnny. Officer Smith approaches Johnny, grabs Johnny's arm and tells Johnny he is under arrest. Johnny protests, but complies with Officer Smith (wow, use of force stops here; imagine that) and is handcuffed. Officer Smith searches Johnny and places Johnny in the rear °of the patrol car. Officer Smith transports Johnny directly to the county jail. Johnny asks Officer Smith why is he under arrest. Officer Smith just smiles and continues to transport Johnny to the jail. Officer Smith follows the intake procedures and turns Johnny over to the jail staff.

© Everett Collection/Shutterstock

Did Officer Smith violate Johnny's constitutional rights? Did Officer Smith have an obligation to read Johnny the Miranda Warnings? Officer Smith never told Johnny why he was placed under arrest. No phone call, nothing but a smile and ride to jail.

Did Officer Smith do anything wrong?

Answers:
Officer Smith, although he probably should explain to Johnny why he placed him under arrest, has no legal obligation to do so. Therefore, no violations of Johnny's constitutional rights occurred.

Officer Smith had no obligation to read Johnny the Miranda Warnings. Discuss why Johnny was not entitled to the Miranda Warnings. Simply, Johnny was never questioned. Further discuss when during or prior to questioning must the Miranda Warnings be read.

The Miranda Warnings
According to the New Jersey Attorney General's Office are as follows

1. You have the right to remain silent.
2. Anything you say can and will be used against you in a court of law.
3. You have the right to talk to a lawyer and have him present with you while you are being questioned.

4. If you cannot afford to hire a lawyer, one will be appointed to represent you before any questioning, if you wish.
5. You can decide at any time to exercise these rights and not answer any questions or make any statements.
6. Do you understand each of these rights I have explained to you?
7. Having these rights in mind, do you wish to talk to us now?

The aforementioned seven statements must be read, word by word; usually from a Miranda Warnings card issued by the Attorney General of the state. Federally, the U.S. Attorney General's Office issues the Miranda Warnings, which are to be read by Federal law enforcement.

What if a suspect makes a statement prior to being asked any questions by the police? Oh well, it is called a spontaneous statement and is fair game for court. Law enforcement agents are advised to ask the suspect to stop and read the suspect the Miranda Warnings.

The Miranda Warnings only apply to questioning a suspect or someone who becomes a suspect about the crime(s) that is being investigated or suspected.

There is no constitutional right to Miranda. The Miranda Warnings encompass the 5th and 6th Amendments to the Constitution.

A police officer can ask a person identification questions without Miranda. General questions concerning the activity of a person, but not if those questions directly relate to a crime they are known to be a suspect.

Discuss the following scenario:

Officer Smith is on the midnight shift in Anytown, USA. Officer Smith is assigned vehicle patrol. At 3 a.m., Officer Smith is notified from dispatch a burglar alarm is activated at a local sport clothing store. An additional unit is dispatched to respond with Officer Smith to the location of the store. The other officer arrives and radios to Officer Smith three unknown persons were running northbound on Main Street upon the other officer's arrival at the alarm. Officer Smith happens to be traveling southbound on Main Street and observes three persons running along the sidewalk. Officer Smith stops and tells the three people to stop. (Does Officer Smith have reasonable suspicion to stop these people?) The three stop running and Officer Smith asks them why are they running down Main Street at 3 a.m. and why would they begin to run when the other officer arrived at the store with the alarm sounding. (Does Officer Smith need to read each of the three persons the Miranda Warnings?) One of the people states they got scared when they heard the alarm and saw the police car arrive. Officer Smith, now with some backup officers ask the three people to sit for a moment. Officer Smith steps away from the three persons and calls the officer at the store. The officer at the store tells Officer Smith the front window was broken, and it appears several sports jerseys are missing from the front display. Officer Smith goes back to the three people (Have the people been lawfully detained?) and takes a long look at them. Officer Smith notices what appear to be broken glass pieces on two of the three people he stopped. Further, Officer Smith notices what appears to be a sports jersey sticking a bit out of the pants of one of the stopped people. Officer Smith asks that person, what is sticking out of your pants (Does Miranda apply here?). The person answers it was an extra shirt they carry. Officer Smith asks to see the shirt (Is this in violation of Miranda, in violation of a pedestrian's rights during a stop?) The person complies and hands Officer Smith the sports shirt. Officer Smith notices a price tag attached to the shirt and this tag has the name of the store in which the alarm sounded, had the front glass broken and what appeared to be missing shirts from the front display.

(Does Officer Smith have reasonable suspicion or probable cause now?) Should Officer Smith ask the three persons anything more or is Miranda now applicable? Would you make an arrest or question them further?

Answers:

Officer Smith now has probable cause to believe a crime has occurred.

Since Officer Smith now has probable cause to believe the three persons were involved in the burglary, any questions relating to the burglary are now protected under the constitution. Therefore, an arrest is warranted and questioning about the burglary should cease.

Marie Kanger Born/Shutterstock.com

Easy, isn't it? Now, the aforementioned scenario was not dynamic, not filled with violence and making a split-second decision of how much force to use and what to do. However, the need to know when it is lawful to stop someone, what can be asked, when Miranda applies, when to make an arrest are all present. A police officer is faced with decisions everyday about potentially violating someone's constitutional rights. When we examine use of force, it is never routine. Each and every situation can become dangerous, in fact, deadly for the officer and/or the suspect(s). A solid foundation of the principles of law is extremely important. Knowledge prevents hesitation. When dealing with force, particularly deadly force, hesitation can be fatal for the officer.

Use of Force Criteria

The building blocks for a use of force can be seen as demonstrated by the New Jersey Attorney General's Guidelines on Use of Force.

Never listed as "steps" but as building blocks to sound decisions and judgement. However, we list them in the following for ease of discussion, we briefly describe them here:

1. Constructive Force—Just the officer's presence, particularly in uniform is constructive force. Although some agencies disagree, an officer (who is justified) pointing a firearm at someone is constructive force. Verbal commands, warnings, gestures, and so on are all constructive force. Not physical contact.
2. Physical Contact—procedural contact with a subject, necessary to accomplish a law enforcement objective; guiding a subject into a vehicle, holding subject's arm while escorting, handcuffing, maneuvering for a pat down are all examples. Note—some agencies place pepper spray (OC Spray) between physical contact and using physical force.
3. Physical Force—contact beyond what is generally used to effect an arrest or other objective, employed to overcome subject's physical resistance, to protect persons or property; grabbing someone, arm lock, striking are examples.
4. Mechanical Force—use of some device or chemical substance (pepper spray/OC is not a chemical), however, some agencies consider pepper spray/OC as mechanical force. These tools are used to overcome subject's resistance; use of a baton, chemical spraying, a canine bite are examples of mechanical force.
5. Deadly Force—Force used with the purpose of causing or which the officer knows to create a substantial risk of causing death or serious bodily harm. Purposely firing at or in the direction of another person, vehicle, building or structure in which another person is believed to be are examples of deadly force.

Key Terms

- **Reasonable Belief**—an objective assessment that is based on how a reasonable officer with comparable training and experience would react or draw inferences from. This assessment is made by facts and circumstances known by the officer at the scene. As you may recall from the Graham decision; officers are often forced to make split second decisions in circumstances that may be tense, unpredictable and rapidly evolving.

pio3/Shutterstock.com

- **Reasonable Force**—Officers can only use reasonable force to accomplish a valid, lawful law enforcement objective. All the events transpiring during the officer's interaction with the subject can be considered in evaluating reasonableness of force used. The use of force can change as circumstances change. "A passing risk to a police officer is not an ongoing license to kill an otherwise unthreatening suspect." (*ABRAHAM CNA v. RASO* 243 96 4884, U.S. 3rd Circuit decision on a New Jersey deadly force incident).

- **Escalation** and **De-Escalation**—An officer may increase or decrease use of force to accomplish a law enforcement objective. Police are not required to desist because the suspect resists. However, once the suspect submits, the officer must stop using force.

- **Imminent Danger**—Threatened actions or outcomes that may occur during an encounter. The threatened harm does not have to be instantaneous; example subject is carrying a weapon and running for cover.

Przemek Tokar/Shutterstock.com

- **Substantial Risk**—Disregard of a foreseeable likelihood that innocent persons will be endangered; firing a weapon into a confined space. When feasible, the officer should identify himself or herself, state purpose of officer's actions but need not do so if it would increase danger to officer or another person.
- **Protection of Property**—Before using physical or mechanical force, the officer should where feasible ask the person to desist unless:

The request would be useless, would be dangerous or substantial harm would be done to property.

Deadly force is not justified solely to protect property.

Use of deadly force:

When the officer reasonably believes it is immediately necessary to protect the officer or another person from imminent threat of death or serious bodily harm.

Factors to consider:

1. Ability—does the subject have physical capacity to cause injury, is there a weapon, is there an imminent threat to the officer or another.
2. Opportunity—does the subject have the opportunity to use his ability to injure or kill the officer or another person.
3. Jeopardy—does the combination of the subject's ability and opportunity provide the officer with a reasonable objective belief that the officer or another person is in imminent physical danger.

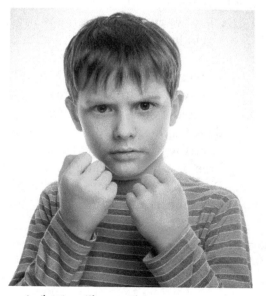

An officer will never be justified in the use of deadly force if the officer reasonably believes that an alternative is available. However, that does not mean an officer must exhaust all possibilities prior to engaging in deadly force, unless it was reasonable to do so.

An alternative is described as allowing the officer to achieve the law enforcement purpose at no increased risk to the officer or another person.

Deadly force is not justified against persons whose conduct is injurious only to

maxim ibragimov/Shutterstock.com

themselves. In New Jersey and some other jurisdictions, the use of less lethal weapons (those which discharge any projectile from a firearm is considered to be deadly force). Example, bean bag ammunition or rubber bullets. New Jersey, as of this writing, considers the Taser in this category and can only be employed if deadly force would be justified.

You may have seen it in the movies or television, but there are no warning shots. Totally against policy in the United States.

In addition, shooting at or from a moving vehicle is against policy unless the officer reasonably believes there exists an imminent threat of death or serious bodily harm to the officer or another person and there are no other means to avert or eliminate the danger. In fact, officers in New Jersey shall not fire a weapon solely to disable moving vehicles. The officer is required to move out of the way of an oncoming vehicle and should not intentionally place himself in the path or an oncoming vehicle.

- **Use of force report forms**—required by most agencies if anything beyond physical control is used. Some agencies place more stringent requirements in the reporting. We examine raw data in this regard later in the text.

Consequences for unconstitutional stops, unlawful search or seizures and excessive force: First and foremost, do not violate someone's Constitutional or Civil Rights. However, mistakes or lapse in judgement can happen. If so, depending on the severity of the infractions, the penalties can range from losing evidence in court to prison time. We briefly outline some of the consequences here:

- **Exclusionary Rule**—a remedy in which evidence against a suspect is suppressed or excluded from court proceedings. Examples of how this can occur:

1. Statements in violation of Miranda—confessions, answers to questions and other such verbal admissions may be excluded from evidence. Often, a case is then "tainted" and most other evidence is then not admissible. The doctrine "Fruits of the Poisonous Tree" is a perfect example.

2. Physical evidence gathered or found unlawfully will be excluded.

The U.S. Supreme Court in *DeShaney v. Winnebago County Dep't of Social Services*, #87–154, 489 U.S. 189 (1989), ruled that there is no Prath/Shutterstock.com general duty under federal civil rights law to protect individuals against private violence or provide police protection against injury in general. Exceptions have been made in some instances where a special relationship—such as having a person in custody, or very specific promises of protection that are reasonably relied on—or the existence of a "state-created danger" is found.

- **Suppression hearing**—A motion to suppress evidence provides relief to a citizen who has had their constitutional rights violated in gaining the evidence. Further, any unlawful evidence will render any subsequent finding of evidence unlawful.

   The defense attorney starts the motion to suppress evidence process by filing formal papers with the court before a trial begins. The prosecutor and defense counsel submit legal arguments in a brief. If there has been an arrest, the prosecutor files the first brief. The prosecutor's brief states the reason for each step taken by the police. The defense attorney responds with a brief explaining how the police violated the defendant's constitutional rights.

- **Civil Liability**—The overall issue of a civil "wrong." Usually, the remedy is compensation. However, under Title 42 U.S. Code § 1983 ("Section 1983"; Civil action for deprivation of rights) a provision for incarceration is present. Much more to discuss in later chapters under Title 42 U.S. Code § 1983 (Civil Liability) and Title 18 U.S. Code § 242 (Criminal Liability).

   In the next chapters, we discuss Federal and State liability claims. However, we must mention immunity. If the federal or state official is protected by immunity, then no civil nor criminal action can be taken against that official or the agency they work for.

IMMUNITY

There are several types of immunity in regard to federal and state civil liability.

1. Sovereign immunity
   Sovereign immunity prevents a sovereign state or person from being subjected to suit without its consent.
   The doctrine of sovereign immunity stands for the principle that a nation is immune from suit in the courts of another country. It was first recognized by U.S. courts in the case of *The Schooner Exchange v. M'Faddon*, 11 U.S. 116 (1812).
2. Governmental tort immunity

Sovereign immunity may also apply to federal, state, and local governments within the United States, protecting these governments from being sued without their consent. The idea behind domestic sovereign immunity—also called governmental tort immunity—is to prevent money judgments against the government, as such judgments would have to be paid with taxpayers' dollars. As an example, a private citizen who is injured by another private citizen who runs a red light generally may sue the other driver for negligence. But under a strict sovereign immunity doctrine, a private citizen who is injured by a city employee driving a city bus has no Cause of Action against the city unless the city, by ordinance, specifically allows such a suit.

Governmental tort immunity is codified at the federal level by the Federal Tort Claims Act (28 U.S.C.A. § 1291 [1946]), and most states and local governments have similar statutes. Courts and legislatures in many states have greatly restricted, and in some cases have abolished, the doctrine of governmental tort immunity.

3. Official immunity

    The doctrine of sovereign immunity has its roots in the law of feudal England and is based on the tenet that the ruler can do no wrong. Public policy grounds for granting immunity from civil lawsuits to judges and officials in the Executive Branch of government survive even today. Sometimes known as official immunity or absolute immunity, the doctrine was first supported by the U.S. Supreme Court in the 1871 case of *Bradley v. Fisher*, 80 U.S. 335. In Bradley, an attorney attempted to sue a judge because the judge had disbarred him. The Court held that the judge was absolutely immune from the civil suit because the suit had arisen from his judicial acts. The Court recognized the need to protect judicial independence and noted that malicious or improper actions by a judge could be remedied by Impeachment rather than by litigation.

    Twenty-five years later, in *Spalding v. Vilas*, 161 U.S. 483 (1896), the Court expanded the doctrine to include officers of the federal Executive Branch. In Spalding, an attorney brought a Defamation suit against the U.S. postmaster general, who had circulated a letter that criticized the attorney's motives in representing local postmasters in a salary dispute. At that time, the postmaster general was a member of the president's cabinet. The Court determined that the proper administration of public affairs by the Executive Branch would be seriously crippled by a threat of civil liability and granted the postmaster general absolute immunity from civil suit for discretionary acts within the scope of the postmaster's authority. Federal courts since Spalding have continued to grant absolute immunity—a complete bar to lawsuits, regardless of the official's motive in acting—to federal executive officials, so long as their actions are discretionary and within the scope of their official duties.

Members of Congress and state legislators are absolutely immune from civil lawsuits for their votes and official actions. The U.S. Supreme Court, in *Bogan v. Scott-Harris*, 523 U.S. 44 U.S. (1998), extended absolute immunity to local legislators (i.e., city council members, and county commissioners) when they act in their legislative, rather than administrative, capacities.

Prosecutors are absolutely immune for their actions during a trial or before a Grand Jury. However, during the investigatory phase, they are only granted qualified immunity. In *Kalina v. Fletcher*, 522 U.S. 118 (1997), the U.S. Supreme Court ruled that a prosecutor was not entitled to absolute immunity with respect to her actions in making an allegedly false statement of fact in an Affidavit supporting an application for an arrest warrant. Policy considerations that merited absolute immunity included both the interest in protecting a prosecutor from harassing litigation that would divert his or her time and attention from official duties and the interest in enabling him or her to exercise independent judgment when deciding which suits to bring and in conducting them in court. These considerations did not apply when a prosecutor became an official witness in swearing to a statement.

However, in *Conn v. Gabbert*, 526 U.S. 286 (1999), the U.S. Supreme Court held that prosecutors cannot be sued for having lawyers searched or for interfering with the ability to advise a client who is appearing before a grand jury. Prosecutors have a qualified immunity in this situation, based on the two-step analysis that the courts apply to qualified-immunity issues. Under this two-part test, an Executive Branch official will be granted immunity if (a) the constitutional right that allegedly has been violated was not clearly established; and (b) the officer's conduct was "objectively reasonable" in light of the information that the officer possessed at the time of the alleged violation. The qualified-immunity test is usually employed during the early stages of a lawsuit. If the standard is met, a court will dismiss the case (summary judgement).

bannosuke/Shutterstock.com

Police and prison officials may be granted qualified immunity. In *Hope v. Pelzer*, 536 U.S. 730 (2002), the U.S. Supreme Court held that Alabama prison officials were not eligible for qualified immunity because they were on notice that their conduct violated established law even in novel factual circumstances. The officials were on notice that tying a prisoner to a hitching post in the prison yard constituted Cruel and Unusual Punishment under the 8th Amendment. Prior court rulings and federal prison policies also made clear that law banning the practice had been clearly established. Therefore, the officials were not qualified for immunity.

In *Saucier v. Katz*, 533 U.S. 194 (2001), the U.S. Supreme Court applied the qualified-immunity test to a claim that a U.S. Secret Service Agent had used excessive force in removing a protester. The Court reasserted its general belief that law officers must be given the benefit of the doubt that they acted lawfully in carrying out their day-to-day activities. Moreover, one of the main goals of qualified immunity is to remove the defendant from the lawsuit as quickly as possible, thereby reducing legal costs. Justice Anthony Kennedy restated the principle that immunity is not a "mere defense" to liability but an "immunity from suit." Therefore, immunity issues must be resolved as early as possible. As to the first step, Kennedy agreed that the case revealed a "general proposition" that excessive force is contrary to the 4th Amendment. However, a more specific inquiry must take place to see whether a reasonable officer "would understand that what he is doing violates that right." As to this second step, Justice Kennedy rejected the idea that because the plaintiff and the officer disputed certain facts, there could be no short-circuiting of this step. He stated that the "concern of the immunity inquiry is to acknowledge that reasonable mistakes can be made as to the legal constraints on particular police conduct." Officers have difficulty in assessing the amount of force that is required in a particular circumstance. If their mistake as to "what the law requires is reasonable, however, the officer is entitled to the immunity defense."

4. Qualified immunity
"Qualified immunity balances two important interests—the need to hold public officials accountable when they exercise power irresponsibly and the need to shield officials from harassment, distraction, and liability when they perform their duties reasonably." *Pearson v. Callahan* (07-751). Specifically, it protects government officials from lawsuits alleging that they violated plaintiffs' rights, only allowing suits where officials violated a "clearly established" statutory or constitutional right. When determining whether or not a right was "clearly

established," courts consider whether a hypothetical reasonable official would have known that the defendant's conduct violated the plaintiff's rights. Courts conducting this analysis apply the law that was in force at the time of the alleged violation, not the law in effect when the court considers the case.

The granting of qualified immunity will be just cause for summary dismissal of claims against an officer. Much balances on "clearly established" law.

NEW JERSEY STATE LAW DISCUSSION POINTS

When a police officer engages in misconduct, the officer, supervising officer and the municipality may be subject to civil liability. City of Oklahoma *City v. Tuttle*, 471 U.S. 808, 85 L.Ed.2d 791, 105 S.Ct. 2427 (1985) (citing *Monell v. Department of Soc. Serv.*, 436 U.S. 658, 98 S.Ct. 2018, 56 L.Ed.2d 611 (1978)); *Schneider v. Simonini*, 163 N.J. 336, 361 (2000), cert. denied, ___U.S. ___, 69 U.S.L.W. 3399 (2001) (adopting "recklessness or deliberate indifference" standard for supervisor liability); *Wildoner v. Borough of Ramsey*, 162N.J. 375 (2000). The officer, supervisor and municipality may be subject to claims under 42 U.S.C.A.§ 1983and the New Jersey Tort Claims Act, N.J.S.A. 59:3-3. Schneider, 163 N.J. at 353; Wildoner, 162 N.J. at 385-87. A police officer may be qualifiedly immune from § 1983 liability if the officer can establish (1) the officer acted with probable cause, or (2) if no probable cause existed, "a reasonable police officer could have believed in its existence." *Kirk v. City of Newark*, 109 N.J. 173, 184 (1988), quoted in, Schneider, 163 N.J. at 355;

Wildoner, 162 N.J. at 389; *Connor v. Powell*, 162 N.J. 397, 408-09, cert. denied, 120 S.Ct. 2220, 147 L.Ed.2d 251 (2000). "The same standard of objective reasonableness that applies in § 1983 actions also governs questions of good faith arising under the Tort Claims Act." Wildoner, 162 N.J. at 387.

Liability arising from a motor vehicle accident, see *Tice v. Cramer*, 133 N.J. 347 (1993).

Here, the Supreme Court held that absent willful misconduct, a police officer is immune from injuries arising from the pursuit of a fleeing vehicle despite discretionary or ministerial negligence of the officer. This immunity also applies to injuries of third-party motorists when an officer responds to police calls. See also *Canico v. Hurtado*, 144 N.J. 361 (officer must establish "good faith" exception to immunity under Tort Claims Act, N.J.S.A. 59:3-3); *Fielder v. Stonack*, 141 N.J. 101.

Liability arising from false arrest, see *Connor v. Powell*, 162 N.J. 397.

In Connor, an officer arrested plaintiff for aggravated assault and possession of a weapon, a plastic fork. Finding no probable cause to arrest defendant, the Supreme Court reversed a dismissal of a § 1983 action for false arrest, false accusation and false imprisonment. See also *Plummer v. Department of Corrections*, 305 N.J. Super. 365 (App. Div. 1997) (finding of immunity for detaining person as suspected inmate).

Liability for failure to act, see *Suarez v. Dosky*, 171 N.J. Super. 1 (App. Div. 1979) (police liable for failure to escort stranded occupants at auto accident, where child and adult were struck and killed by passing vehicles), certif. denied, 82 N.J. 300 (1980). For failure to provide medical treatment, see *Del Tufo v. Township of Old Bridge*, 147 N.J. 90, 101 (1996) (the police have a reasonable duty of care to provide emergent medical assistance). It is plaintiff's burden to establish that the police were indifferent "to serious known medical needs." Id. The court found "common sense dictates that a police officer is not obligated to seek medical treatment for every arrestee involved in an automobile accident." Id. at 101. See also *Battista v. Olson*, 213 N.J. Super. 137 (App. Div. 1986) (officer's failure to provide prompt medical assistance despite knowing about defendant's perilous condition resulted in liability); *Hake v. Manchester Township*, 98 N.J.

Rainer Lesniewski/Shutterstock.com

Marsan/Shutterstock.com

302 (1985) (matter remanded for jury to consider if police's failure to provide prompt medical assistance to arrestee, who committed suicide, deprived the arrestee of a chance to be revived).

Liability under Domestic Violence Act, N.J.S.A. 2C:25-22, see Wildones, 162 N.J. at 387-89 (claim of false arrest and imprisonment in a husband-wife domestic violence situation); cf. *Campbell v. Campbell*, 294 N.J. Super. 18 (Law Div. 1996) (found liable for failure to make arrest under a domestic violence order). State law only provides for the State to indemnify police officers and pay for counsel fees in civil suits, not criminal suits. N.J.S.A. 59:10-1 et. seq; *Chasin v. Montclair State University*, 159 N.J. 418, 463-64 (1999) (citing *Helduser v. Kimmelman*, 191 N.J. Super. 493 (App. Div. 1983) (discretion of Attorney General to defend criminal actions)); *Querques v. City of Jersey City*, 198 N.J. Super. 566 (App. Div.) (where officer acquitted of criminal charges not arising from or incidental to official duties, officer not entitled to statutory reimbursement by the city for his legal fees and expenses), certif. denied, 101 N.J. 242 (1985).

THE USE OF FORCE

The U.S. Supreme Court addressed the topic of police use of deadly force in *Tennessee v. Garner*, 471 U.S. 1, 105 S.Ct. 1694, 85 L.Ed.2d 1 (1985). Garner states that the use of deadly force to apprehend a suspect is a "seizure" under the 4th Amendment and therefore requires a balancing test, assessing whether the totality of the circumstances justified the use of deadly force to seize the suspect. *Tennessee v. Garner*, 471 U.S. at 7-8, 105 S.Ct. at 1699. The use of deadly force to prevent escape of an unarmed criminal suspect is constitutionally unreasonable if the suspect poses no immediate threat to the officer or to others. Before using deadly force, the officer must have probable cause to believe that the suspect poses a threat of serious physical harm, either to the officer or to others and the use of deadly force must be necessary to prevent the escape, and state a warning if possible. 471 U.S. at 11-12, 105 S.Ct. at 1701. The use of deadly force is also permissible to prevent escape if the officer has "probable cause to believe that the suspect has committed a violent crime, involving the infliction or threatened infliction of serious physical harm." Id. Furthermore, deadly force cannot be justified solely to prevent the escape of an unarmed felon who poses no physical danger to himself or others, or solely on the basis that a felony, such as a nighttime burglary of a dwelling, has been committed. Id. at 21, 105 S.Ct. at 1706.

Police use of force in the performance of their duties is governed by N.J.S.A. 2C:3-7. Under the Code, deadly force is justified to prevent the escape of a criminal suspect if the officer makes known the purpose of the arrest, if feasible, and if the officer reasonably believes that such force creates "no substantial risk of injury to innocent persons"; the person is suspected of committing, attempting to commit or committed the crime of homicide, kidnaping, sexual assault, criminal sexual contact, aggravated sexual assault, aggravated criminal sexual contact, arson, robbery, burglary of a dwelling; and there is an imminent threat of deadly force to the officer or another. N.J.S.A. 2C:3-7. In 1989, the U.S. Supreme Court examined the police use of excessive force in the course of arrest. *Graham v. O'Connor*, 490 U.S. 386, 109 S.Ct. 1865, 104 L.Ed.2d 443 (1989). The use of excessive force is also analyzed under the 4th Amendment as a "seizure." Id.at 393-94, 109 S.Ct. at 1870-71 (1989).

The totality of the circumstances includes "the severity of the crime at issue, whether the suspect poses an immediate threat to the safety of the officers or others, and whether he is actively resisting arrest or attempting to evade arrest by flight." Id. at 396, 109 S.Ct. at 1871-72. See generally, *Abraham v. Raso*, 183 F. 3d 279 (3d Cir. 1999); *Groman v. Township of Manalapan*, 47 F. 3d 628 (3d Cir. 1995); *Hill v. Algor*, 85 F. Supp. 2d 391, 403 (D.N.J. 2000) (arrestee subject to 4th Amendment protection up to prearraignment); *Ridgeway v. City of Woolwich Township Police Dept.*, 924 F. Supp. 653 (D.N.J. 1996); cf. *Clark v. Buchko*, 936 F. Supp. 212 (D.N.J. 1996) (accidental shooting not seizure under 4th Amendment). In June of 2000, the New Jersey Attorney General issued a revision on the Use of Force policy in Directives to Police Enforcement. The Attorney General's policy directive places greater restrictions on police use of deadly force. The officer cannot use deadly force if the officer reasonably believes that an alternative exists to avert danger. The officer cannot use a firearm solely to disable a moving vehicle. The officer can only fire at a moving vehicle if there is an imminent danger of death or serious bodily injury, and it is the only means to eliminate the danger. The directive also sets up a protocol in an officer's show or unholstering of a firearm, placing a restriction of appropriate show of constructive authority. The directive also sets forth a reporting requirement upon the use of deadly force or when an injury results from a discharge of a firearm.

Summary

As one can see, the road to lawful searches, seizures, arrests, motor vehicle stops, pat downs, and many other law enforcement functions is mired in case law and evolving procedures to meet constitutional requirements. Therefore, if the law enforcement officer violates a citizen's constitutional right(s), consequences occur. Arrestees are let go, pretrial detainees are released, evidence is suppressed, cases compromised, credibility lost. Beyond all the arrest and trial consequences, beyond losing cases and credibility (which can lead to loss of employment for the law enforcement officer), the civil rights violations bring the most severe consequences one could ever imagine. In Chapter 4, we discuss civil liability. Suffice it to say, if a law enforcement officer is found guilty of civil rights violations, the consequences are monetary and possibly incarceration.

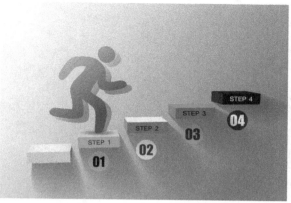

vector work/Shutterstock.com

Discussion Points

1. Should there be a requirement for a use of force "step ladder"? In effect, should police be required to exhaust all options prior to "moving on" to another force level?
   - Is deadly force always the final option for use of force? Should it be?
   - Should the police be required to remove themselves from a potentially dangerous situation involving a person suffering from a mental illness and call in mental health experts, prior to resorting to the use of force?
2. Often police perform warrantless searches and seizures. Do you believe the founders of the Constitution intended this?
   - Why should probable cause be a pivotal factor in a warrantless search/seizure?
   - Should verbal/written consent even be an exception to the warrant requirement?

This form must be completed and turned in for credit. No copies or other format will be accepted.

Student Name _____ Date _____

Course Section _____ Chapter _____

What is the prevailing case law regarding use of force and the violation of civil rights (2); discuss the case and include the four things officers must consider when using force, how does a jury and/or judge instructed to review use of force.

_____

_____

_____

_____

_____

_____

_____

_____

_____

_____

_____

_____

_____

_____

Student Name _____ Date _____

Course Section _____ Chapter _____

What SCOTUS case was the first to put a standard on lethal force; in considering the use of force, the officer must be able to specifically articulate what three things; for the use of force to be valid, the officer must be accomplishing what; when using force, the officer must use force that is the least amount for the situation – what are the three terms we used to define this amount of force?

_____

_____

_____

_____

_____

_____

_____

_____

_____

_____

_____

_____

_____

_____

LEGAL PRECEDENTS AND CASE LAW

Law is nothing else but the best reason of wise men applied for ages to the transactions and business of mankind.

—Abraham Lincoln

David Evison/Shutterstock.com

Key Terms

The U.S. Supreme Court, Legal Precedence, "Objective Reasonableness," Search, Seizure, Reasonable Suspicion, Custodial Interrogation, Exclusionary Rule, Totality of the Circumstances, *Weeks v. United States*, *Mapp v. Ohio*, *Miranda v. Arizona*

Learning Objectives

After exploring Chapter 3, the student will be able to:

1. Define the purpose of the U.S. Supreme Court.
2. Explain Legal Precedence.
3. Describe the "objective reasonableness standard" as applied to police use of force.
4. Describe the uniqueness of *Terry v. Ohio* regarding the establishment of reasonable articulable suspicion.
5. Define "custodial interrogation."
6. Explain the "totality of the circumstances relating to the training and experience of a police officer.

To harvest a true understanding of police use of force in America, we must review federal case law decisions that rule on basic and complex police behavior. These fundamental judgments guide police procedure nationwide providing guidance for departmental policy, prosecutors, judges, and the complete criminal justice structure. The final appellate court in the United States of America that rules on a variety of issues, including the legality of police behavior, is the Supreme Court of the United States of America. The Supreme Court takes cases typically connecting to the "constitutionality" of a certain issue that has been appealed from a lower court's original decision. Legal precedents are conclusions made in past that are appealed to when attempting to resolve a similar case. They provide a reason for deciding similar cases in the same manner (Landes & Posner, 1976). When the Supreme Court selects a case and renders a verdict, they set precedence above all courts in the nation. When a precedent is set on the federal level, State Supreme Courts and local benches must adapt their versions of comparable law to the decisions made by the Supreme Court of the United States (Tarr & Porter, 1988).

Examining the relevant cases of the past illustrates the precedence set for police procedure and ultimately demonstrates what is, and what is not "constitutional" regarding the use of force by police in America. There are many cases decided by the U.S. Supreme Court ruling on police behavior. Let's examine some of the milestones of police work, the distinctive cases and judgments that resonate in everyday policing and echo frequently in cities and small towns across the nation.

The following case descriptions can be viewed in their entirety from the Federal Law Enforcement Training Centers in at https://www.fletc.gov/legal-division-reference-book-pdf.

Graham v. Connor
490 U.S. 386, 109 S. Ct. 1865 (1989)

FACTS: Graham, a diabetic, felt the onset of an insulin reaction and desired to purchase some orange juice to counteract the reaction. Berry, a friend of the Graham's, drove him to a convenience store. Graham, concerned about the number of people ahead of him at the checkout line, rushed out of the store and returned to Berry's automobile. He asked Berry to take him to a friend's house. Officer Connor observed Graham hastily enter and leave the store and became suspicious. Officer Connor made an investigative stop of the automobile. Although Berry explained that his friend was suffering from a "sugar reaction," the officer ordered Berry and Graham to wait while he found out what happened in the convenience store. When the officer returned to his patrol car to call for backup, Graham got out of the car, ran around it twice, and sat down on the curb, where he passed out briefly. A number of other police officers responded to the officer's request for backup. One of the officers rolled Graham over on the sidewalk and cuffed his hands tightly behind his back, ignoring Berry's pleas to get him some sugar. Another officer said "I've seen a lot of people with sugar diabetes that never acted like this. Ain't nothing wrong with the M. F. but drunk. Lock the S.B. up." Several officers then lifted Graham up from behind, carried him over to Berry's car, and placed him face down on its hood. Regaining consciousness, Graham asked the officers to check in his wallet for a diabetic decal that he carried. One of the officers told him to "shut up" and shoved his face down against the hood of the car. Four officers grabbed Graham and threw him headfirst into the police car. A friend of Graham's brought some orange juice to the car, but the officers refused to let him have it. After receiving a report that Graham had done nothing wrong at the convenience store, the officers drove him home and released him.

GMEVIPHOTO/Shutterstock.com

Graham sustained a broken foot, cuts on his wrists, a bruised forehead, and an injured shoulder; he also claimed to have developed a permanent loud ringing in his right ear. He sued the officers under Title 42 U.S.C. § 1983, alleging that they had used excessive force in making the investigatory stop.

ISSUE: Whether the constitutional standard governs a citizen's claim that a law enforcement officer used excessive force is reasonableness?

HELD: Yes. Claims of excessive use of force in the course of making an arrest, investigatory stop, or other seizure of a person are examined under the 4th Amendment's "objective reasonableness" standard.

DISCUSSION: When an excessive force claim arises in the context of an arrest or investigatory stop, it is most properly characterized as one invoking the protections of the 4th Amendment, which guarantees citizens the right "to be secure in their persons . . . against unreasonable . . . seizures." Accordingly, all claims that law enforcement officers have used excessive force—deadly or not—in the course of an arrest, investigatory stop, or other seizure should be analyzed under the 4th Amendment and its "reasonableness" standard. Further, the "reasonableness" of a particular seizure depends not only on when it is made, but also on how it is carried out. The Supreme Court has long recognized that the right to make an arrest or investigatory stop necessarily carries with it the right to use some degree of physical coercion or threat thereof to affect it.

In determining whether the use of force in a given situation was "reasonable," courts consider all of the facts and circumstances of each particular case, including the severity of the crime at issue, whether the suspect poses an immediate threat to the safety of the officers or others, and whether he is actively resisting arrest or attempting to evade arrest by flight. The "reasonableness" of a particular use of force must be judged from the perspective of a reasonable officer on the scene, rather than with the 20/20 vision of hindsight. For example, the 4th Amendment is not necessarily violated by an arrest based on probable cause, even though the wrong person is arrested, nor by the mistaken execution of a valid search warrant on the wrong premises. With respect to a claim of excessive force, the same standard of reasonableness at the moment applies. Not every push or shove, even if it may later seem unnecessary in the peace of a judge's chambers, violates the 4th Amendment. The calculus of reasonableness must embody allowance for the fact that police officers are often forced to make split-second judgments—in circumstances that are tense, uncertain, and rapidly evolving—about the amount of force that is necessary in a particular situation. Finally, as in other 4th Amendment contexts, the "reasonableness" inquiry in an excessive force case is an objective one: the question is whether the officers' actions are "objectively reasonable" in light of the facts and circumstances confronting them, without regard to their underlying intent or motivation.

Ultimately, the *Graham* (1989) decision held that the use of force to seize a free person should be scrutinized under the 4th Amendment's "objective reasonableness" standard. All declarations of excessive force in rendering a stops or a seizure will be examined under the 4th Amendment. This was a break from previous cases regarding the use of force, which used the 14th Amendment under a "due process" evaluation to decide on cases of alleged excessive force. Graham changed the landscape, holding that excessive force claims would be judged under the 4th Amendment's "objective reasonableness" criterion. There are some police practitioners who believe the "objective reasonableness" standard should function as the only factor in determining use of force in police procedure manuals (Peters & Brave, 2006). However, in the ever-evolving climate of policing, lawmakers and legal minds consistently appraise the policies of the past and the forecasts for the future in police procedure.

Discuss the following scenario:

Mr. Smith, who suffers from bi-polar disorder, swiftly sprints out of a jewelry store in a local downtown area near the Delaware River in New Jersey. Mr. Smith is 6'4, approximately 250 lbs. Officer Schwartz observed him run into his vehicle parked in front of the store and quickly drive off. Officer Schwartz is 5'8, approximately 175 lbs. After the vehicle departs, Officer Schwartz sees a store clerk emerge from the storefront looking down the road toward the fleeing vehicle, looks at Officer Schwartz and ardently points at the bolting vehicle. Officer Schwartz follows the vehicle operated by Mr. Smith onto a local bridge crossing the Delaware River where he conducts a motor vehicle stop with his mounted emergency lights and audible siren.

When Officer Schwartz approaches the vehicle, Mr. Smith abruptly exits his vehicle and runs toward Officer Schwartz screaming for help. Officer Schwartz yells for Mr. Smith to stop multiple times. Mr. Smith continues to sprint at Officer Schwartz. Officer Schwartz engages his expandable baton and strikes him in the thigh several times until he falls to the ground and wrestles with him for approximately one minute until a backup officer arrives and Smith is placed in handcuffs. He is placed in the rear of the patrol vehicle and an ambulance is called to treat Smith for his injuries. Mr. Smith sustained a broken leg and some facial injuries during the scuffle.

u3d/Shutterstock.com.

While the ambulance squad is treating Mr. Smith, an additional responding officer who spoke with the store clerk notifies Officer Schwartz that the clerk was simply trying to return a credit card to Mr. Smith and was getting his attention to assist. Additionally, Officer Schwartz is made aware that Mr. Smith, who is bi-polar, has a significant fear of bridges. Officer Schwartz apologizes to Mr. Smith and arranges for transport to the hospital to treat his injuries.

With the *Graham* decision in mind, is this a violation of the 4th Amendment under the "objective reasonableness" standard? Why?

Scott v. Harris
127 S. Ct. 1769 (2007)

FACTS: In an effort to stop a speeding motorist, a police officer activated his blue flashing lights. The suspect sped away and the officer radioed for assistance and gave chase. The pursuit resulted in dangerous maneuvers by the suspect, including damage to one of the officers' vehicles. Six minutes and nearly 10 miles after the chase had begun, a police officer attempted a maneuver designed to cause the fleeing vehicle to spin to a stop. The result, however, was that the officer applied his bumper to the rear of the suspect's vehicle, who lost control of his vehicle and crashed. The suspect was "badly injured and was rendered a quadriplegic."

ISSUE: Whether it is reasonable for an officer to take actions that place a fleeing motorist at risk of serious injury or death in order to stop the motorist's flight from endangering the lives of innocent bystanders?

HELD: Yes. "A police officer's attempt to terminate a dangerous high-speed car chase that threatens the lives of innocent bystanders does not violate the 4th Amendment, even when it places the fleeing motorist at risk of serious injury or death."

DISCUSSION: The defendant's actions "posed an actual and imminent threat to the lives of any pedestrians who might have been present, to other civilian motorists, and to the officers involved in the chase." The officers were justified in taking some action. The Court asked "how does a court go about weighing the perhaps lesser probability of injuring or killing numerous bystanders against the perhaps larger probability of injuring or killing a single person?" An appropriate analysis includes taking "into account not only the number of lives at risk, but also their relative culpability." In this instance, the defendant's actions place a significant number of persons in danger, and the officers' range of reasonable responses was limited. In this instance, ramming the vehicle was reasonable under the 4th Amendment.

Discuss the following scenario:

Officer Johnson observes a motorist who is not wearing his seatbelt driving down a county highway in daylight on a clear, pleasant day in a rural New Jersey township. Officer Johnson activates her emergency lights and audible siren to conduct a motor vehicle stop for the seatbelt violation, which is a motor vehicle offense of the state traffic code in New Jersey. The motorist continues on at normal speed and does not stop or yield to Officer Johnson's emergency lights. The driver is not driving "erratically" or offending any "moving violations." Officer Johnson advises the dispatcher to run the vehicle registration for the vehicle, which will not stop for the obvious police emergency lights. The information relayed to Officer Johnson matches the description of the motorist, which Officer Johnson observed for quite some time now as the motorist will not halt for the officer.

Along with the detail information transmitted to Officer Johnson, it is revealed that the motorist's driver's license is suspended for failure to pay surcharges from a drunk driving offense, complemented by a traffic warrant for failure to appear at the trial for driving while intoxicated (DWI). At this point, Officer Johnson observes the motorist increasing speeds and driving erratically in attempt to flee. Officer Johnson broadcasts to the dispatchers that she is attempting to pursue the motorist who is driving at fast speeds in a residential area with several vehicles and pedestrians in the area. Sergeant Shaughnessy gets on the radio and discontinues the pursuit, ordering all officers to discontinue tracking the offender allowing them to escape.

After examining the *Scott v. Harris* case argued in front of the U.S. Supreme Court, do you think Officer Johnson would have been justified in putting the motorist at risk of serious injury or death in attempt to stop the motorist from fleeing a lawful motor vehicle stop?

Terry v. Ohio
392 U.S. 1, 88 S. Ct. 1868 (1968)

FACTS: Police Detective McFadden had been a police officer for 39 years. He served 35 years of those years as a detective and 30 of those years walking a beat in downtown Cleve-land. At approximately 2:30 p.m. on October 31, 1963, Officer McFadden was patrolling in plain clothes. Two men, Chilton and the defendant, standing on a corner, attracted his attention. He had never seen the men before, and he was unable to say precisely what first drew his eye to them. His interest aroused, Officer McFadden watched the two men. He saw one man leave the other and walk past several stores. The suspect paused and looked in a store window, then walked a short distance, turned around and walked back toward the corner, pausing again to look in the same store window. Then the second suspect did the same. This was repeated approximately a dozen times. At one point, a third man approached the suspects, engaged them in a brief conversation, and left. Chilton and the defendant resumed their routine for another 10 to 12 minutes before leaving to meet with the third man.

Officer McFadden testified that he suspected the men were "casing a job, a stick-up," and that he feared "they may have a gun." Officer McFadden approached the three men, identified himself and asked for their names. The suspects "mumbled something" in response. Officer McFadden grabbed the defendant,

spun him around and patted down the outside of his clothing. Officer McFadden felt a pistol in the defendant's left breast pocket of his overcoat, which he retrieved. Officer McFadden then patted down Chilton. He felt and retrieved another handgun from his overcoat. Officer McFadden patted down the third man, Katz, but found no weapon. The government charged Chilton and the defendant with carrying concealed weapons.

ISSUES:
1. Whether the detective's actions amounted to a seizure?
2. Whether the detective's actions amounted a search?

HELD:
1. Yes. Detective McFadden seized the defendant when he grabbed him.
2. Whether the detective's actions amounted a search?
3. Yes. Detective McFadden searched the defendant when he put his hands on the defendant's person.

DISCUSSION: The Constitution only prohibits unreasonable searches and seizures. An officer "seizes" a person when he or she restrains their freedom to walk away. Likewise, there is a "search" when an officer makes a careful exploration of outer surfaces of person's clothing to attempt to find weapons. These searches and seizures must be reasonable to justify them under the 4th Amendment.

In justifying any particular intrusion, the government must be able to point to specific and articulable facts that, taken with rational inferences from those facts, reasonably warrant that intrusion. Searches and seizures must be based on more than hunches. Simple good faith on part of the officer is not sufficient.

The Court permitted Detective McFadden to conduct the limited intrusions of stopping the suspects based on articulable (reasonable) suspicion that criminal activity was afoot. The Court also found that Detective McFadden demonstrated reasonable suspicion that the men were armed and dangerous. Therefore, the Court allowed his limited intrusion onto their persons in search of weapons. While both standards are less than probable cause, the Court acknowledged that limited intrusions, based on articulated, reasonable suspicion can be reasonable.

Discuss the following scenario:

Officer Cooney has been a police officer for 15 years. He's been working as a criminal investigator in the detective bureau in the last five years. Prior to being assigned as a detective, Officer Cooney worked in the Guns, Gangs, and Narcotics Unit (GGN) purging his community of weapons and dangerous drugs. Officer Cooney is walking in a downtown area known for transactions of controlled dangerous substances (CDS). Officer

Photographee.eu/Shutterstock.com.

Cooney observes a subject he has arrested for the possession of crack cocaine. The person leaves a street corner that is being surveyed drug distribution and walks down a dilapidated alley. Officer Cooney follows the subject down the alley and approaches the subject.

Officer Cooney advised the person to put his hands behind his head so he can conduct a pat down (Terry Frisk). While Officer Cooney is patting down the outer areas of the subjects clothing, he immediately detects a substance that in his experience feels like a CDS, specifically crack cocaine. With this is mind, Officer Cooney retrieves the familiar rock-like substance that field tests positive for cocaine. Officer Cooney arrests and charges the person with possession of a CDS. The arrestee appeals to the court to suppress the evidence on the grounds of an illegal search under the 4th Amendment of the U.S. Constitution.

Under *Terry v. Ohio*, was this frisk of the outer clothing a lawful search and seizure and should the evidence be introduced into a court of law?

Miranda v. Arizona
384 U.S. 436, 86 S. Ct. 1602 (1966)

FACTS: The defendant was arrested at his home for a rape and taken to the police station. While there, the victim identified him as the rapist. The police took the defendant to an interrogation room, where he was questioned by two police officers. These officers later testified at trial that the defendant was not advised that he had a right to have an attorney present during his questioning. The officers also testified that the defendant was not told that he had a right to be free from self-incrimination. The defendant signed a statement that contained a pre-prepared clause stating that he had "full knowledge" of his "legal rights." At trial, the written confession was admitted against the defendant and he was convicted.

ISSUE: Whether the written confession given by the defendant was obtained in violation of the defendant's 5th Amendment right to be free from compulsion?

HELD: Yes. The written confession by the defendant was obtained in violation of the defendant's 5th Amendment privilege against compulsory self-incrimination.

DISCUSSION: The Court held that "the prosecution may not use statements, whether exculpatory or inculpatory, stemming from custodial interrogation of the defendant unless it demonstrates the use of procedural safeguards effective to secure the privilege against self-incrimination." The Court defined a "custodial interrogation" as "questioning initiated by law enforcement officers after a person has been taken into custody or otherwise deprived of his freedom of action in any significant way [underline added]." The procedural safeguards required by the Court consisted of four warnings that must be provided to the suspect before a custodial interrogation can take place. First, the suspect must be notified that he has the right to remain silent. Second, the suspect must be notified that any statement made may be used as evidence against him. Third, the suspect has the right to consult with a lawyer and have the lawyer present during the questioning. And fourth, the suspect must be informed that if he cannot afford to retain a lawyer, one will be appointed to represent him prior to any questioning.

Once these warnings have been given, then and only then, can the individual voluntarily, knowingly, and intelligently waive these rights. However, "if the individual indicates in any manner that he wishes to remain silent, the interrogation must cease. Similarly, if the individual states that he wants an attorney, the interrogation must cease until an attorney is present."

Discuss the following scenario:

Officers Mantone and Wray are investigating a spree of motor vehicle burglaries that have occurred in a small suburban town. Both officers obtained pawn slips in a neighboring jurisdiction indicating that the defendant sold various amounts of property from several motor vehicle burglaries to a pawn outlet. Officers Mantone and Wray go to the defendant's home and knock on the door. The defendant answers and Officer Mantone says, "I need to speak with you about some property you sold to a pawn shop, do you mind coming to the police department with me to talk about it." The defendant replies, "Sure, I've got nothing to hide."

Officers Mantone and Wray transport the defendant to the local police department, which has sealed, locked doors only accessible to be authorized personnel. Officers Mantone and Wray escort the defendant to an interview room and say, "There are no charges against you at this time, we just want to talk, we will be back in a minute."

In terms of *Miranda*, are Officers Mantone and Wray obligated to inform the defendant of Miranda Warnings per the 5th Amendment of the U.S. Constitution?

Weeks v. United States
232 U.S. 383, 34 S. Ct. 341 (1914)

FACTS: Police officers arrested the defendant without a warrant at his place of employment. Other police officers went to his home. After a neighbor told the officers where the defendant kept a key, they entered the house. The officers searched and found evidence of gambling paraphernalia that they turned over to the U.S. Marshal. Later that day, the Marshal returned to the house and found additional evidence. Neither the Marshal nor the police had a search warrant. The government used this evidence to convict the defendant of using the mails to transport gambling paraphernalia.

ISSUE: Whether the evidence seized by the U.S. Marshal was admissible?

HELD: No. As the evidence was obtained through unconstitutional means, it was not admissible.

Elnur/Shutterstock.com

DISCUSSION: An official of the United States seized the evidence acting under the color of office in direct violation of the constitutional rights of the defendant. The Supreme Court held that the federal government could not use unreasonably obtained evidence in a federal courtroom. However, the fruit of the first search conducted by the state officers was admissible. "As the 4th Amendment is not directed to the individual misconduct of such officials, "the fruits of the state search were admissible in a federal trial.

Note: The 4th Amendment would not be completely applicable to state actions until the *Mapp v. Ohio* decision in 1961.

Discuss the following scenario:

Trooper Austin has information that a local business owner is distributing child pornography. She has a reliable confidential informant, who has provided significant information in the past to support the arrest and conviction of many felons. This informant says he was approached by the defendant to purchase this illegal material and even observed it in the defendant's place of business. The infor-

a katz/Shutterstock.com.

mant quickly contacts Trooper Austin and tells her the child pornography in the store now and he saw the owner place it in a drawer behind his desk. The informant said the Trooper must hurry, because the pornography will be sold and gone shortly. Trooper Austin rushes to the store and retrieves the child pornography from the drawer and arrests the business owner for possession and distribution of child pornography. This reliable confidential informant once again assists Trooper Austin in arresting a dangerous criminal.

Was Trooper Austin's search and seizure constitutional under the 4th Amendment and do you think the child pornography can be introduced in a criminal trial?

Elkins v. United States
364 U.S. 206, 80 S. Ct. 1437 (1960)

FACTS: State officers, having received information that the defendants possessed obscene motion pictures, obtained a search warrant for the defendant's house. The officers did not find any obscene pictures but they found various paraphernalia they believed was used to make illegal wiretaps. A state court held that the search was illegal under state law. During these state proceedings, federal officers, acting under a federal search warrant, obtained the items in state custody. Shortly after that, state officials abandoned their case and federal agents obtained a federal indictment.

ISSUE: Whether evidence obtained because of an unreasonable search and seizure by state officers, without involvement of federal officers, is admissible in a federal criminal trial?

HELD: No. Evidence obtained because of an unreasonable search and seizure by state officers is inadmissible in a federal criminal trial.

DISCUSSION: The Supreme Court created the exclusionary rule to prevent, not repair. Its purpose is to deter unreasonable activity—to compel respect for the constitutional guarantee to be free from unreasonable searches in the only effective way—by removing the incentive to disregard it. Evidence obtained by state officers during a search that, if conducted by federal officers, would have violated the 4th Amendment, is inadmissible in a federal criminal trial.

Discuss the following scenario:

Municipal police officers are investigating a group of individuals involved in selling illegal narcotics. During their investigation, they conduct two "controlled buys" of heroin and prepare an affidavit for a search warrant. The affidavit is approved by the prosecutor then presented to a Superior Court

Judge. The judge authorizes execution of the search warrant. During the warrant execution, officers located several bundles of heroin, wax folds (packaging materials), and scales. In the scope of their search, they uncover materials for pirating movies and cloning DVDs and Blue Rays. Through an interview with an occupant of the house, who was in custody but not mirandized, information is gained to charge the leader of the drug network with video piracy. During the trial, the drug leader is charged with the distribution of narcotics; however, he is found not guilty of video piracy because the confession was obtained with the absence of a required Miranda Warning, and hence the charge was dismissed. Federal prosecutors pick up the case to charge the drug leader with video piracy, using the evidence obtained from the original municipal search warrant.

Will the video piracy materials be allowed to be introduced as evidence in a Federal Court?

Mapp v. Ohio
367 U.S. 643, 81 S. Ct 1684 (1961)

FACTS: Three police officers arrived at the defendant's home pursuant to information that "a person [was] hiding out in the home, who was wanted for questioning in connection with a recent bombing, and that there was a large amount of policy paraphernalia being hidden in the home." The officers knocked on the door and demanded entry. The defendant, after telephoning her attorney, refused to admit them without a search warrant.

Three hours later, the officers (now with four additional officers) again sought entry. When the defendant did not immediately come to the door, the officers forcibly opened at least one door to the house. It appeared that the defendant was halfway down the stairs from the upper floor when the officers broke into the house. She demanded to see the search warrant. One officer held up a paper claimed to be a warrant. The defendant grabbed the "warrant" and placed it in her bosom. A struggle followed in which the officers recovered the piece of paper. They handcuffed the defendant because she had been "belligerent" in resisting their _official rescue of the "warrant" from her person. Running roughshod over the defendant, a police officer "grabbed" her, "twisted" [her] hand, and she "yelled [and] pleaded with him because it was hurting." The officers discovered the obscene materials for which she was ultimately convicted of possessing in the course of a widespread search. At trial, the officers produced no search warrant, nor was the failure to produce one explained.

hafakot/Shutterstock.com

ISSUE: Whether the 4th Amendment applies to state actions?

HELD: Yes. The Supreme Court made the 4th Amendment and the exclusionary rule applicable to the states.

DISCUSSION: The 4th Amendment right of privacy is enforceable against the states through the due process clause of the 14th Amendment. All evidence obtained by searches and seizures in violation of the Constitution is inadmissible in both federal a state court.

Discuss the following scenario:

New Jersey State Troopers stop a motor vehicle on the New Jersey Turnpike that was speeding. Upon the approach to the vehicle, the driver steps out of the car and says, "I have the right to remain silent and I want my attorney now!" The troopers place the driver under arrest and search the vehicle for contraband based on the driver's strange behavior. After a thorough

val lawless/Shutterstock.com.

search, the troopers locate explosive material, bomb vests, ignition switches, and plans for detonating the munitions on the George Washington Bridge.

With an understanding of *Mapp v. Ohio*, is the evidence the troopers seized admissible in state or federal courts?.

Tennessee v. Garner
471 U.S. 1, 105 S. Ct. 1694 (1985)

FACTS: At about 10:45 p.m., two police officers were dispatched to answer a "prowler inside call." Upon arriving at the scene, they saw a woman standing on her porch and gesturing toward the adjacent house. She told them she had heard glass breaking and that "they" or "someone" was breaking in next door. While one of the officers radioed the dispatcher to say that they were on the scene, the second officer went behind the house. He heard a door slam and saw someone run across the backyard. The fleeing suspect, the defendant, stopped at a 6-feet-high chain link fence at the edge of the yard. With the aid of a flashlight, the officer was able to see his face and hands. He saw no sign of a weapon, and, though not certain, was "reasonably sure" and "figured" that the defendant was unarmed. The officer testified he thought the defendant was 17 or 18 years old and about 5'5" or 5'7 tall. In fact, the defendant, an eighth-grader, was 15. He was 5'4" tall and weighed somewhere around 100 or 110 pounds. While the defendant was crouched at the base of the fence, the officer called out "police, halt" and took a few steps toward him. The defendant began to climb over the fence. Convinced that if he made it over the fence he would elude capture, the officer shot him. The bullet hit the defendant in the back of the head. The defendant later died at a hospital. In using deadly force to prevent the escape, the officer was acting under the authority of a state statute and pursuant to his department's policy. The statute provided that "[if], after notice of the intention to arrest the defendant, he either flee or forcibly resist, the officer may use all the necessary means to effect the arrest." The department policy was slightly more restrictive than the statute, but still allowed the use of deadly force in cases of burglary. The defendant's father brought suit under Title 42 U.S.C. § 1983, alleging, among other things, that his son's 4th Amendment rights had been violated by the use of deadly force in this situation.

ISSUE: Whether deadly force may be used to prevent the escape of an apparently unarmed suspected felon?

HELD: No. Deadly force may not be used unless it is necessary to prevent the escape and the officer has probable cause to believe that the suspect poses a significant threat of death or serious physical injury to the officer or others.

DISCUSSION: Whenever an officer restrains the freedom of a person to walk away, he has "seized" that person. Apprehension by the use of deadly force is a seizure subject to the reasonableness requirement of the 4th Amendment. To determine the constitutionality of a seizure, a court must balance the nature and quality of the intrusion on the individual's 4th Amendment interests against the importance of the governmental interests alleged to justify the intrusion. The "reasonableness" of a seizure depends on not only when a seizure is made, but also how it is carried out.

Notwithstanding probable cause to seize a suspect, an officer may not always do so by killing him. The use of deadly force to prevent the escape of all felony suspects, without considering the circumstances, is constitutionally unreasonable. It is not better that all felony suspects die than that they escape. Where the suspect poses no immediate threat to the officer and no threat to others, the harm resulting from failing to apprehend him does not justify the use of deadly force to do so. It is unfortunate when a suspect who is in sight escapes, but the fact that the police arrive a little late or are a little slower afoot does not always justify killing the suspect. A police officer may not seize an unarmed, non-dangerous suspect by shooting him dead. For this reason, the state statute was found to be unconstitutional insofar as it authorized the use of deadly force against such fleeing suspects.

It was not, however, unconstitutional on its face. Where an officer has probable cause to believe that the suspect poses a threat of serious physical harm, either to the officer or to others, it is not constitutionally unreasonable to prevent escape by using deadly force. Thus, if the suspect threatened the officer with a weapon or there is probable cause to believe that he has committed a crime involving the infliction or threatened infliction of serious physical harm, deadly force may be used if necessary to prevent escape, and if, where feasible, some warning has been given.

In this case, the officer could not reasonably have believed that the defendant—young, slight, and unarmed—posed any threat. Indeed, the officer never attempted to justify his actions on any basis other than the need to prevent an escape. While the defendant was suspected of burglary, this fact could not, without regard to the other circumstances, automatically justify the use of deadly force. The officer did not have probable cause to believe that Garner, whom he correctly believed to be unarmed, posed any physical danger to himself or others.

Discuss the following scenario:

Officers from a local police department are called to a local convenience store where there is a report of two adults physically assaulting each other in the parking lot. While two officers are turning onto the road the convenience store is located, a third-party caller advises dispatchers that one of the males fighting has brandished a silver handgun and fired one shot missing the other person fighting. As the officers pull up, one male runs down the street and another stays on the scene. The quickly speak to the other party involved in fight, who tells them he fired a shot at him but missed. The officers begin to chase the fleeing involved person who is believed to be carrying a handgun. The officers catch up with the aid of their patrol vehicle. As the officers approach this individual, who has his back turned to the officers, the person swiftly turns around and points his arm at the officers. The two officers fire a total of five shots at the individual knocking him to the ground, motionless. When the officers approach the individual to disarm him and render aid, they recognize he is dead. Also, they observe he is unarmed.

With the knowledge of *Tennessee v. Garner* and *Graham v. Connor*, was the use of deadly force a "reasonable" seizure under the precepts of the 4th Amendment?

Hudson v. Michigan
126 S. Ct. 2159 (2006)

FACTS: Police officers obtained a search warrant for the defendant's home to look for controlled substances. Before entering, they announced their presence, but waited only three to five seconds before using force to enter.

ISSUE: Whether a violation of the "knock-and-announce" rule requires the suppression of all evidence found in the search.

HELD: No.

DISCUSSION: The Court commented that "[S]uppression of evidence, however, has always been our last resort, not our first impulse." It should only be applied when other options are ineffective. The Court also stated that "[T]he interests protected by the knock-and-announce requirement are quite different" and do not include the shielding of potential evidence from the government's eyes." As the knock-and-announce does not protect one's reasonable expectation of privacy the Court concluded that the exclusionary rule is inapplicable in cases where the rule is violated.

PhotosbyAndy/Shutterstock.com

The government obtains little advantage in its endeavors to ferret out criminal activity by ignoring the knock-and-announce requirement. The possible prevention of the destruction of evidence or the avoidance of violence by occupants of the premises is the likely result, but no new evidence. Therefore, the Court found that "civil liability is an effective deterrent" to address violations of the knock-and-announce rule.

Discuss the following scenario:

Officers from a County Special Weapons and Tactics (SWAT) Team are briefed by local detectives and their commander about an approved search warrant for the collection of evidence in a drug trafficking ring at 3:30 a.m. The search warrant includes a "knock-and-announce" clause, which mandates officers knock and announce their presence prior to making entry. The SWAT team checks their gear, learns their assignments, and runs through some practice drills for the 4:45 search warrant execution. The team loads up into their vehicle and routes itself to the target residence. The point man approaches the front door with various members of the team behind her. She knocks on the door and yells, "Police, search warrant!" She then immediately breaches the front door with a ram. The occupants of the residents are detained and placed in handcuffs and zip ties. The search yields several ounces of heroin, three automatics weapons, journals consistent with drug sales, and packaging materials.

Does the *Hudson v. Michigan* decision allow for this evidence to be suppressed in court for being "fruits of the poisonous tree?"

Silverthorne Lumber Co. v. United States
251 U.S. 385, 40 S. Ct. 182 (1920)

FACTS: Silverthorne was indicted and arrested. While he was being detained, DOJ representatives and the U.S. Marshal went to his corporate office. Without authority, they confiscated and copied his records.

The federal trial court held that the officers unconstitutionally obtained the records and ordered their return. Based on the copies, the government obtained a new indictment, and served the defendant a subpoena for the original records.

Casimiro PT/Shutterstock.com

ISSUE: 1. Whether the government can use information obtained from an illegal search and seizure to secure other evidence?

ISSUE: 2. Whether the 4th Amendment protects corporations against unlawful searches and seizures?

HELD 1: No. The government may not use illegally obtained evidence to gain additional evidence.

HELD 2: Yes. Corporations enjoy 4th Amendment protections.

DISCUSSION: Information gained by the government's unlawful search and seizure may not be used as a basis to subpoena that information. The essence of a rule prohibiting the acquisition of evidence in an illegal way is that it cannot be used at all. This is the "Fruit of the Poisonous Tree" doctrine. This doctrine prohibits law enforcement officers from doing indirectly what they are prohibited from doing directly. Also, the Court held that corporations enjoy a right be free from unreasonable searches and seizures.

Discuss the following scenario:

Officers from a local New Jersey police department arrest an owner of a residential bar in one of their precincts for theft and money laundering offenses. While she is arrested, local detectives respond to the bar and demand employment lists and accounting documents without a warrant. The detectives believe, this information will improve their case against the bar owner in the money laundering case.

In this case, are the officers gaining evidence that can be directly obtained by a search warrant, thus avoiding dismissal by "fruits of the poisonous tree."?

Photographee.eu/Shutterstock.com.

Delaware v. Prouse
440 U.S. 648, 99 S. Ct. 1391 (1979)

FACTS: A police officer stopped a vehicle occupied by the defendant. The officer testified that, prior to the stop, he had observed neither traffic or equipment violations, nor any other suspicious activity. Instead, he made the stop only to check the driver's license and the vehicle's registration documents. In making the stop, the officer was not acting pursuant to any standards, guidelines, or procedures promulgated by either his department or the State Attorney General. Upon approaching the vehicle, the officer smelled marijuana. He later seized marijuana in plain view on the floor of the car.

ISSUE: Whether the officer's stop of the vehicle without reasonable suspicion violated of the 4th Amendment?

HELD: Yes. The officer may not stop a vehicle without establishing that an articulable reason exists to suspect that criminal activity is afoot.

DISCUSSION: While the State has an interest in ensuring the safety of its roadways, an individual still retains a reasonable expectation of privacy in a vehicle, despite significant governmental regulation of vehicles. If an individual was subjected to unrestricted governmental intrusion every time he or she entered a vehicle, the 4th Amendment prohibition against unreasonable searches and seizures would be severely undermined. Instead, except in those situations in which there is at least articulable and reasonable suspicion that a motorist is unlicensed or that an automobile is not registered, or that either the vehicle or an occupant is otherwise subject to seizure for violation of law, stopping an automobile and detaining the driver in order to check his driver's license and the registration of the vehicle are unreasonable under the 4th Amendment.

Discuss the following scenario:

Officer Shaughnessy is patrolling the downtown of a small municipality at 2:00 a.m. He observes a vehicle leave the rear of a local jewelry store and proceed onto Main Street. He runs the vehicle's license plate and learns the vehicle has a valid registration. Shortly afterward, an alarm call is dispatched for the jewelry store where this vehicle left. Officer Shaughnessy conducts a motor vehicle stop on the vehicle that left from behind the store. He has not observed any motor vehicle violations.

Is this a reasonable seizure under the 4th Amendment?

United States v. Arvizu
534 U.S. 266; 122 S. Ct. 744 (2002)

FACTS: A Border Patrol Agent received information that a vehicle sensor had been triggered in a remote area. The agent suspected that the vehicle could be attempted to evade a checkpoint as the timing corresponded with a shift change, leaving the area unpatrolled. The agent located the vehicle, a minivan. He obtained a visual vantage point by pulling off to the side of the road at an angle so he could see the oncoming vehicle as it passed by. The agent observed (1) the vehicle slow considerably as it approached his position, (2) the driver appear stiff and rigid, (3) the driver seemed to pretend the agent was not there, (3) the knees of the passengers (children) in the very back seat were unusually high (as if their feet were elevated by something on the floor). The agent followed the vehicle for a short distance and observed (4) the children, while facing forward, wave at the agent in an abnormal fashion, (5) the strange waving continued intermittently for four to five minutes, (6) the driver signaled for a turn, turned the signal off,

Michael Dechev/Shutterstock.com

then suddenly signaled and turned the vehicle, (7) the turn was the last that would allow the vehicle to avoid the checkpoint, (8) the road is rough and usually utilized by four-wheel-drive vehicles, (9) the vehicle did not appear to be part of the local traffic, and (10) there were no recreation areas associated with this road. The agent requested vehicle registration information via the radio and learned that (11) the vehicle was registered to an address four blocks north of the border in an area known for alien and narcotics smuggling. At this point, the agent decided to conduct a traffic stop.

ISSUE: Whether the agent could articulate reasonable suspicion to conduct a Terry stop considering all observed factors had innocent explanations?

HELD: Yes. Reasonable suspicion is determined by the totality of the circumstances.

DISCUSSION: The Court stated that—[W]hen discussing how reviewing courts should make reasonable-suspicion determinations, we have said repeatedly that they must look at the "totality of the circumstances" of each case to see whether the detaining officer has a particularized and "objective basis for suspecting legal wrongdoing." In doing so, it is imperative that the officer be allowed to use—their own experience and specialized training to make inferences about a circumstance. Otherwise innocent actions, considered together, may warrant a further look by a law enforcement officer.

Discuss the following scenario:

Officer DeMarco is a one-man patrol unit. He is patrolling and an apartment complex high-rise building, an area of his jurisdiction known for high crime, specifically the distribution of CDS. At approximately 3:00 a.m., Officer DeMarco observes an SUV pull up to a corner known for drug sales. Three people surround the vehicle, a short exchange is made, and the vehicle pulls away. As Officer DeMarco follows the vehicle, he observes a burst of light in the interior of the vehicle, which in his experience he determines is the flame of a lighter. While Officer DeMarco continues to follow the vehicle, they stop at a traffic light, which happens to be a well-lit area.

Paul Matthew Photography/Shutterstock.com.

At this point, Officer DeMarco realizes the passenger is alerted to his presence, and the passenger ducks down in the front seat. At this point, Officer DeMarco activates his emergency lights to conduct a motor vehicle stop to investigate further. Officer DeMarco did not observe any motor vehicle violations.

With the Arvizu decision in mind, do you think Officer DeMarco had "reasonable suspicion" to conduct a Terry stop?

Federal case law guides what the police can do, and what they cannot do. These landmark cases serve as "models" for making decisions about the admissibility of evidence and upholding basic protections provided by the U.S. Constitution. Alternatively, the decisions outline the tools police have to carry out their missions and enforce the law. The criminal justice system is repetitively preserving this balance of personal rights and the maintenance of order in society.

These important decisions guide policies in policing; however, the procedures are not always so clear. Many of the concepts discussed, such as "reasonable suspicion," and "probable cause," are to be determined on an individual case-by-case basis. These concepts are organic and can only be applied exclusively to the facts presented in a given circumstance.

Many police use of force cases are traced back to the genesis of the police intrusion, generally the motor vehicle stop, the pedestrian stop, the call for service, etc. The origin of the police encounter and the detailed events that follow are indispensible when examining the use of force on free citizens and concluding whether the force applied is lawful or unlawful.

It is widely known that *Graham v. Connor* decision is the milestone, currently, governing the analysis of use of force legitimacy in American policing. The clear fact remains today, and strengthened by judicial precedence, is that use of force decisions will be openly viewed in terms of whether the officer acted with "objective reasonableness" in light of the surrounding circumstances presented to him or her when the level of force was employed.

Discussion Points

1. Why is *Graham v Connor* still the standard when articulating the necessity to use force?
   - "Objective reasonableness" and "totality of the circumstances" are extremely key in determining the lawful application of force, why?
2. How is "clearly established law' so important when factoring the legality of use of force?
   - Why is there no requirement for absolute certainty in the use of deadly force?

References

Landes, W. M., & Posner, R. (1976). Legal precedent: A theoretical and empirical analysis *Journal of Law and Economics, 19*(2), 249–307.

Peters, J., & Brave, M. (2006). Force continuums: Are they still needed. *Police and Security News, 22*(1), 1–5.

Tarr, G. A., & Porter, M. C. (1988). *State supreme courts in state and nation* (pp. 124–183). New Haven, CT: Yale University Press.

Student Name _____ Date _____

Course Section _____ Chapter _____

For any use of force to be lawful, what two things must occur first; to stop a person, what must the police demonstrate; to stop a motor vehicle, what case law prevails and what level of evidence must the police articulate; in patting down a person, what case law prevails and what is the officer specifically looking for under this case law:

_____

_____

_____

_____

_____

_____

_____

_____

_____

_____

_____

_____

_____

_____

CIVIL LIABILITY

The time is always right to do what's right.

—Martin Luther King

"The security of one's privacy against arbitrary intrusion by the police—which is at the core of the Fourth Amendment—is basic to a free society."

Wolf v. Colorado, 338 U.S. 25 (1949).

Key Terms

1983 Lawsuit, Federal Tort Claims Act, Title 18 Section 241 and 242, Bivens Action, Damages, "Under color of the law," Respondeat Superior, Vicarious Liability, Deliberate Indifference, Failure to Train, Qualified Immunity

Learning Objectives

After exploring Chapter 4, the student will be able to:

1. Explain the civil implications if law enforcement agents violate a citizen's constitutional rights.
2. Understand the federal and state lawsuit remedies.
3. Describe violations of excessive force.
4. Detail vicarious liability and deliberate indifference.
5. List the requirements for a successful lawsuit under Title 18 and Title 42 of the U.S. Code.
6. Describe qualified immunity.

THE START OF FEDERAL CIVIL LIABILITY

Bivens, Brady, Graham, and several other landmark case names can make a police administrator cower in fear. If you are the federal officer charged, criminally or (in this chapter) civilly; your day, week, month, and life can be turned upside down.

There is a definite need for a free society to have recourse and remedies for violations of their civil rights. Without question, a free society must have protections against unreasonable law enforcement practices, against excessive or improper force, against the lack of due process and lack of fairness in the criminal justice system. In this chapter, we focus on federal civil liability. In the next chapter, we will focus on state civil liability.

Rawpixel.com/Shutterstock.com

However, before discussing the parameters, constraints, rules, and constitutionality of actions, we must have a basic understanding of civil law. To begin, Tort liability must be examined. All law is tort law. The United States is a common law country. Torts, a civil wrong, allow recovery for personal injury and arise out of situations between private parties (normally). Tort law has no clear definition and is loosely structured. Major differences exist between criminal law and tort law:

Torts can be seen as private injuries or wrongful acts that result in injury or harm between individuals or their property. In a civil action, an individual may seek a

Components of Criminal Law	**Components of Tort Law**
A Public Offense	Private or Civil Wrong
State vs. Individual	Individual vs. Individual
Fines, Probation, Incarceration, Death	Monetary Sanctions
Guilt Beyond a Reasonable Doubt	Preponderance of the Evidence
Acquittal Normally Not Appealable by the State	Both Parties May Appeal
The State Receives Fines and Restitution Goes to Victim	Plaintiff Receives Monetary Damages as Compensation
Both criminal law and tort law seek to control behavior and impose sanctions	

remedy for a private injury. The plaintiff seeks compensation from the defendant. Usually, the compensation is punitive or strictly compensatory. Punitive damages are set by a judge or jury to "punish" or "deter" the behavior from occurring again. On a personal level, an award of several thousands of dollars would certainly punish most people. On a corporate level, an award can be in the millions or even billions.

hafakot/Shutterstock.com

The legal standard needed to prevail in a civil action is that of "a preponderance of the evidence." In terms of percentages of how "wrong or guilty" a person can be viewed as 51%, more likely than not they are culpable. As you know, in a criminal action, "proof beyond a reasonable doubt" is the standard to be met. Percentages in a criminal case should be near to 99.9% as possible. Why is there a difference?

Torts can be divided into three major categories: intentional, negligent, and strict liability. Intentional torts are behaviors that are highly likely to cause injury to another. Intent in the context of tort means to bring about some physical or mental harm, either through omission or commission by the actor. In order to prevail in the case, the plaintiff must prove behavior was intentional.

Negligence is the breach of common law or statutory duty to act reasonably toward those who may foreseeably be harmed. There are two categories:

1. Simple negligence means failure to exercise reasonable care in performance of duties which then leads to injury.
2. Gross negligence means a performance of duties with reckless disregard of consequences that cause harm. Gross negligence is normally required in order for plaintiff to prevail.

State Civil Rights Laws—provide sanctions for violations and are implemented as federal rights laws at the state level.

<u>Criminal:</u>
<u>Title 18 U.S. Code § 242 (Criminal Liability for Deprivation of Civil Rights)—an officer must have acted under color of law, acted intentionally to deprive the person of a protected right, and person must actually have been deprived of that right.</u>
<u>§ 241 (Conspiracy to Deprive a Person of Rights)—punishes the violation for conspiracy to commit the act, which requires at least two participants.</u>
<u>Civil Liability:</u>
<u>42 U.S. Code § 1983 - Civil action for deprivation of rights -an officer must have acted under color of law, acted intentionally to deprive the person of a protected right, and person must actually have been deprived of that right.</u>

The Supreme Court defined the concept of color of law as it pertains to § 1983 actions in the case of *West v. Atkins*, 487 U.S. 42 (1988). The traditional definition of acting under color of state law requires that the defendant in a § 1983 action have exercised power "possessed by virtue of state law and made possible only because the wrongdoer is clothed with the authority of state law." *United States v. Classic*, 313 U.S. 299 (1941). *Accord, Monroe v. Pape*, 365 U.S. 167 (1961). In *Lugar v. Edmondson Oil Co., supra*, the Court made clear that, if a defendant's conduct satisfies the state action requirement of the 14th Amendment, "that conduct [is] also action under color of state law and will support a suit under § 1983." Id. at 457 U.S. 935. Accord, *Rendell-Baker v. Kohn*, 457 U.S. 830 (1982); *United States v. Price*, 383 U.S. at 383 U.S. 794, n. 7. In such circumstances, the defendant's alleged infringement of the plaintiff's federal rights is "fairly attributable to the State." Lugar, 457 U.S. at 457 U.S. 937. Therefore, state employment is generally sufficient to render the defendant a state actor, while acting in his official capacity or while exercising his responsibilities pursuant to state law.

In federal civil liability, we focus on Title 18 U.S. Code § 242 and 241. However, we will look at some of the federal acts and statutes that give purview to the Department of Justice to investigate claims of excessive force, prosecutorial abuse, and other forms of violations of a citizen's Constitutional Rights.

ibreakstock/Shutterstock.com

Section 210401 of the Violent Crime Control and Law Enforcement Act of 1994—grants the Department of Justice extremely broad investigative powers and prosecutorial authority in cases of alleged use of excessive force.

Sections 14141 and 14142 permit the Department of Justice to investigate patterns or practices of misconduct in local police departments and require the collection of statics of police abuse. Gives the Department of Justice authority to file civil actions on behalf of citizens to obtain declaratory or equitable relief. Ensures that the rights of institutionalized persons are protected from unconstitutional conditions.

Title 42 U.S.C. § 1997—permits the Attorney General to bring civil lawsuits against state institutions regarding the civil rights of those housed in the facility.

(1) Discretionary authority of Attorney General; preconditions, Whenever the Attorney General has reasonable cause to believe that any state or political subdivision of a state, official, employee, or agent thereof, or other person acting on behalf of a State or political subdivision of a state is subjecting persons residing in or confined to an institution, as defined in § 1997 of this title, to egregious or flagrant conditions which deprive such persons of any rights, privileges, or immunities secured or protected by the Constitution or laws of the United States causing such persons to suffer grievous harm, and that such deprivation is pursuant to a pattern or practice of resistance to the full enjoyment of such rights, privileges, or immunities, the Attorney General, for or in the name of the United States, may institute a civil action in any appropriate U.S. district court against such party for such equitable relief as may be appropriate to insure the minimum corrective measures necessary to insure the full enjoyment of such rights, privileges, or immunities, except that such equitable relief shall be available under this subchapter to persons residing in or confined to an institution as defined in § 1997(1)(B)(ii) of this title only insofar as such persons are subjected to conditions which deprive them of rights, privileges, or immunities secured or protected by the Constitution of the United States. (2) Discretionary award of attorney fees in any action commenced under this section, the court may allow the prevailing party, other than the United States, a reasonable attorney's fee against the United States as part of the costs. (3) Attorney General to personally sign complaint—The Attorney General shall personally sign any complaint filed pursuant to this section.

Plaintiff suing a federal officer must base their action on a complaint arising out of the scope of the federal officer's employment and must file his or her complaint in accordance with the Federal Tort Claims Act (FTCA).

Under the FTCA, the federal government acts as a self-insurer, and recognizes liability for the negligent or wrongful acts or omissions of its employees acting within the scope of their official duties. The United States is liable to the same extent an individual would be in like circumstances. The statute substitutes the United States as the defendant in such a suit and the United States—not the individual employee—bears any resulting liability.

Making a Claim Under the FTCA: Individuals who are injured or whose property is damaged by the wrongful or negligent act of a federal employee acting in the scope of his or her official duties may file a claim with the government for reimbursement for that injury or damage. In order to state a valid claim, the claimant must demonstrate that:

alexmillos/Shutterstock.com

1. He was injured or his property was damaged by a federal government employee.
2. The employee was acting within the scope of his official duties.
3. The employee was acting negligently or wrongfully.
4. The negligent or wrongful act proximately caused the injury or damage of which he complains.

Basic ideas under Federal Civil Liability (encompasses the fundamentals of state and local civil liability):

1. May be brought against federal employees and not the federal government.
2. Specifically upheld by the Supreme Court for violations of the 5th Amendment's due process clause and for federal prisoners claiming 8th Amendment violations.
3. Plaintiff must file claim within 2 years of violation.
4. 1866 Congress enacted the Civil Rights Act that provided federal criminal penalties for state and local officials who violate guaranteed rights of citizens.
5. Section 1983, passed in 1871, provided vehicle for citizens to sue for violations of constitutional rights.
6. Prior to § 1983, the only option for redressing a violation of a constitutional right was through the common law, and those actions were heard in state court.
7. Lay dormant between 1871 and 1961 was used in 24 cases during that period; further defined:
   - Person filing suit must be a protected person within the meaning of the act.
   - **The defendant must have been acting under "color of law"** or acting within the scope of their authority at the time of the constitutional deprivation.

- "Every person" means every individual public official and governmental entity may be liable for constitutional deprivations.
- **A constitutionally protected right must have been violated.**

Generally accepted principles for Federal Civil Liability:

1. *Monroe v. Pape*—The Supreme Court defined "person" as an individual officer.
2. *Monell v. Department of Social Services of the City of New York*—The Supreme Court expanded definition of "person" to include local governments and their employees.
3. The Dictionary Act, enacted in 1871, instructs courts to apply to all federal statutes definitions of certain common words (including "person") and basic rules of grammatical construction (such as the rule that plural words include the singular) "unless context indicates otherwise." Therefore, allowed "person" to be applied to political bodies.
4. Acting under "color of law."
5. Normally means that an officer or official misused his or her official powers granted by law in the office he or she was sworn to uphold.
6. Actions that exceed the law and the scope of authority also constitute acting under "color of law."
7. The off-duty actions of an officer cannot be the basis of litigation unless the officer uses police equipment or uses their authority as an "official" employee.
8. A determination of the "nature of the officer's act, not simply his duty status," is needed.
9. The court may declare that a state statute or regulation is unconstitutional.
10. In federal court, declaratory relief is discretionary.
11. Injunctive relief goes a step further in providing redress to the plaintiff.
12. Section 1983 does not require the awarding of attorney's fees and is at the discretion of the court.
13. Prevailing plaintiffs, not defendants, sued under § 1983 can recover attorney's fees.
14. The situation may or may not be within the scope of the officer's duties depending on the situation.

Lyudmyla Kharlamova/Shutterstock.com

Damages can be awarded for prevailing plaintiffs:

1. Compensatory damages—compensation for plaintiff's injury caused by defendant's breach of duty
2. Punitive damages—assessed primarily to punish errant officer and send a message to others that the court will not tolerate such misconduct
3. Nominal damages—awarded as symbolic gesture, recognizing plaintiff prevailed in civil action but did not sustain an actual injury

SOME APPLICABLE CASE LAW

Bivens v. Six Unknown Named Agents of the Federal Bureau of Narcotics, 403 U.S. 388 (1971)

FACTS: Bivens sued federal agents under Title 42 U.S.C. § 1983 after they entered his apartment without a warrant. The agents searched his apartment and then placed him under arrest for violating narcotics laws. They placed Bivens in manacles in the presence of his wife and children. They also threatened to arrest his family. The agents took Bivens to the courthouse, then their headquarters. He was interrogated, fingerprinted, photographed, subjected to a visual strip search, and booked.

The charges against Bivens were ultimately dismissed. Bivens alleged the search and his arrest were conducted—in an unreasonable manner. Initially, the court dismissed Bivens' lawsuit because Title 42 U.S.C. § 1983 was inapplicable to actions performed by federal officials. This ruling was affirmed by the court of appeals, and Bivens appealed to the Supreme Court.

The 4th Amendment guarantees to citizens of the United States the absolute right to be free from unreasonable searches and seizures carried out by virtue of federal authority. And where federally protected rights have been violated, it has been the rule from the beginning that courts will be alert to adjust their remedies so as to grant the necessary relief to those who have been victimized. While the 4th Amendment does not provide for its enforcement by an award of money damages for the consequences of its violation, it is well settled that where legal rights have been invaded, and a federal statute provides for a general right to sue for such invasion, federal courts may use any available remedy to make good the wrong done. Here, Bivens' complaint stated a cause of action under the 4th Amendment, and he was entitled to recover money damages for any injuries he suffered as a result of the agents' violation of that Amendment.

Brady v. Maryland, 373 U.S. 83 (1963)

The crime in question was murder committed in the perpetration of a robbery. Punishment for that crime in Maryland is life imprisonment or death, the jury being empowered to restrict the punishment to life by addition of the words "without capital punishment." 3 Md.Ann.Code, 1957, Art. 27, § 413. In Maryland, by reason of the state constitution, the jury in a criminal case is "the Judges of Law, as well as of fact." Art. XV, § 5. The question presented is whether petitioner was denied a federal right when the Court of Appeals restricted the new trial to the question of punishment.

We agree with the Court of Appeals that suppression of this confession was a violation of the Due Process Cla use of the 14th Amendment. The Court of Appeals relied, in the main, on two decisions from the Third Circuit Court of Appeals United States ex rel. *Almeida v. Baldi*, 195 F.2d 815, 33 A.L.R.2d 1407, and United States ex rel. *Thompson v. Dye*, 221 F.2d 763 which, we agree, state the correct constitutional rule.

This ruling is an extension of *Mooney v. Holohan*, 294 U.S. 103, 112, where the Court ruled on what nondisclosure by a prosecutor violates due process:

"It is a requirement that cannot be deemed to be satisfied by mere notice and hearing if a state has contrived a conviction through the pretense of a trial which, in truth, is but used as a means of depriving a defendant of liberty through a deliberate deception of court and jury by the presentation of testimony known to be perjured. Such a contrivance by a state to procure the conviction and imprisonment of a defendant is as inconsistent with the rudimentary demands of justice as is the obtaining of a like result by intimidation."

In *Pyle v. Kansas*, 317 U.S. 213, 215–216, we phrased the rule in broader terms:

"Petitioner's papers are inexpertly drawn, but they do set forth allegations that his imprisonment resulted from perjured testimony, knowingly used by the State authorities to obtain his conviction, and from the deliberate suppression by those same authorities of evidence favorable to him. These allegations sufficiently charge a deprivation of rights guaranteed by the Federal Constitution, and, if proven, would entitle petitioner to release from his present custody. *Mooney v. Holohan*, 294 U.S. 103."

We now hold that the suppression by the prosecution of evidence favorable to an accused upon request violates due process where the evidence is material either to guilt or to punishment, irrespective of the good faith or bad faith of the prosecution.

Evlakhov Valeriy/Shutterstock.com

- Further examples about the impetus of civil rights violations (both federal and state law enforcement are impacted)

There is no bright-line rule to determine when an investigatory stop becomes an arrest. *United States v. Parr*, 843 F.2d 1228, 1231 (9th Cir. 1988). Rather, in determining whether stops have turned into arrests, courts consider the "totality of the circumstances." *United States v. Del Vizo*, 918 F.2d 821, 824 (9th Cir. 1990) (quoting *United States v. Baron*, 860 F.2d 911, 914 (9th Cir. 1988), cert. denied, 490 U.S. 1040, 109 S.Ct. 1944, 104 L.Ed.2d 414 (1989)). As might be expected, the ultimate decision in such cases is fact specific.

Baker v. McCollan, No. 78-752 (1979)

For 1983 imposes civil liability only upon one "who, under color of any statute, ordinance, regulation, custom, or usage, of any State or Territory, subjects, or causes to be subjected, any citizen of the United States or other person within the jurisdiction thereof to the deprivation of any rights, privileges, or immunities secured by the Constitution and laws . . ."

The first inquiry in any 1983 suit, therefore, is whether the plaintiff has been deprived of a right "secured by the Constitution and laws." If there has been no such deprivation, the state of mind of the defendant is wholly immaterial. We think that respondent has failed to satisfy this threshold requirement of 1983 and thus defer once again consideration of the question whether simple negligence can give rise to 1983 liability.

The 14th Amendment does not protect against all deprivations of liberty. It protects only against deprivations of liberty accomplished "without due process of law."

A reasonable division of functions between law enforcement officers, committing magistrates, and judicial officers—all of whom may be potential defendants in a 1983 action—is entirely consistent with "due process of law." Given the requirements that arrest be made only on probable cause and that one detained be accorded a speedy trial, we do not think a sheriff executing an arrest warrant is required by the constitution [443 U.S. 137, 146] to investigate independently every claim of innocence, whether the claim is based on mistaken identity or a defense such as lack of requisite intent. Nor is the official charged with maintaining custody of the accused named in the warrant required by the Constitution to perform an error-free investigation of such a claim. The ultimate determination of such claims of innocence is placed in the hands of the judge and the jury.

Monroe v. Pape, 365 U.S. 167 (1961)

Held: The complaint stated a cause of action against the police officers under § 1979; but the City of Chicago was not liable under that section. Pp. 168–192.

   Section 1979 came onto the books as § 1 of the Ku Klux Act of April 20, 1871. 17 Stat. 13. It was one of the means whereby Congress exercised the power vested in it by § 5 of the Fourteenth Amendment to enforce the provisions of that Amendment.

1. Allegation of facts constituting a deprivation under color of state authority of the guaranty against unreasonable searches and seizures, contained in the Fourth Amendment and made applicable to the States by the Due Process Clause of the Fourteenth Amendment, satisfies to that extent the requirement of § 1979. Pp. 170–171.

2. In enacting § 1979, Congress intended to give a remedy to parties deprived of constitutional rights, privileges and immunities by an official's abuse of his position. Pp. 171–187.

   a. The statutory words "under color of any statute, ordinance, regulation, custom, or usage, of any State or Territory" do not exclude acts of an official or policeman who can show no authority under state law, custom or usage to do what he did, or even who violated the state constitution and laws. Pp. 172–187. [p168]

   b. One of the purposes of this legislation was to afford a federal right in federal courts because, by reason of prejudice, passion, neglect, intolerance, or otherwise, state laws might not be enforced and the claims of citizens to the enjoyment of rights, privileges and immunities guaranteed by the Fourteenth Amendment might be denied by state agencies. Pp. 174–180.

    c. The federal remedy is supplementary to the state remedy, and the state remedy need not be sought and refused before the federal remedy is invoked. P. 183.

    d. Misuse of power possessed by virtue of state law and made possible only because the wrongdoer is clothed with the authority of state law is action taken "under color of" state law within the meaning of § 1979. *United States v. Classic*, 313 U.S. 299; *Screws v. United States*, 325 U.S. 91. Pp. 183–187.

3. Since § 1979 does not contain the word "willfully," as does 18 U.S.C. § 242 and § 1979 imposes civil liability, rather than criminal sanctions, actions under § 1979 can dispense with the requirement of showing a "specific intent to deprive a person of a federal right." P. 187.

4. The City of Chicago is not liable under § 1979, because Congress did not intend to bring municipal corporations within the ambit of that section. Pp. 187–192.

False Arrest

"Arrest" is defined as taking a person into custody against his or her will for the purpose of criminal prosecution or interrogation.

An arrest only occurs when there is a governmental termination of freedom of movement through means intentionally applied. A conclusion that is used to describe a complex series of events that have taken place. In order for an arrest to be valid, the officer must have probable cause. The officer must have the intent to take the person into custody. The officer must have the authority to restrict the person's liberty. The person must come under the control and custody of the officer, via voluntary submission or use of force. In a false arrest claim, the plaintiff asserts that the arresting officer or officers deprived her of her liberty without proper authority. The plaintiff will generally allege that the officer acted without probable cause.

Brodnicki v. City of Omaha, 874 F.Supp. 1006 (1995)

A warrantless arrest without probable cause violates the Constitution and forms the basis for a § 1983 claim. If there was probable cause for the officers' actions, however, they cannot be held liable. *Hannah v. Overland*, 795 F.2d 1385 (8th Cir. 1986). When the facts are not in dispute, whether probable cause existed is a question of law, and summary judgment is appropriate. *White v. Pierce County*, 797 F.2d 812, 815 (9th Cir. 1986).

The U.S. Supreme Court articulated the test for probable cause in *Beck v. Ohio*, 379 U.S. 89 (1964):

> Whether [an] arrest was constitutionally valid depends . . . upon whether, at the moment the arrest was made, the officers had probable cause to make it—whether at that moment the facts and circumstances within their knowledge and of which they had reasonably trustworthy information were sufficient to warrant a prudent man in believing that the [person arrested] had committed . . . an offense.

Id. at 91, 85 S.Ct. at 225. The Supreme Court has acknowledged that it is inevitable that law enforcement officials will from time to time reasonably but mistakenly conclude that probable cause is present, but should nevertheless not be held liable. *Anderson v. Creighton*, 483 U.S. 635 (1987). As the U.S. Court of Appeals for the Second Circuit has stated, "[e]vidence before the court might be insufficient to sustain a finding of probable cause for the [arrest], yet be adequate for the judge to conclude it was reasonable for [the officer] to believe he had a good basis for his actions." *Magnotti v. Kuntz*, 918 F.2d 364, 367 (2d Cir. 1990). Probable cause does require overwhelmingly convincing evidence, but only "reasonably trustworthy information." Beck, 379 U.S. at 91, 85 S.Ct. at 225. Probable cause "is to be viewed from the vantage point of a prudent, reasonable, cautious police officer on the scene at the time of the arrest guided by his experience and training." *United States v. Davis*, 458 F.2d 819, 821 (D.C.Cir. 1972); see also *United States v. Ortiz*, 422 U.S. 891 (1975). The Court must therefore consider the facts and circumstances within the officers' knowledge and of which they had reasonably trustworthy information at the time of arrest.

Washington v. Lambert, No. 94-56685 (9th Cir. 1996)
Facts and Procedural History

Around midnight on June 25, 1991, Washington, a picture editor with Sports Illustrated, and Hicks, a senior program analyst at the Bank of New York, who were visiting the Los Angeles area from New York, were returning from a baseball game at Dodger Stadium. Perhaps not reflecting the best gustatory judgment, they decided to stop at a Carl's Jr. restaurant in Santa Monica to get some food to take back to their hotel. Their decision proved to be an unfortunate one. Skystone Lambert, a uniformed Santa Monica police officer, had also chosen to visit Carl's Jr. that evening. He observed Hicks and Washington and thought they resembled the description of two suspects being sought for 19 armed robberies, most of which had taken place in the western part of the vast Los Angeles metropolitan area. Lambert also thought that

Washington appeared nervous. None of the robberies had occurred in the City of Santa Monica, and the most recent had occurred six days earlier.

Police knowledge of the suspects in the robberies consisted of the following. They were described as two African–American males, aged 20–30, one tall (6' to 6'2") and 150–170 pounds, and the other short (5'5" to 5'7") and 170–190 pounds. They were known to have driven a variety of get-away cars—including a Porsche 911, a BMW and a stolen, white Oldsmobile Cutlass. The police bulletin also stated that they were considered armed and dangerous.

Neither Washington nor Hicks fit the specifics of the descriptions of the suspects. Washington was 6'4" and weighed 235 pounds. He was taller and far heavier than the "tall suspect." Hicks was 5'7 1/212" and weighed 135–140 pounds. He was much thinner than the "short suspect."

Based principally on what appeared to him to be physical similarities between Washington and Hicks and the two suspects, Lambert called for back-up and followed Washington and Hicks out of the fast-food restaurant. Hicks noticed they were being followed and told Washington. Washington and Hicks entered a white Plymouth Dynasty, which bore a rental car company sticker on the back bumper and drove off. Lambert followed in his squad car. A second police car soon joined Lambert in following Hicks and Washington. Washington looked back several times, which Lambert found suspicious. While following the car, Lambert requested a check on the license plate, which revealed that it had not been reported stolen.

Washington and Hicks reached their hotel and entered the underground parking garage. Lambert did not immediately follow them into the garage because he did not observe them make the turn into the garage entrance. Thus, the police cars did not arrive until Washington and Hicks were preparing to get out of their car. The officers shone spotlights on the two men and pointed their guns at them. Using the police vehicle's speaker system, Lambert ordered Hicks to open the car door and get out, raise his hands and interlock his fingers behind his head, face the wall, and close the car door with his feet. Lambert repeated the instructions for Washington. He ordered Washington and Hicks one by one, to walk backward toward him. He then handcuffed their hands behind their backs, patted them down, and placed them in separate police cars. Washington and Hicks complied with all orders and offered no resistance.

The officers searched the rental car and opened up Hicks' fanny-pack/pouch where he found identification. Lambert then reached into Washington's pants and retrieved his wallet. The officers looked at the men's identification and may have run a computer check. If so, it failed to reveal any outstanding warrants or other problems. In any event, shortly after the officers concluded their investigation, they released the two men.

In total, three or four police cars gathered in the hotel garage in order that the officers assigned to them could help detain Washington and Hicks. Washington estimated that there were about seven officers at the scene. Sergeant Grant, a supervisor who arrived at the end of the incident, testified that he believed that four officers were present when he arrived. No one disputes that one of the policemen was a K–9 officer with a police dog in tow.

Washington and Hicks filed suit under 42 U.S.C. § 1983 alleging a violation of their Fourth Amendment rights. Defendant Lambert moved for summary judgment on the basis of qualified immunity. The district judge, the Honorable Harry L. Hupp, denied the motion. The case went to trial, and on the third day of trial, Judge Hupp again denied defendant's motion for a judgment of qualified immunity, granted a directed verdict for the plaintiffs, and left only the issue of damages for the jury. The district judge believed he was bound under this circuit's precedent to grant the directed verdict because, on the undisputed facts, the detention constituted an arrest, the officers lacked probable cause, and the law was clearly established. The jury deadlocked and was unable to reach a verdict on damages. The defendants subsequently filed a motion to reconsider the previous order denying dismissal on the basis of qualified immunity. The district judge denied the motion as to Officer Lambert, again rejecting his argument that he had only performed a Terry stop and finding instead that he had made what a reasonable officer should have known was an arrest without probable cause.

Some of the first modern judicial review of racial profiling entered into this case:

In balancing the interests in freedom from arbitrary government intrusion and the legitimate needs of law enforcement officers, we cannot help but be aware that the burden of aggressive and intrusive police action falls disproportionately on African–American, and sometimes Latino, males. Notwithstanding the views of some legal theoreticians, as a practical matter neither society nor our enforcement of the laws is yet color-blind. Cases, newspaper reports, books, and scholarly writings all make clear that the experience of being stopped by the police is a much more common one for black men than it is for white men. See, e.g., Kolender v. Lawson, 461 U.S. 352, 354, 103 S.Ct. 1855, 1856, 75 L.Ed.2d 903 (1983) (Lawson, a law abiding African–American man, was stopped or arrested fifteen times in primarily white neighborhoods in a 22–month period); Jeff Brazil and Steve Berry, Color of Driver is Key to Stops in I–95 Videos, Orl. Sent., Aug. 23, 1992, at A1 and Henry Curtis, Statistics Show Pattern of Discrimination, Orl. Sent. Aug. 23, 1992 at A11 (videotapes show that 70% of stops made by drug interdiction unit on portion of I–95 in Florida are of African–Americans or Hispanics, although they made up only 5% of the drivers on that stretch of the interstate. Only about 5% of these stops lead to arrests); Michael Schneider, State Police I–95 Drug Unit Found to Search Black Motorists 4 Times More Often Than White, Balt. Sun, May 23, 1996, at B2 (reporting similar statistics in Maryland four years later); David A. Harris, Factors for Reasonable Suspicion: When Black and Poor Means Stopped and Frisked, 69 Ind. L.J. 659, 679–80 (1994); Elizabeth A. Gaynes, The Urban Criminal Justice System: Where Young + Black + Male = Probable Cause, 20 Ford. Urb. L.J. 621, 623–25 (1993); Tracey Maclin, Black and Blue Encounters—Some Preliminary Thoughts About Fourth Amendment Seizures: Should Race Matter?, 26 Val. U.L.Rev. 243, 250–57 (documenting incidents); Developments in the Law—Race and the Criminal Process, 101 Harv. L.Rev. 1472, 1505 (1988) ("[P]olice often lower their standards of investigation when a suspect has been described as a minority, thus intruding upon a greater number of individuals who meet the racial description than if the suspect had been described as white.").

Although much of the evidence concerns the disproportionate burden police action imposes on African–American males who are young and poor, there is substantial evidence that the experience of being stopped by police is also common both for older African–Americans and for those who are professionals—lawyers, doctors, businessmen, and academics.10 E.g., Schneider, I–95 Drug Unit, at B2 (reporting complaints of an African–American couple in their mid-sixties whose minivan was pulled over and searched for drugs on their 40th wedding anniversary); Gaynes, Probable Cause, 20 Ford. Urb. L.J. at 625 ("Most black professionals can recount at least one incident of being stopped, roughed up, questioned, or degraded by white police officers."). For example, Deval Patrick, formerly a partner in a prestigious Boston law firm and now an Assistant Attorney General of the United States and head of the Civil Rights Division at the Department of Justice, recently reported that "I still get stopped if I'm driving a nice car in the 'wrong' neighborhood." Deval Patrick, Have Americans Forgotten Who They Are?, L.A. Times, Sept. 2, 1996, at B5. Christopher Darden, a suddenly well-known prosecutor, recently wrote that he is stopped by police five times a year because "I always seem to get pulled over by some cop who is suspicious of a black man driving a Mercedes." Christopher Darden, In Contempt 110 (1996). Henry L. Gates, Jr. has written, poignantly, "[n]or does [University of Chicago Professor] William Julius Wilson wonder why he was stopped near a small New England town by a policeman who wanted to know what he was doing in those parts. There's a moving violation that many African–Americans know as D.W.B.: Driving While Black." Thirteen Ways of Looking at a Black Man, New Yorker, Oct. 23, 1995 at 59; see also Michael A. Fletcher, Driven to Extremes; Black Men Take Steps to Avoid Police Stops, Wash. Post, March 29, 1996, at A1 (reporting frequent stops by police of black professionals). These encounters are humiliating, damaging to the detainees' self-esteem, and reinforce the reality that racism and intolerance are for many African–Americans a regular part of their daily lives. See, e.g., Charles N. Jamison, Jr., Racism: The Hurt That Men Won't Name, Essence, Nov. 1992 at 64; Patrick, Have Americans Forgotten?.

The Court went on to include the following:

In recent years, police in the Los Angeles area have unlawfully detained Hall of Fame baseball player Joe Morgan at the Los Angeles airport. Morgan v. Woessner, 997 F.2d 1244, 1254 (9th Cir.1993) (affirming district court holding that Morgan's seizure on basis of tip that "made all black men suspect" and Morgan's walking away from police was illegal). The police have also erroneously stopped businessman and former Los Angeles Laker star Jamaal Wilkes in his car and handcuffed him, and stopped 1984 Olympic medalist Al Joyner twice in the space of twenty minutes, and once forcing him out of his car, handcuffing him and making him to lie spread-eagled on the ground at gunpoint. A Foul on 'Silk', L.A. Times, March 2, 1991; John Schwada, Track Olympian Settles False–Arrest Lawsuit, L.A. Times, February 8, 1995. Similarly, actor Wesley Snipes was taken from his car at gunpoint, handcuffed, and forced to lie on the ground while a policeman kneeled on his neck and held a gun to his head. John L. Mitchell, Four Actors Allege Abuse by Police, L.A. Times, April 13, 1991. Actor Blair Underwood was also stopped in his car and detained at gunpoint. Id. We do not know exactly how often this happens to African–American men and women who are not celebrities and whose brushes with the police are not deemed newsworthy. It is clear, however, that African–Americans are stopped by the police in disproportionate numbers. See also discussion infra, at 1187–88. We believe that there is much truth to Justice Jackson's statement, made almost fifty years ago in Brinegar v. United States, 338 U.S. 160, 181, 69 S.Ct. 1302, 1313–14, 93 L.Ed. 1879 (1949), that "there are[ ] many unlawful searches of homes and automobiles of innocent people which turn up nothing incriminating, in which no arrest is made, about which courts do nothing, and about which we never hear." (Jackson, J., dissenting).

In looking at the totality of the circumstances, the Court will consider both the intrusiveness of the stop, that is, the aggressiveness of the police methods and how much the plaintiff's liberty was restricted, United States v. Robertson, 833 F.2d 777, 780 (9th Cir. 1987) ("Whether an arrest has occurred depends on all the surrounding circumstances, including the extent to which liberty of movement is curtailed and the type of force or authority employed."), and the justification for the use of such tactics, that is, whether the officer had sufficient basis to fear for his safety to warrant the intrusiveness of the action taken. For example, *United States v. Jacobs*, 715 F.2d 1343, 1345–46 (9th Cir. 1983) (per curiam). In short, <u>the Court will decide whether the police action constitutes a Terry stop or an arrest by evaluating not only how intrusive the stop was, but also whether the methods used were reasonable given the specific circumstances.</u> See Del Vizo, 918 F.2d at 824–25. As a result, the Court has held that while certain police actions constitute an arrest in certain circumstances, for example, where the "suspects" are cooperative, those same actions may not constitute an arrest where the suspect is uncooperative or the police have specific reasons to believe that a serious threat to the safety of the officers exists. "The relevant inquiry is always one of reasonableness under the circumstances." *Allen v. City of Los Angeles*, 66 F.3d 1052, 1057 (9th Cir. 1995) (quoting *United States v. Sanders*, 994 F.2d 200, 206 (5th Cir.)

The Ninth Circuit Court stated in *Washington v. Lambert* "Whether we deem a particular detention a Terry stop or an arrest is of great importance because the decision we make will frequently determine whether the police conduct was lawful or not. <u>If we conclude that the detention was only a 'stop' it will be lawful even though there was no probable cause. If, under the same circumstances, we term it an arrest, it will not be lawful in the absence of such cause. In the latter case, the evidence seized will be excludable and the arresting officer may be liable for damages.</u> It would be far simpler, and on the surface far more logical, to base the decision as to whether an arrest occurred solely on the determination of how intrusive the stop and eventual detention was, on how severely the police action infringed on the suspect's liberty. If we were to do so, we could set forth simple rules as to how intrusive police action must be before a suspect is deemed to have been arrested. There are, however, valid reasons why the law has developed differently."

Targn Pleiades/Shutterstock.com

Continuing—"Although our doctrine lacks the simplicity and logic of a bright-line rule, the analytical course we have chosen proved necessary to accommodate our compelling and legitimate concerns for the safety of law enforcement personnel. In proclaiming the law of unlawful arrests, we must always keep in mind two important concerns: the safety of those who serve the public by enforcing the law and the constitutionally guaranteed 'right of the people to be secure in their persons against unreasonable searches and seizures.' U.S. Const. amend. IV. <u>Accordingly, when we evaluate whether the police conduct was lawful or unlawful, we must do so in light of the dangerousness of the particular situation that confronted the police.</u> Sometimes, an investigatory stop may involve more than the ordinary risks inherent in any contact between police officers and suspects. Even though the officers may not have sufficient cause to make an arrest, they may have to take particular measures to protect themselves during the course of the stop. As a result, we allow intrusive and aggressive police conduct without deeming it an arrest in those circumstances when it is a reasonable response to legitimate safety concerns on the part of the investigating officers."

The complexity of this doctrinal scheme—that is, that the identical police action can be an arrest under some circumstances and not in others—originated with *Terry v. Ohio* and subsequent decisions allowing the police to stop suspects for "investigatory detentions" with less than probable cause. When the investigatory stop became an accepted part of police procedure, courts began allowing police, in certain circumstances, to take intrusive steps to protect themselves as part of a Terry stop, while recognizing that in other circumstances the use of those same methods in connection with such a stop might turn it into an arrest. This doctrinal flexibility allows officers to take the steps necessary to protect themselves when they have adequate reason to believe that stopping and questioning the suspect will pose particular risks to their safety. See generally Terry, 392 U.S. at 23, 88 S.Ct. at 1881 ("Certainly it would be unreasonable to require that police officers take unnecessary risks in the performance of their duties."); see also Jacobs, 715 F.2d at 1346.

<u>"It is because we consider both the inherent danger of the situation and the intrusiveness of the police action, that pointing a weapon at a suspect and handcuffing him, or ordering him to lie on the ground, or placing him in a police car will not automatically convert an investigatory stop into an arrest that requires probable cause."</u> Del Vizo, 918 F.2d at 825; see also Allen, 66 F.3d at 1056.

Free Wind 2014/Shutterstock.com

Although we are mindful that those who serve the public by taking on the dangerous job of enforcing the criminal laws are not required by the 4th Amendment to take unreasonable risks, we also recognize that, by their choice of a profession, they have knowingly agreed to subject themselves to some physical jeopardy. That is inherent in the job of a law enforcement officer. In fact, it is the nature of a democratic society that all of us, especially the police, take some risks in the interest of preserving freedom. While we must not compel police officers to take unnecessary risks, total security is possible, if at all, only in a society that puts a much lesser premium on freedom than does ours. Therefore, in determining whether a stop was lawful or unlawful, we must consider the risk to the police officers inherent in the situation, but we must also consider the liberty interests all Americans cherish—"specifically the freedom from unreasonable searches and seizures guaranteed by the Fourth Amendment to our Constitution."

Continuing—"In this nation, all people have a right to be free from the terrifying and humiliating experience of being pulled from their cars at gunpoint, handcuffed, or made to lie face down on the pavement when insufficient reason for such intrusive police conduct exists. The police may not employ such tactics every time they have an 'articulable basis' for thinking that someone may be a suspect in a crime. The infringement on personal liberty resulting from so intrusive a type of investigatory stop is simply too great. <u>Under ordinary circumstances, when the police have only reasonable suspicion to make an investigatory stop, drawing weapons and using handcuffs and other restraints will violate the 4th Amendment.</u> Del Vizo, 918 F.2d at 825; *United States v. Delgadillo–Velasquez,* 856 F.2d 1292, 1295 (9th Cir. 1988).

In fact, even markedly less intrusive police action has been held to constitute an arrest when the inherent danger of the situation does not justify the intrusive police action. For example, *United States v. Ricardo D.*, 912 F.2d 337, 340–42 (9th Cir. 1990) (finding arrest occurred where police held suspect in patrol car for twenty minutes without drawing weapons or handcuffing him); Robertson, 833 F.2d at 781 (numerous police officers drew guns and detained suspect, neither handcuffed nor in a police car, for 5–15 minutes); id. at 787 (Noonan, J., dissenting) (acknowledging that

nobeastsofierce/Shutterstock.com

if the police had ordered suspect to 'prone out' it probably would have constituted an arrest even if the police did not handcuff or touch the suspect); *Kraus v. County of Pierce*, 793 F.2d 1105, 1109 (9th Cir. 1986) (holding that arrest occurred where police used guns and searchlights but neither handcuffed suspects nor restrained them in a police car)."

False Imprisonment

The unlawful confining of a person, which deprives that person of their liberty

- Includes prolonged detention

Brady v. Dill, No. 98-2293 (1999)

This appeal poses an intriguing question of constitutional law. Suppose that the following scenario exists: (1) the police arrest a person pursuant to a facially valid warrant, supported by probable cause; (2) the person, though named in the warrant, asserts that he is actually innocent; and (3) the police come to believe that claim. In those circumstances, can the officers be held liable under 42 U.S.C. § 1983 for their refusal unilaterally to release the person whom they have arrested?

<u>When qualified immunity is at issue, an inquiring court first must ask whether the Constitution recognizes the right asserted by the plaintiff.</u> See *Conn v. Gabbert*, 526 U.S. 286, —, 119 S.Ct. 1292, 1295, 143 L.Ed.2d 399 (1999).

1. Warrantless searches incident to a valid arrest are limited to the person and the surrounding area.
2. A search is any governmental intrusion into a person's reasonable and justifiable expectation of privacy.
3. *Minnesota v. Dickerson*, 508 U.S. 366 (1993): expanded stop-and-frisk to seizure of contraband detected through an officer's sense of touch.

Howe v. State 916 P.2d 153 (1996) Reasoning and explanation from the Court:
    "The Fourth Amendment to the United States Constitution forbids unreasonable searches and seizures. U.S. Const. amend. IV." Warrantless searches and seizures in a home are presumptively unreasonable. "*Doleman v. State*, 107 Nev. 409, 413, 812 P.2d

1287, 1289 (1991) (citing *Payton v. New York*, 445 U.S. 573, 587, 100 S. Ct. 1371, 1380, 63 L. Ed. 2d 639 (1980))." However, warrantless searches are permitted if based upon both probable cause and exigent circumstances. "Id. Consent also exempts a search from the probable cause and warrant requirements of the Fourth Amendment. *Schneckloth v. Bustamonte*, 412 U.S. 218, 93 S. Ct. 2041, 36 L. Ed. 2d 854 (1973); *Davis*

Andrey_Popov/Shutterstock.com

v. State, 99 Nev. 25, 656 P.2d 855 (1983). When considering our citizens' constitutional right to be secure in their homes and free from unreasonable searches and seizures," this court, on review, must be careful not to permit the exception to swallow the rule. "*Phillips v. State*, 106 Nev. 763, 765–66, 801 P.2d 1363, 1365 (1990) (quoting *Nelson v. State*, 96 Nev. 363, 365, 609 P.2d 717, 719 [1980])". The 4th Amendment protects the individual's privacy in a variety of settings. In none is the zone of privacy more clearly defined than when bounded by the unambiguous physical dimensions of an individual's home, a zone that finds its roots in clear and specific constitutional terms: "The right of people to be secure in their. . . houses . . . shall not be violated." That language unequivocally establishes the proposition that "[a]t the very core [of the Fourth Amendment] stands the right of a man to retreat into his own home and there be free from unreasonable governmental intrusion." *Silverman v. United States*, 365 U.S. 505, 511 [81 S. Ct. 679, 683, 5 L. Ed. 2d 734 (1961)]. In terms that apply equally to seizures of property and to seizures of persons, the 4th Amendment has drawn a firm line at the entrance to the house. Absent exigent circumstances, that threshold may not reasonably be crossed without a warrant. Exigent circumstances are "those circumstances that would cause a reasonable person to believe that entry (or other relevant prompt action) was necessary to prevent physical harm to the officers and other persons, the destruction of relevant evidence, the escape of the suspect, or some other consequence improperly frustrating legitimate law enforcement efforts." *Doleman v. State*, 107 Nev. 409, 414, 812 P.2d 1287, 1290 (1991) (quoting *United States v. McConney*, 728 F.2d 1195, 1199 (9th Cir.), cert. denied, 469 U.S. 824, 105 S. Ct. 101, 83 L. Ed. 2d 46 (1984)). "[I]n the absence of a showing, by the State, of a true necessity that is, an imminent and substantial threat to life, health, or property the constitutionally guaranteed right to privacy must prevail." *Nelson v. State*, 96 Nev.

363, 366, 609 P.2d 717, 719 (1980). <u>The state bears the burden of showing that the exigencies of the situation required intrusion without a warrant.</u> *State v. Hardin*, 90 Nev. 10, 13, 518 P.2d 151, 153 (1974).

An Area of Debate

Racial profiling: stopping a person based solely on their perceived race or ethnicity instead of individualized suspicion

Diminished expectation of privacy in public transportation facilities (e.g., airports); individuals may be singled out for scrutiny (*United States v. Drayton*, 1999)

Profiling—in and of itself, profiling is a valid and lawful law enforcement tool. Can help an officer with articulation of an individualized suspicion. Must be objective reasonable and not based solely on race or ethnicity.

To every violation and charge, there will be a defense.
Each of these defenses bars recovery of damages by plaintiffs:

1. <u>Absolute immunity</u>
   Courtroom testimony to include perjury by the police officer.
   The courts have recognized that there are other sanctions to include criminal perjury.
   Therefore, officers who intentionally provide perjured testimony are immune from civil liability but may be charged and convicted of a criminal offense.
2. <u>Qualified immunity</u>
   Qualified immunity extends to police officers who are performing duties of a discretionary nature.
   Duties that require deliberation or judgment.
   To protect "all but the plainly incompetent or those who knowingly violate the law"
   - Determined by a two-part analysis
   - Breech of a clearly established constitutional right.
   - Was the officers' conduct objectively reasonable?
   The Individual Defense:
   - Objectively reasonable mistakes
   - Not a "Good Faith" defense
   - Lost when violating a clearly established Constitutional right

"In determining whether an officer is entitled to qualified immunity, we consider (1) whether there has been a violation of a constitutional right; and (2) whether that right was clearly established at the time of the officer's alleged misconduct." *Lal v. California*, 746 F.3d 1112, 1116 (9th Cir. 2014) (citing *Pearson v. Callahan*, 555 U.S. 223, 232 (2009)). While we have discretion to decide which prong to address first, here we address both. Id. Graham provides the framework for reviewing excessive force claims. Its nonexhaustive list of factors for evaluating reasonableness include: (1) the severity of the crime at issue; (2) whether the suspect posed an immediate threat to the safety of the officers or others; and (3) whether the suspect actively resisted arrest or attempted to escape. Graham, 490 U.S. at 396; see also *George v. Morris*, 736 F.3d 829, 837–38 (9th Cir. 2013) (discussing Graham and *Tennessee v. Garner*, 471 U.S. 1 [1985]). We must judge the reasonableness of a particular use of force "from the perspective of a reasonable officer on the scene, rather than with the 20/20 vision of hindsight," Graham, 490 U.S. at 396, keeping in mind that the "most important' factor under Graham is whether the suspect posed an 'immediate threat to the safety of the officers or others,'" George, 736 F.3d at 838 (internal quotation marks omitted) (quoting *Bryan v. MacPherson*, 630 F.3d 805, 826 (9th Cir. 2010)). "*[S]ummary judgment should be granted sparingly in excessive force cases. This principle applies with particular force where the only witness other than the officers was killed during the encounter.*" *Gonzalez v. City of Anaheim, 747 F.3d 789, 795 (9th Cir. 2014) (en banc)*.

"A Government official's conduct violates clearly established law when, at the time of the challenged conduct, '[t]he contours of [a] right [are] sufficiently clear' that every 'reasonable official would have understood that what he is doing violates that right.'" *Ashcroft v. al-Kidd*, 131 S. Ct. 2074, 2083 (2011) (alteration in original) (quoting *Anderson v. Creighton*, 483 U.S. 635, 640 [1987]). "We do not require a case directly on point, but existing precedent must have placed the . . . constitutional question beyond debate." Id.; see also *Brosseau v. Haugen*, 543 U.S. 194, 198 (2004) (per curiam) (explaining that the qualified immunity inquiry "must be undertaken in light of the specific context of the case, not as a broad general proposition" (quoting *Saucier v. Katz*, 533 U.S. 194, 201 [2001]).

Gonzalez, 747 F.3d at 793–98 (reversing the district court's grant of summary judgment on excessive force claim where officer shot driver of a minivan after driver accelerated vehicle with officer inside and refused commands to stop); Glenn, 673 F.3d at 871–78 (reversing the district court's grant of summary judgment on excessive force claim where officers shot and killed individual who did not comply with orders to put down a knife for approximately three minutes); George, 736 F.3d at 837–39 (affirming the district court's denial of summary judgment on excessive force claim where officer shot and killed an armed individual and there were triable issues as to whether the individual had the gun "trained on the ground"). Brosseau, 543 U.S. at 200–01 (holding that officer was entitled to qualified immunity where the cases relied on by plaintiffs did not "squarely govern[]" the constitutionality of shooting a "disturbed felon, set on avoiding capture through vehicular flight, when persons in the immediate area [were] at risk from that flight"); *Blanford v. Sacramento* County, 406 F.3d 1110, 1119 (9th Cir. 2005) (holding that deputies were entitled to qualified immunity because they "would not have found fair warning in Garner, Graham, or any other Supreme Court or circuit precedent at the time that they could not use deadly force to prevent someone with an edged sword, which they had repeatedly commanded him to drop and whom they had repeatedly warned would otherwise be shot, from accessing a private residence where they or people in the house or yard might be seriously harmed").

3. Probable cause
   Police officers who face false arrest or unlawful search are afforded qualified immunity if they can show probable cause.
   Probable cause in this sense is defined as reasonable good faith belief in the legality of the action taken.
   Officers are therefore entitled to immunity if a reasonable officer could have believed that probable cause existed to arrest.

4. Good faith
   In effect argues that at the time the act was committed the officer could not have reasonably known that the act was unconstitutional or against the law.
   Arresting on a valid warrant that later is determined to be invalid is an example.

4th Amendment—Reasonableness

Brower v. Inyo, No. 87-248 (1989)

1. Consistent with the language, history, and judicial construction of the 4th Amendment, a seizure occurs when governmental termination of a person's movement is effected through means intentionally applied. Because the complaint

alleges that Brower was stopped by the instrumentality set in motion or put in place to stop him, it states a claim of 4th Amendment "seizure." (pp. 595–599).

2. Petitioners can claim the right to recover for Brower's death because the unreasonableness alleged consists precisely of setting up the roadblock in such a manner as to be likely to kill him. On remand, the Court of Appeals must determine whether the District Court erred in concluding that the roadblock was not "unreasonable." (pp. 599–600).

3. In *Tennessee v. Garner*, 471 U.S. 1 (1985), all Members of the Court agreed that a police officer's fatal shooting of a fleeing suspect constituted a 4th Amendment "seizure." See id., at 7; id., at 25. We reasoned that <u>"[w]henever an officer restrains the freedom of a person to walk away, he has seized that person."</u> Id., at 7. While acknowledging Garner, the Court of Appeals here concluded that no "seizure" occurred when Brower collided with the police roadblock because "[p]rior to his failure to stop voluntarily, his freedom of movement was never arrested or restrained" and because "[h]e had a number of opportunities to stop his automobile prior to the impact." 817 F.2d, at 546. Essentially the same thing, however, could have been said in Garner. Brower's independent decision to continue the chase can no more eliminate respondents' responsibility for the termination of his movement effected by the roadblock than Garner's independent decision to flee eliminated the Memphis police officer's responsibility for the termination of his movement effected by the bullet.

4. The Court of Appeals was impelled to its result by consideration of what it described as the "analogous situation" of a police chase in which the suspect unexpectedly loses control of his car and crashes. See *Galas v. McKee*, 801 F.2d 200, 202–203 (CA6 1986) (no seizure in such circumstances). We agree that no unconstitutional seizure occurs there, but not for a reason that has any application to the present case. [489 U.S. 593, 596] <u>Violation of the 4th Amendment requires an intentional acquisition of physical control. A seizure occurs even when an unintended person or thing is the object of the detention or taking,</u> see *Hill v. California*, 401 U.S. 797, 802–805 (1971); cf. *Maryland v. Garrison*, 480 U.S. 79, 85–89 (1987), but <u>the detention or taking itself must be willful.</u> This is implicit in the word "seizure," which can hardly be applied to an unknowing act. The writs of assistance that were the principal grievance against which the 4th Amendment was directed, see *Boyd v. United States*, 116 U.S. 616, 624–625 (1886); T. Cooley, Constitutional Limitations *301–*302, did not involve unintended consequences of government action. Nor did the general warrants issued by Lord Halifax in the 1760s, which produced "the first and only major litigation in the English courts in the field of search and seizure," T. Taylor, Two Studies in Constitutional

Interpretation 26 (1969), including the case we have described as a "monument of English freedom" "undoubtedly familiar" to "every American statesman" at the time the Constitution was adopted, and considered to be "the true and ultimate expression of constitutional law," Boyd, supra, at 626 (discussing *Entick v. Carrington*, 19 How. St. Tr. 1029, 95 Eng. Rep. 807 (K. B. 1765)). In sum, the 4th

Andy Dean Photography/Shutterstock.com

Amendment addresses "misuse of power," *Byars v. United States*, 273 U.S. 28, 33 (1927), not the accidental effects of otherwise lawful government conduct.

14th Amendment—Shocks the Conscience and case law for immunity/summary judgement

COUNTY OF SACRAMENTO v. LEWIS
(96-1337), 98 F.3d 434

"only a purpose to cause harm unrelated to the legitimate object of arrest will satisfy the element of arbitrary conduct shocking to the conscience, necessary for a due process violation."

After petitioner James Smith, a county sheriff's deputy, responded to a call along with another officer, Murray Stapp, the latter returned to his patrol car and saw a motorcycle approaching at high speed, driven by Brian Willard, and carrying Philip Lewis, respondents' decedent, as a passenger. Stapp turned on his rotating lights, yelled for the cycle to stop, and pulled his car closer to Smith's in an attempt to pen the cycle in, but Willard maneuvered between the two cars and sped off. Smith immediately switched on his own emergency lights and siren and began high-speed pursuit. The chase ended after the cycle tipped over. Smith slammed on his brakes, but his car skidded into Lewis, causing massive injuries and death. Respondents brought this action under 42 U.S.C. §

1983, alleging a deprivation of Lewis's 14th Amendment substantive due process right to life. The District Court granted summary judgment for Smith, but the Ninth Circuit reversed, holding, inter alia, that the appropriate degree of fault for substantive due process liability for high-speed police pursuits is deliberate indifference to, or reckless disregard for, a person's right to life and personal security.

HELD: A police officer does not violate substantive due process by causing death through deliberate or reckless indifference to life in a high-speed automobile chase aimed at apprehending a suspected offender. (Pp. 713–1721). (a) The "more-specific-provision" rule of *Graham v. Connor*, 490 U.S. 386, 395, 109 S.Ct. 1865, 1871, 104 L.Ed.2d 443, does not bar respondents' suit. <u>Graham simply requires that if a constitutional claim is covered by a specific constitutional provision, the claim must be analyzed under the standard appropriate to that specific provision, not under substantive due process.</u> For example, *Lanier v. United States*, 520 U.S. 259, —, n. 7, 117 S.Ct. 1219, 1228, n. 7, 137 L.Ed.2d 432 (1997). Substantive due process analysis is therefore inappropriate here only if, as amici argue, respondents' claim is "covered by" the 4th Amendment. It is not. That Amendment covers only "searches and seizures," neither of which took place here. No one suggests that there was a search, and this Court's cases foreclose finding a seizure, since Smith did not terminate Lewis's freedom of movement through means intentionally applied. For example, *Brower v. County of Inyo*, 489 U.S. 593, 597, 109 S.Ct. 1378, 1381, 103 L.Ed.2d 628. (Pp. 1714–1716).

(b) Respondents' allegations are insufficient to state a substantive due process violation. Protection against governmental arbitrariness is the core of due process, for example, *Hurtado v. California*, 110 U.S. 516, 527, 4 S.Ct. 111, 116–117, 28 L.Ed. 232, including substantive due process, see, for example, *Daniels v. Williams*, 474 U.S. 327, 331, 106 S.Ct. 662, 665, 88 L.Ed.2d 662, but only the most egregious executive action can be said to be "arbitrary" in the constitutional sense, for example, *Collins v. Harker Heights*, 503 U.S. 115, 129, 112 S.Ct. 1061, 1071, 117 L.Ed.2d 261; the cognizable level of executive abuse of power is that which shocks the conscience, for example, id., at 128, 112 S.Ct., at 1070; *Rochin v. California*, 342 U.S. 165, 172–173, 72 S.Ct. 205, 209–210, 96 L.Ed. 183. The conscience-shocking concept points clearly away from liability, or clearly toward it, only at the ends of the tort law's culpability spectrum: Liability for negligently inflicted harm is categorically beneath the *1711 constitutional due process threshold, see, for example, *Daniels v. Williams*, 474 U.S., at 328, 106 S.Ct., at 663, while conduct deliberately intended to injure in some way unjustifiable by any government interest is the sort of official action most likely to rise to the conscience-shocking level, see id., at 331, 106 S.Ct., at 665. Whether that level is reached when culpability falls between negligence and intentional conduct is a matter for closer calls. The Court has recognized that deliberate indifference is egregious enough to state a substantive due process claim in one context, that of deliberate indifference to the medical needs of pretrial detainees, see *City of Revere v. Massachusetts Gen. Hospital*, 463 U.S. 239, 244, 103 S.Ct. 2979, 2983, 77 L.Ed.2d 605; cf. *Estelle v. Gamble*, 429 U.S. 97, 104, 97 S.Ct. 285, 291, 50 L.Ed.2d 251, but rules of due process are not subject to mechanical application in unfamiliar territory, and the need to preserve the constitutional proportions of substantive due process demands an exact analysis of context and circumstances before deliberate indifference is condemned as conscience-shocking, cf. *Betts v. Brady*, 316 U.S. 455, 462, 62 S.Ct. 1252, 1256, 86 L.Ed. 1595. Attention to the markedly different circumstances of normal pretrial custody and high-speed law enforcement chases shows why the deliberate indifference that shocks in the one context is less egregious in the other. <u>In the circumstances of a high-speed chase aimed at apprehending a suspected offender, where unforeseen circumstances demand an instant judgment on the part of an officer who feels the pulls of competing obligations, only a purpose to cause harm unrelated to the legitimate object of arrest will satisfy the shocks-the-conscience test.</u> Such chases with no intent to harm suspects physically or to worsen their legal plight do not give rise to substantive due process liability. Cf. *Whitley v. Albers*, 475 U.S. 312, 320–321, 106 S.Ct. 1078, 1084–1085, 89 L.Ed.2d 251. The fault claimed on Smith's part fails to meet this test. Smith was faced with a course of lawless behavior for which the police were not to blame. They had done nothing to cause Willard's high-speed driving in the first place, nothing to excuse his flouting of the commonly understood police authority to control traffic, and nothing (beyond a refusal to call off the chase) to encourage him to race through traffic at breakneck speed. Willard's outrageous behavior was practically instantaneous, and so was Smith's instinctive response. While prudence would have repressed the reaction, Smith's instinct was to do his job, not to induce Willard's lawlessness, or to terrorize, cause harm, or kill. Prudence, that is, was subject to countervailing enforcement considerations, and while Smith exaggerated their demands, there is no reason to believe that they were tainted by an improper or malicious motive. (pp. 1716–1721).

The issue in this case is whether a police officer violates the 14th Amendment's guarantee of substantive

hafakot/Shutterstock.com

due process by causing death through deliberate or reckless indifference to life in a high-speed automobile chase aimed at apprehending a suspected offender. We answer no and <u>hold that in such circumstances only a purpose to cause harm unrelated to the legitimate object of arrest will satisfy the element of arbitrary *1712 conduct shocking to the conscience, necessary for a due process violation.</u>

As in any action under § 1983, the first step is to identify the exact contours of the underlying right said to have been violated. See *Graham v. Connor*, 490 U.S. 386, 394, 109 S.Ct. 1865, 1870–1871, 104 L.Ed.2d 443 (1989). The District Court granted summary judgment to Smith on the basis of qualified immunity, assuming without deciding that a substantive due process violation took place but holding that the law was not clearly established in 1990 so as to justify imposition of § 1983 liability. We do not analyze this case in a similar fashion because, as we have held, the better approach to resolving cases in which the defense of qualified immunity is raised is to determine first whether the plaintiff has alleged a deprivation of a constitutional right at all. Normally, it is only then that a court should ask whether the right allegedly implicated was clearly established at the time of the events in question. See *Siegert v. Gilley*, 500 U.S. 226, 232, 111 S.Ct. 1789, 1793, 114 L.Ed.2d 277 (1991) ("A necessary concomitant to the determination of whether the constitutional right asserted by a plaintiff is 'clearly established' at the time the defendant acted is the determination of whether the plaintiff has asserted a violation of a constitutional right at all, 'and courts should not' assum[e], without deciding, this preliminary issue").

Because we have "always been reluctant to expand the concept of substantive due process," *Collins v. Harker Heights*, supra, at 125, 112 S.Ct., at 1068, we held in *Graham v. Connor* that "[w]here a particular amendment provides an explicit textual source of constitutional protection against a particular sort of government behavior, that Amendment, not the more generalized notion of substantive due process, must be the guide for analyzing these claims." *Albright v. Oliver*, 510 U.S. 266, 273, 114 S.Ct. 807, 813, 127 L.Ed.2d 114 (1994) (plurality opinion of REHNQUIST, C.J.) (quoting *Graham v. Connor*, 490 U.S. 386, 395, 109 S.Ct. 1865, 1871, 104 L.Ed.2d 443 [1989]) (internal quotation marks omitted). Given the rule in Graham, we were presented at oral argument with the threshold issue raised in several *1715 amicus briefs, [FN6] whether facts involving a police chase aimed at apprehending suspects can ever support a due process claim. The argument runs that in chasing the motorcycle, Smith was attempting to make a seizure within the meaning of the 4th Amendment, and, perhaps, even that he succeeded when Lewis was stopped by the fatal collision. <u>Hence, any liability must turn on an application of the reasonableness standard governing searches and seizures, not the due process standard of liability for constitutionally</u>

arbitrary executive action. See *Graham v. Connor*, supra, at 395, 109 S.Ct., at 1871 ("all claims that law enforcement officers have used excessive force—deadly or not—in the course of an arrest, investigatory stop, or other 'seizure' of a free citizen should be analyzed under the Fourth Amendment and its 'reasonableness' standard, rather than under a 'substantive due process' approach"); *Albright v. Oliver*, 510 U.S., at 276, 114 S.Ct., at 814 (GINSBURG, J., concurring); id., at 288, n. 2, 114 S.Ct., at 820 (SOUTER, J., concurring in judgment). One Court of Appeals has indeed applied the rule of Graham to preclude the application of principles of generalized substantive due process to a motor vehicle passenger's claims for injury resulting from reckless police pursuit. See *Mays v. East St. Louis*, 123 F.3d 999, 1002–1003 (C.A.7 1997).

"does not hold that all constitutional claims relating to physically abusive government conduct must arise under either the Fourth or Eighth Amendments; rather, Graham simply requires that if a constitutional claim is covered by a specific constitutional provision, such as the Fourth or Eighth Amendment, the claim must be analyzed under the standard appropriate to that specific provision, not under the rubric of substantive due process." *United States v. Lanier*, 520 U.S. 259, —, n. 7, 117 S.Ct. 1219, 1228, n. 7, 137 L.Ed.2d 432 (1997).

Adwo/Shutterstock.com

The 4th Amendment covers only "searches and seizures," U.S. Const., Amdt. 4, neither of which took place here. No one suggests that there was a search, and our cases foreclose finding a seizure. We held in *California v. Hodari D.*, 499 U.S. 621, 626, 111 S.Ct. 1547, 1550–1551, 113 L.Ed.2d 690 (1991), that a police pursuit in attempting to seize a person does not amount to a "seizure" within the meaning of the 4th Amendment. And in *Brower v. County of Inyo*, 489 U.S. 593, 596–597, 109 S.Ct. 1378, 1381, 103 L.Ed.2d 628 (1989), we explained "that a Fourth Amendment seizure does not occur whenever there is a governmentally caused termination of an individual's freedom of movement (the innocent passerby), nor even whenever there is a governmentally caused and governmentally desired termination of an individual's freedom of movement (the fleeing felon), but only when there is a governmental termination of freedom of movement through means intentionally applied." We illustrated the point by saying that no 4th Amendment seizure would take place where a "pursuing police car sought to stop the suspect only by the show of authority represented by flashing lights and continuing pursuit," but accidentally stopped the suspect by crashing into him. Id., at 597, 109 S.Ct., at 1381–1382. That is exactly this case. See, for example, *Campbell v. White*, 916 F.2d 421, 423 (C.A.7 1990) (following Brower and finding no seizure where a police officer accidentally struck and killed a fleeing motorcyclist during a high-speed pursuit), cert. denied, 499 U.S. 922, 111 S.Ct. 1314, 113 L.Ed.2d 248 (1991). Graham's more-specific-provision rule is therefore no bar to respondents' suit. See, for example, *Frye v. Akron*, 759 F.Supp. 1320, 1324 (N.D.Ind.1991) (parents of a motorcyclist who was struck and killed by a police car during a high-speed pursuit could sue under substantive due process because no *1716 4th Amendment seizure took place); *Evans v. Avery*, 100 F.3d, at 1036 (noting that "outside the context of a seizure, . . . a person injured as a result of police misconduct may prosecute a substantive due process claim under section 1983"); *Pleasant v. Zamieski*, 895 F.2d 272, 276, n. 2(CA6) (noting that Graham "preserve[s] fourteenth amendment substantive due process analysis for those instances in which a free citizen is denied his or her constitutional right to life through means other than a law enforcement official's arrest, investigatory stop or other seizure"), cert. denied, 498 U.S. 851, 111 S.Ct. 144, 112 L.Ed.2d 110 (1990). [FN7]

"The principal and true meaning of the phrase has never been more tersely or accurately stated than by Mr. Justice Johnson, in *Bank of Columbia v. Okely*, 17 U.S. 235, 4 Wheat. 235–244, 4 L.Ed. 559 [(1819)]: 'As to the words from Magna Charta, incorporated into the Constitution of Maryland, after volumes spoken and written with a view to their exposition, the good sense of mankind has at last settled down to this: that they were intended to secure the individual from the arbitrary exercise of the powers of government, unrestrained by the established principles of private right and distributive justice." *Hurtado v. California*, 110 U.S. 516, 527, 4 S.Ct., at 117 (1884).

We have emphasized time and again that "[t]he touchstone of due process is protection of the individual against arbitrary action of government," *Wolff v. McDonnell*, 418 U.S. 539, 558, 94 S.Ct. 2963, 2976, 41 L.Ed.2d 935 (1974), whether the fault lies in a denial of fundamental procedural fairness, see, for example, *Fuentes v. Shevin*, 407 U.S. 67, 82, 92 S.Ct. 1983, 1995, 32 L.Ed.2d 556 (1972) (the procedural due process guarantee protects against "arbitrary takings"), or in the exercise of power without any reasonable justification in the service of a legitimate governmental objective, see, for example, *Daniels v. Williams*, 474 U.S., at 331, 106 S.Ct., at 664 (the substantive due process guarantee protects against government power arbitrarily and oppressively exercised). While due process protection in the substantive sense limits what the government may do in both its legislative, see, for example, *Griswold v. Connecticut*, 381 U.S. 479, 85 S.Ct. 1678, 14 L.Ed.2d 510 (1965), and its executive capacities, see, for example, *Rochin v. California*, 342 U.S. 165, 72 S.Ct. 205, 96 L.Ed. 183 (1952), criteria to identify what is fatally arbitrary differ depending on whether it is legislation or a specific act of a governmental officer that is at issue.

Gts/Shutterstock.com

To this end, for half a century now we have spoken of the cognizable level of executive abuse of power as that which shocks the conscience. We first put the test this way in *Rochin v. California*, supra, at 172–173, 72 S.Ct., at 209–210, where we found the forced pumping of a suspect's stomach enough to offend due process as conduct "that shocks the conscience" and violates the "decencies of civilized conduct." In the intervening years, we have repeatedly adhered to Rochin's benchmark. See, for example, *Breithaupt v. Abram*, 352 U.S. 432, 435, 77 S.Ct. 408, 410, 1 L.Ed.2d 448 (1957) (reiterating that conduct that "'shocked the conscience' and was so 'brutal' and 'offensive' that it did not comport with traditional ideas of fair play and decency" would violate substantive due process); *Whitley v. Albers*, 475 U.S. 312, 327, 106 S.Ct. 1078, 1088, 89 L.Ed.2d 251 (1986) (same); *United States v. Salerno*, 481 U.S. 739, 746, 107 S.Ct. 2095, 2101, 95 L.Ed.2d 697 (1987) ("So-called 'substantive due process' prevents the government from engaging in conduct that 'shocks the conscience,' . . . or interferes with rights 'implicit in the concept of ordered liberty'") (quoting *Rochin v. California*, supra, at 172, 72 S.Ct., at 209–210, and *Palko v. Connecticut*, 302 U.S. 319, 325–326, 58 S.Ct. 149, 151–152, 82 L.Ed. 288 (1937)). Most recently, in *Collins v. Harker Heights*, supra, at 128, 112 S.Ct., at 1070, we said again that the substantive component of the Due Process Clause is violated by executive action only when it "can properly be characterized as arbitrary, or conscience shocking, in a constitutional sense." While the measure of what is conscience-shocking is no calibrated yard stick, it does, as Judge Friendly put it, "poin[t] the way." *Johnson v. Glick*, 481 F.2d 1028, 1033 (C.A.2), cert. denied, 414 U.S. 1033, 94 S.Ct. 462, 38 L.Ed.2d 324 (1973). [FN8]

"[W]hen the State takes a person into its custody and holds him there against his will, the Constitution imposes upon it a corresponding duty to assume some responsibility for his safety and general well-being. The rationale for this principle is simple enough: when the State by the affirmative exercise of its power so restrains an individual's liberty that it renders him unable to care for himself, and at the same time fails to provide for his basic human needs—e.g., food, clothing, shelter, medical care, and reasonable safety—it transgresses the substantive limits on state action set by the . . . Due Process Clause." *DeShaney v. Winnebago County Dept. of Social Servs.*, 489 U.S., at 199–200, 109 S.Ct., at 1005.

But just as <u>the description of the custodial prison situation shows how deliberate indifference can rise to a constitutionally shocking level, so too does it suggest why indifference may well not be enough for liability in the different circumstances</u> of a case like this one. We have, indeed, found that deliberate indifference does not suffice for constitutional liability (albeit under the 8th Amendment) even in prison circumstances when a prisoner's claim arises not from normal custody but from response to a violent disturbance. Our analysis is instructive here:

"[I]n making and carrying out decisions involving the use of force to restore order in the face of a prison disturbance, prison officials undoubtedly must take into account the very real threats the unrest at 1720 presents to inmates and prison officials alike, in addition to the possible harms to inmates against whom force might be used. . .. In this setting, a deliberate indifference standard does not adequately capture the importance of such competing obligations, or convey the appropriate hesitancy to critique in hindsight decisions necessarily made in haste, under pressure, and frequently without the luxury of a second chance." *Whitley v. Albers*, 475 U.S., at 320, 106 S.Ct., at 1084.

We accordingly held that a much higher standard of fault than deliberate indifference has to be shown for officer liability in a prison riot. In those circumstances, liability should turn on "whether force was applied in a good faith effort to maintain or restore discipline or maliciously and sadistically for the very purpose of causing harm." Id., at 320–321, 106 S.Ct., at 1085 (internal quotation marks omitted). The analogy to sudden police chases (under the Due Process Clause) would be hard to avoid.

[8] <u>Like prison officials facing a riot, the police on an occasion calling for fast action have obligations that tend to tug against each other. Their duty is to restore and maintain lawful order, while not exacerbating disorder more than necessary to do their jobs.</u> They are supposed to act decisively and to show restraint at the same moment, and their decisions have to be made "in haste, under pressure, and frequently without the luxury of a second chance." Id., at 320, 106 S.Ct., at 1084; cf. *Graham v. Connor*, 490 U.S., at 397, 109 S.Ct., at 1872 ("police officers are often forced to make split-second judgments—in circumstances that are tense, uncertain, and rapidly evolving"). A police officer deciding whether to give chase must balance on one hand the need to stop a suspect and show that flight from the law is no way to freedom, and, on the other, the high-speed threat to everyone within stopping range, be

they suspects, their passengers, other drivers, or bystanders.

To recognize a substantive due process violation in these circumstances when only mid-level fault has been shown would be to forget that liability for deliberate indifference to inmate welfare rests upon the luxury enjoyed by prison officials of having time to make unhurried judgments, upon the chance for repeated reflection, largely uncomplicated by the pulls of competing obligations. When such extended opportunities to do better are teamed with pro-

Dirk Ercken/Shutterstock.com

tracted failure even to care, indifference is truly shocking. But when unforeseen circumstances demand an officer's instant judgment, even precipitate recklessness fails to inch close enough to harmful purpose to spark the shock that implicates "the large concerns of the governors and the governed." *Daniels v. Williams*, 474 U.S., at 332, 106 S.Ct., at 665. Just as a purpose to cause harm is needed for 8th Amendment liability in a riot case, so it ought to be needed for Due Process liability in a pursuit case. Accordingly, we hold that high-speed chases with no intent to harm suspects physically or to worsen their legal plight do not give rise to liability under the 14th Amendment, redressible by an action under § 1983. [FN13]

FN13. Cf. *Checki v. Webb*, 785 F.2d 534, 538 (C.A.5 1986) ("Where a citizen suffers physical injury due to a police officer's negligent use of his vehicle, no section 1983 claim is stated. It is a different story when a citizen suffers or is seriously threatened with physical injury due to a police officer's intentional misuse of his vehicle") (citation omitted).

[9] The fault claimed on Smith's part in this case accordingly fails to meet the shocks-the-conscience test. In the count charging him with liability under § 1983, respondents' complaint alleges a variety of culpable states of mind: "negligently responsible in some manner," (App. 11, Count one, ¶ 8), "reckless and careless" (id., at 12, ¶ 15), "recklessness, gross negligence and conscious disregard for [Lewis's] safety" (id., at 13, ¶ 18), and "oppression, fraud and malice" (Ibid.) The subsequent summary judgment proceedings revealed that the height of the fault actually claimed was "conscious disregard," the malice allegation having been made in aid of a request

for punitive damages, but unsupported either in allegations of specific conduct or in any affidavit of fact offered on the motions for summary judgment. The Court of Appeals understood the *1721 claim to be one of deliberate indifference to Lewis's survival, which it treated as equivalent to one of reckless disregard for life. We agree with this reading of respondents' allegations, but consequently part company from the Court of

Jack Dagley Photography/Shutterstock.com

Appeals, which found them sufficient to state a substantive due process claim, and from the District Court, which made the same assumption arguendo. [FN14]

FN14. To say that due process is not offended by the police conduct described here is not, of course, to imply anything about its appropriate treatment under state law. See *Collins v. Harker Heights*, 503 U.S. 115, 129, 112 S.Ct. 1061, 1070, 117 L.Ed.2d 261 (1992) (decisions about civil liability standards that "involve a host of policy choices . . . must be made by locally elected representatives [or by courts enforcing the common law of torts], rather than by federal judges interpreting the basic charter of Government for the entire country"). Cf. *Thomas v. City of Richmond*, 9 Cal.4th 1154, 40 Cal.Rptr.2d 442, 892 P.2d 1185 (1995) (en banc) (discussing municipal liability under California law for injuries caused by police pursuits).

Whether, in a police pursuit case, the legal standard of conduct necessary to establish a violation of substantive due process under the 14th Amendment is "shocks the conscience" . . . or "deliberate indifference," or "reckless disregard." Pet. for Cert. i.

When defendants in a § 1983 action argue in the alternative (a) that they did not violate the Constitution, and (b) that in any event they are entitled to qualified immunity because the constitutional right was not clearly established, the opinion in *Siegert v. Gilley*, 500 U.S. 226, 111 S.Ct. 1789, 114 L.Ed.2d 277 (1991), tells us that we should address the constitutional question at the outset. That is sound advice when the answer to the constitutional question is clear. When, however, the question is both difficult and unresolved, I believe it wiser to adhere to the policy of avoiding the unnecessary adjudication of constitutional questions. Because I consider this, such a case, I would reinstate the judgment of the District Court on the ground that the relevant law was not clearly defined in 1990.

The Court expresses concern that deciding the immunity issue without resolving the underlying constitutional question would perpetuate a state of uncertainty in the law. Ante, at 1714 n. 5. Yet the Court acknowledges, as it must, that a qualified immunity defense is unavailable in an action against the municipality itself. Id. Sound reasons exist for encouraging the development of new constitutional doctrines in adversarial suits against municipalities, which have a substantial stake in the outcome and a risk of exposure to damages liability even when individual officers are plainly protected by qualified immunity.

Supervisory Liability

Respondeat Superior: A master is responsible for the actions of a servant

In *Monell v. New York City Dep't of Social Services*, 436 U.S. 658, 98 S.Ct. 2018, 56 L.Ed.2d 611 (1978), the Supreme Court determined in what circumstances a municipality could be held liable under § 1983 for deprivations of constitutional rights suffered at the hands of municipal employees. It held that:

Sam72/Shutterstock.com

a municipality cannot be held liable solely because it employs a tortfeasor—or, in other words, a municipality cannot be held liable under § 1983 on a respondeat superior theory.

Official policymaker: Supervisor is not liable because employee violated the individual's constitutional rights, but may be liable for failing in his or supervisory responsibilities (*Monell v. Department of Social Services*, 1978)

Directly participated in the action

After learning about the violation for a report or compliant, failed to remedy a wrong

Created a policy or custom under which unconstitutional practices occurred or allowed such a police or custom to continue

Was grossly negligent in managing the subordinates who cause the unlawful condition or event

Some supervisory liability categories are as follows:

Negligent hiring

1. Asserts that constitutional violation would not have occurred had the administrator properly performed a thorough screening of the errant officer prior to hiring him or her
2. *Board of Commissioners of Bryan County v. Brown* (1997): Plaintiff must show a strong connection between the background of the particular applicant and the specific violation alleged

Negligent assignment

1. Assigning an employee to a job without ascertaining his or her competence, or retaining an employee on a job who is known to be incapable of performing the job

Negligent entrustment

1. Failure to properly supervise or control an employee's custody, use, or supervision of equipment or facilities entrusted to him or her
2. Goes beyond incompetence in performing a job

Failure to direct

1. Failure to inform employees of the special requirements and limits of the job
2. Includes failure to promulgate policies and procedures

Failure to supervise subordinates

1. Abdication of the responsibility to oversee employees
2. Tolerating a pattern of physical abuse of arrestees or prisoners, racial discrimination, and pervasive deprivation of individual rights and privileges

Negligent failure to discipline/negligent retention

1. Failure to investigate complaints about employees and take appropriate action as warranted

2. A supervisor has a duty to take all necessary and proper steps to discipline or terminate a subordinate who is obviously unfit for employment

Failure to train

1. Clarified the standard for failure to train supervisory liability
2. Standard raised from gross negligence to deliberate indifference

Deliberate indifference factors:
The training must be adequate to the tasks the employee must perform.
The identified deficiency must be directly related to the injury.
The training need not be unconstitutional.
Improper training must not be an isolated incident but a pattern.
The training must address regular and ongoing tasks that officers routinely face.
The degree of training required need only be adequate to address a particular matter.

Medical Care

Not a specific duty of the police, absent a "special relationship"
A government agency must provide medical care to people who have been injured while being apprehended by the police.

Frequently a major allegation in excessive force claims, pursuits, arrests of intoxicated or mentally impaired individuals, and injuries sustained while in detention.

Includes: impact weapons, flashlights, aerosol sprays

871 F. 2d 1151—*Bordanaro v. McLeod City of Everett*

Instead, it is when execution of a government's policy or custom, whether made by its lawmakers or by those whose edicts or acts may fairly be said to represent official policy, inflicts the injury that the government as an entity is responsible under § 1983.

42 U.S.C. § 1983 (emphasis added). In defining the parameters of the terms "custom" and "usage," the Court has instructed that:

"Congress included customs and usages [in § 1983] because of the persistent and wide-spread discriminatory practices of state officials . . . Although not authorized by written law, such practices of state officials could well be so permanent and well settled as to constitute 'custom or usage' with the force of law."

Following this teaching, courts have established two requirements for plaintiffs to meet in maintaining <u>a § 1983 action grounded upon an unconstitutional municipal custom. First, the custom or practice must be attributable to the municipality.</u> In other words, it must be so well settled and widespread that the policymaking officials of the municipality can be said to have either actual or constructive knowledge of it yet did nothing to end the practice. See *Spell v. McDaniel*, 824 F.2d 1380, 1386–88 (4th Cir.), cert. denied, — U.S. —, 108 S.Ct. 752, 98 L.Ed.2d 765 (1988); see also Praprotnik, 108 S.Ct. at 925–26; Tuttle, 471 U.S. at 818–20, 105 S.Ct. at 2433–35; *Voutour v. Vitale*, 761 F.2d 812, 820 (1st Cir. 1985), cert. denied, 474 U.S. 1100, 106 S.Ct. 879, 88 L.Ed.2d 916 (1986). <u>Second, the custom must have been the cause of and the moving force behind the deprivation of constitutional rights.</u> See Tuttle, 471 U.S. at 819, 105 S.Ct. at 2434; Monell, 436 U.S. at 694–95, 98 S.Ct. at 2037–38; Kibbe, 777 F.2d at 809–10; see also City of Canton, — U.S. at —, 109 S.Ct. at 1206; Annotation, What Constitutes Policy or Custom for Purposes of Determining Liability of Local Government Unit under 42 U.S.C. § 1983—Modern Cases, 81 A.L.R.Fed. 549, 561–66, 571–83 (1987) (collecting and assessing various municipal policy/custom cases) [hereinafter Annotation, § 1983].

Additional support for the <u>existence of such a practice can be inferred from the event itself.</u> This incident involved the joint actions of the entire night watch of the Everett Police Department. A reasonable inference to draw from this is that all of the officers involved were operating under a shared set of rules and customs. The fact that all of these officers <u>acted in concert</u> are further evidence that there was a preexisting practice of breaking down doors when apprehending felons. Absent such a norm, it is highly unlikely such unanimity of action could occur. While it is true that evidence of a single event alone cannot establish a municipal custom or policy, see, for example, Tuttle, 471 U.S. at 823–24, 105 S.Ct. at 2436–37 (opinion of Rehnquist, J.), where other evidence of the policy has been presented and the "single incident" in question involves the concerted action of a large contingent of individual municipal employees, the event itself provides some proof of the existence of the underlying policy or custom.5 See Kibbe, 777 F.2d at 805–06; Grandstaff, 767 F.2d at 171–72; Annotation, § 1983, 81 A.L.R.Fed. 549, 569–70 (1987).

The evidence is sufficient to prove <u>that the Chief should have known of the unconstitutional arrest practice.</u> The Chief's own testimony and that of others was that he oversaw the operations of the department and set much of its policy. The evidence showed that the Chief utilized an extensive report review process to monitor the conduct of his officers and to ensure their compliance with the rules of the department. Such a review process would alert the Chief to practices that transgressed department policy. Knowledge of the practice may thus be imputed to the Chief. And <u>allowing this custom to continue amounted to a deliberate indifference to the rights of the citizens</u> of Everett, making a constitutional violation "almost bound to happen, sooner or later." Spell, 824 F.2d at 1391; see also *City of Canton v. Harris*, — U.S. at —, 109 S.Ct. at 1205. In this case, the jury

pockygallery/Shutterstock.com

could conclude that there was "supervisory encouragement, condonation and even acquiescence" in the unconstitutional practice. Voutour, 761 F.2d at 820 (noting absence of supervisory acquiescence in that case). Chief Bontempo's <u>failure to eradicate this facially unconstitutional practice from the police department attributes that custom to the municipality</u>.

The Causal Link. <u>The Supreme Court has declared that to support liability under § 1983, a municipal custom must have been the "moving force" behind the plaintiff's injury.</u> See Tuttle, 471 U.S. at 819, 105 S.Ct. at 2434; Monell, 436 U.S. at 694–95, 98 S.Ct. at 2037–38; *Polk County v. Dodson*, 454 U.S. 312, 326, 102 S.Ct. 445, 454, 70 L.Ed.2d 509 (1981); *Milligan v. City of Newport News*, 743 F.2d 227, 230 (4th Cir. 1984). There must be <u>some "affirmative link" between the municipal custom and the constitutional deprivation</u>. See Tuttle, 471 U.S. at 824–25 and n. 8, 105 S.Ct. at 2436–37 and n. 8 (opinion of Rehnquist, J.); Kibbe, 777 F.2d at 808; Voutour, 761 F.2d at 819–20; see also City of Canton, — U.S. at —, 109 S.Ct. at 1206.

Municipal Liability Based on a Deficient Custom or Policy in the Recruitment, Training, Supervision or Discipline of Everett Police Officers.

The city was also found liable under § 1983 for having a policy of inadequate recruitment, training, supervision, or discipline of its police officers. The jury found that this policy <u>evidenced gross negligence amounting to deliberate indifference to the constitutional rights of those with whom the police would come into contact</u>.

After the case at bar had been decided below, the Supreme Court issued its decision in *City of Canton v. Harris*, — U.S. —, 109 S.Ct. 1197. The issue presented to the Court in that case was whether a municipality could be held liable under § 1983 "for constitutional violations resulting from its failure to train municipal employees." City of Canton, at —, 109 S.Ct. at 1199. The Court held that <u>"only where a municipality's failure to train its employees in a relevant respect evidences a 'deliberate indifference' to the rights of its inhabitants can such a</u>

shortcoming be properly thought of as a city 'policy or custom' that is actionable under Sec. 1983." At —, 109 S.Ct. at 1205.

The Court then addressed what type of evidence was necessary to establish such deliberate indifference. It stated: Monell's rule that a city is not liable under § 1983 unless a municipal policy causes a constitutional deprivation will not be satisfied by merely alleging that the existing training program for a class of employees, such as police officers, represents a policy for which the city is responsible. That much may be true. The issue in a case like this one, however, is whether that training program is adequate; and if it is not, the question becomes whether such inadequate training can justifiably be said to represent "city policy." It may seem contrary to common sense to assert that a municipality will actually have a policy of not taking reasonable steps to train its employees. But it may happen that in light of the duties assigned to specific officers or employees the need for more or different training is so obvious, and the inadequacy so likely to result in the violation of constitutional rights, that the policymakers of the city can reasonably be said to have been deliberately indifferent to the need. In that event, the failure to provide proper training may fairly be said to represent a policy for which the city is responsible, and for which the city may be held liable if it actually causes injury.

THE EXISTENCE OF THE POLICY: The evidence adduced at trial supports the finding that the City of Everett failed to provide minimally acceptable standards of recruitment, training, supervision, or discipline of its police force. In the instant action, the jury was not asked to infer the existence of this policy based solely on the incident at the King Arthur Motel. "Rather, there was direct evidence presented to the jury of the City of [Everett's] failure to train and supervise its officers in a number of key areas of law enforcement and of its indifference to the circumstances of [the plaintiffs' beatings]." Wierstak, 789 F.2d at 975.

The jury had solid evidentiary grounds for finding that the failure of the Mayor and the Chief of Police to institute a minimally acceptable program of recruitment, training, supervision, or discipline amounted to a deliberate indifference to the constitutional rights of the city's inhabitants. See City of Canton, — U.S. at —, 109 S.Ct. at 1206. The consequence of this policy was that the Everett police force was ill-prepared and ill-equipped to perform the obvious and recurring duties of police officers. See id., at — - —, 109 S.Ct. at 1205–06; id. at —, 109 S.Ct. at 1208 (O'Connor, J., concurring in part and dissenting in part). The "do nothing policy" of the Mayor and the Chief exposed the citizens of Everett to imminent police misconduct, and was attributable to the municipality. See id. at — - —, 109 S.Ct. at 1204–05.

The Causal Link. In order to hold the city liable for their injuries under § 1983, the plaintiffs must also establish that there was a direct causal connection between the policy of inadequate recruitment, training, supervision, or discipline and the deprivations of their constitutional rights. This connection needs to rise above a mere but/for coupling between cause and effect, see City of Canton, at — - —, 109 S.Ct. at 1204–05; Tuttle, 471 U.S. at 823, 105 S.Ct. at 2436 (opinion of Rehnquist, J.); for "[i]n every instance where a person has had his or her constitutional rights violated by a city employee, a § 1983 plaintiff will be able to point to something the city 'could have done' to prevent the unfortunate incident. See Oklahoma City v. Tuttle, supra, 471 U.S. at 823, 105 S.Ct. at 2436 (opinion of Rehnquist, J.)." City of Canton, — U.S. at —, 109 S.Ct. at 1205. <u>To form the basis for liability under § 1983, a municipal policy must be affirmatively linked to and the moving force behind the constitutional violation.</u> See Monell, 436 U.S. at 694, 98 S.Ct. at 2037; Polk County v. Dodson, 454 U.S. 312, 326, 102 S.Ct. 445, 454, 70 L.Ed.2d 509 (1981). See also id. The evidence was sufficient to prove such a causal connection.

Police officers must comport themselves in accordance with the laws that they are sworn to enforce and behave in a manner that brings honor and respect for rather than public distrust of law enforcement personnel. They are required to do more than refrain from indictable conduct. Police officers are not drafted into public service; rather, they compete for their positions. In accepting employment by the public, they implicitly agree that they will not engage in conduct which calls into question their ability and fitness to perform their official responsibilities.

Ivelin Radkov/Shutterstock.com

Davis v. Mason County, 927 F.2d 1473 (9th Cir. 1991)

In § 1983 action against county, its sheriff and several deputies, the U.S. District Court, Western District of Washington, Robert J. Bryan, J., entered judgment on jury verdict finding defendants liable for damages for excessive use of force used while arresting citizens in four separate incidents. Defendants appealed. The Court of Appeals, Pregerson, Circuit Judge, held that: (1) sheriff was official policymaker regarding law enforcement practices; (2) county's failure to adequately train its deputies as to constitutional limits of use of force was deliberate indifference to safety of county inhabitants as matter of law for purposes of § 1983 liability; (3) evidence supported award of punitive damages; and (4) evidence supported determination that plaintiff was "seized" when deputy's wife ordered him down from hay wagon and put him in patrol vehicle.

To establish municipal liability under § 1983, it must be shown that the decision maker possesses final authority to establish municipal policy with respect to the action ordered. Pembaur v. City of Cincinnati, 475 U.S. 469, 481, 106 S.Ct. 1292, 1299, 89 L.Ed.2d 452 (1986) (plurality opinion). Because "municipalities often spread policy-making authority among various officers," a particular officer may have authority to establish binding policy with respect to particular matters, but not others. Id. at 483, 106 S.Ct. at 1300.

The issue is not whether the officers had received any training—most of the deputies involved had some training, even if it was minimal at best—rather the issue is the adequacy of that training. City of Canton, 489 U.S. at 390, 109 S.Ct. at 1205. More importantly, while they may have had some training in the use of force, they received no training in the constitutional limits of the use of force. The Supreme Court in City of Canton declared: if "the need for more or different training is so obvious, and the inadequacy so likely to result in the violation of constitutional rights, . . . the policymakers of the city can reasonably be said to have been deliberately indifferent to the need." Id. The Court went on to say in a footnote that "the need to train officers in the constitutional limitations on the use of deadly force can be said to be 'so obvious,' that failure to do so could properly be characterized as 'deliberate indifference' to constitutional rights." Id. at 390 n. 10, 109 S.Ct. at 1205 n. 10 (citation omitted).

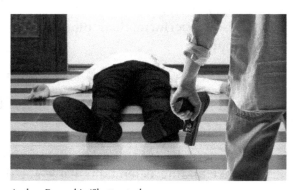

In the case at bar, the deprivation of plaintiffs' 4th Amendment rights was a direct consequence of the inadequacy of the training the deputies received. Mason County's failure to train its officers in the legal limits of the use of force constituted "deliberate indifference" to the safety of its

Andrey Burmakin/Shutterstock.com

inhabitants as a matter of law. [FN5] Moreover, there was certainly more than enough evidence presented regarding the inadequacy of training in order to survive Mason County's motion for a directed verdict on the issue of municipal liability.

George v. Morris, 736 F. 3d 829—Court of Appeals, 9th Circuit 2013

This is not to say that the 4th Amendment always requires officers to delay their fire until a suspect turns his weapon on them. If the person is armed—or reasonably suspected of being armed—a furtive movement, harrowing gesture, or serious verbal threat might create an immediate threat. On this interlocutory appeal, though, we can neither credit the deputies' testimony that Donald turned and pointed his gun at them, nor assume that he took other actions that would have been objectively threatening. Given that version of events, a reasonable fact finder could conclude that the deputies' use of force was constitutionally excessive. Contrary to the dissent's charge, we are clear-eyed about the potentially volatile and dangerous situation these deputies confronted. Yet, we cannot say they assuredly stayed within constitutional bounds without knowing "[w]hat happened at the rear of the George residence during the time Mr. George walked out into the open on his patio and the fatal shot." Dissent 839*839 at 848. That is, indeed, "the core issue in this case." Id.

Moreover, the majority opinion misperceives an important aspect of the doctrine of qualified immunity as explained by the Supreme Court in Scott v. Harris, 550 U.S. 372, 127 S.Ct. 1769, 167 L.Ed.2d 686 (2007), an aspect since embraced by the Third, Fourth, Sixth, Eighth, Tenth, and Eleventh Circuits—not to mention our own. The Court's holding in Scott v. Harris and the principle upon which it rests ensures that government officials will not be required to defend themselves in court if it appears to an appellate court from the record taken as a whole that the plaintiff has no case, and therefore as a matter "of law," id. at 381 n. 8, 127 S.Ct. 1769 (emphasis added), the lawsuit cannot survive summary judgment. Thus, the majority opinion inadvertently dilutes an essential public interest the doctrine protects: the ability of government officials to perform their responsibilities without paralyzing fear of inappropriate personal lawsuits and potential civil liability.

1. *United States v. Martinez*, 406 F.3d 1160, 1164 (9th Cir. 2005) (emphasis supplied). The volatility of situations involving domestic violence makes them particularly well suited for an application of the emergency doctrine. When officers respond

to a domestic abuse call, they understand that "violence may be lurking 847*847 and explode with little warning." *Fletcher v. Clinton*, 196 F.3d 41, 50 (1st Cir. 1999). Indeed, "more officers are killed or injured on domestic violence calls than on any other type of call." Hearings before Senate Judiciary Committee, 1994 WL 530624 (F.D.C.H.) (Sept. 13, 1994) (statement on behalf of National Task Force on Domestic Violence).

2. *United States v. Brooks*, 367 F.3d 1128, 1137 (9th Cir. 2004).

Brooks contends that even if there were probable cause and exigent circumstances to justify Perez's warrantless entry, once Perez heard from Bengis that she was unharmed, the exigency dissipated and Perez, by staying to question longer, violated Brooks's 4th Amendment rights.

We disagree. In Perez's experience, as he testified in the district court, it was "very common" for victims of domestic abuse initially to deny that they had been assaulted. This view could be credited by the district court. We, too, agree that a victim of domestic violence may deny an assault, especially when an abuser is present. Perez's decision to stay and ask more questions was a reasonable police procedure. A potential victim in Bengis's situation with justification may fear that by complaining to police, he or she might expose himself or herself to likely future harm at the hands of a hostile aggressor who may remain unrestrained by the law.

3. *Tierney v. Davidson*, 133 F.3d 189, 198 (2nd Cir. 1998) (emphasis added).

Indeed, it may have been a dereliction of duty for Davidson to have left the premises without ensuring that any danger had passed. See Barone, 330 F.2d at 545. And Davidson could not tell that the danger had passed unless he found the other participant in the dispute. See *State v. Raines*, 55 Wash.App. 459, 778 P.2d 538, 542–43 (1989) ("[T]he fact that the occupants appeared to be unharmed when the officers entered did not guarantee that the disturbance had cooled to the point where their continued safety was assured. Until they had an opportunity to observe [the boyfriend] and talk to him, they had no knowledge of his condition and state of mind.").

4. *Fletcher v. Town of Clinton*, 196 F.3d 41, 50–51 (1st Cir. 1999).

The balanced choice the officers must make is protected by qualified immunity . . . Such immunity is given not only for the protection of the officers, but also to protect victims of crime. <u>In the domestic violence context, immunity is given so that officers will not have strong incentives to do nothing when they believe a domestic abuse victim is in danger</u>. Permitting suit against officers who have acted reasonably when there is reason to fear would create exactly the wrong incentives. Indeed, if the officers had done nothing, and Fletcher had been injured, they would have faced the threat of suit. In either event, their choice <u>would be protected if it was objectively reasonable in light of clearly settled law</u>.

5. *Fletcher v. Town of Clinton*, 196 F.3d 41, 52 (1st Cir. 1999).

In domestic violence situations, officers may reasonably consider whether the victim is acting out of fear or intimidation, or out of some desire to protect the abuser, both common syndromes. See *United States v. Bartelho*, 71 F.3d 436, 438 (1st Cir. 1995) (noting that officers are often trained not to take the statements of abuse victims at face value, but instead to consider whether the victims are acting out of fear). Indeed, one commentator has estimated that domestic violence victims are uncooperative 848*848 in eighty to ninety percent of attempted criminal prosecutions against their batterers.

More on Qualified Immunity

<u>*The essence of the concept is that, because police officers are often called upon to make difficult decisions, sometimes with only split seconds to respond, they ought not to face civil liability or the burden of the litigation process, including discovery and trial, in circumstances where they have not acted in violation of clearly established law.*</u>

Because the immunity involved offers the officer relief not just from civil liability, but also from the burdens of litigation, a trial court's denial of a defendant officer's motion for qualified immunity is, with some exceptions, subject to immediate appeal. See *Anderson v. Creighton*, No. 85–1520, 483 U.S. 635 (1987) and *Mitchell v. Forsyth*, No. 84-335, 472 U.S. 511 (1985).

<u>*In circumstances where the defense of qualified immunity is upheld, an officer will not be found liable, even if their conduct, such as the use of deadly force, actually could be said to have violated the plaintiff's federal civil rights, so long as an objectively reasonable officer could have believed, under the circumstances, that the conduct was lawful.*</u>

A U.S. Supreme Court decision, *Brosseau v. Haugen*, No. 03-1261, 543 U.S. 194 (2004), illustrates the application of this principle in the context of the use of deadly force, and ruled that an officer who shot a fleeing felon motorist in the back was entitled to qualified immunity, when prior case law did not clearly establish that her conduct violated his 4th Amendment rights.

In this case, an officer learned that a man was wanted on a felony no-bail warrant for drugs and other offenses, and heard a report of a "ruckus" at his mother's house. The suspect attempted to flee in a vehicle, getting into a jeep, and trying to start it.

The officer ran to the jeep with her handgun drawn and ordered him to stop. As the suspect fumbled with his keys, she hit the driver's side window several times with her handgun and, on the third or fourth try, broke the window. She had mace and a baton, but allegedly did not use them, instead trying to grab the car keys.

Just after she broke the window, the suspect succeeded in starting the jeep.

Either before he pulled away, or just after he started to do so (the evidence being conflicting), the officer shot him in the back. Because he did not stop, the officer believed she had missed him, but she did not take a second shot, believing the risk to be too great as he began to drive away and others being in the potential line of fire. The driver subsequently pulled over and passed out.

A federal appeals court ruled that the officer who shot the suspect did not act reasonably if there was no evidence that he posed a threat of serious harm to others or was armed with a weapon, overturning a grant of qualified immunity to the officer by the trial court. *Haugen v. Brosseau*, No. 01-35954, 339 F.3d 857 (9th Cir. 2003).

The U.S. Supreme Court disagreed and ruled that the officer was, indeed, entitled to qualified immunity.

Qualified immunity shields an officer from suit when she makes a decision that, even if constitutionally deficient, reasonably misapprehends the law governing the circumstances she confronted. Because the focus is on whether the officer had fair notice that her conduct was unlawful, reasonableness is judged against the backdrop of the law at the time of the conduct. If the law at that time did not clearly establish that the officer's conduct would violate the Constitution, the officer should not be subject to liability or, indeed, even the burdens of litigation.

The Supreme Court noted that the parties had pointed to only a "handful of cases" relevant to the issue of whether shooting a disturbed felon, set on avoiding capture through vehicular flight, when persons in the immediate area are at risk from that flight was reasonable.

In two of the cases, the courts found no 4th Amendment violation when an officer shot a fleeing suspect who presented a risk to others, including on the basis of the possibility that a speeding vehicle being used to flee could endanger others or that the suspect had proven that they would do almost anything to avoid capture. In a third case, the court found summary judgment inappropriate on a 4th Amendment claim involving a fleeing suspect, ruling that the threat created by the fleeing suspect's failure to brake when an officer suddenly stepped in front of his just-started car was not a sufficiently grave threat to justify the use of deadly force.

The Court found that these three cases taken together "undoubtedly show that this area is one in which the result depends very much on the facts of each case," and that none of them "squarely governs the case here," while suggesting that the officer's actions fell in the "hazy border" between excessive and acceptable force.

bikeriderlondon/Shutterstock.com

Since it was not "clearly established" that the officer's conduct violated the 4th Amendment, she was entitled to qualified immunity.

The Court in Brosseau was applying the method for determining qualified immunity previously established in *Saucier v. Katz*, No. 99-1977, 533 U.S. 194 (2001).

Under that method, a trial court should first inquire, in response to a motion for qualified immunity, whether a constitutional right would have been violated on the facts alleged by the plaintiff, because if no right would have been violated, there is then no need for any further inquiry. Second, if a violation could be made out, based on the facts alleged, the court must then determine whether the right involved was clearly established.

The most important ruling in Saucier is that this second inquiry must be made in light of the case's specific facts and context, not as a "broad general" proposition. The Court in Brosseau, in applying this approach, therefore, focused its inquiry not on whether there was a broad general right clearly established not to be subjected to unreasonable use of deadly force, which, of course, there is, but whether it would be clear to a reasonable officer, in the specific circumstances confronted, that her conduct was unlawful in those circumstances.

In circumstances where the officer or officers who used deadly force seek qualified immunity, but there is a genuine issue of disputed material fact essential to the determination of whether there is or is not a constitutional violation, a federal appeals court will often rule that it cannot determine whether or not the officers were entitled to qualified immunity until the disputed factual issue is first decided.

In some instances, the suspect may not even be in actual possession of a weapon or other dangerous instrumentality, but instead simply be engaged in apparently threatening conduct, combined with the potential to obtain such a weapon. In *Henning v. O'Leary*, No. 06-2378, 477 F.3d 492 (7th Cir. 2007), the court found that officers acted reasonably in shooting and killing an arrestee who had refused to submit to their attempts to handcuff him, when they believed that he had his hands on or near one officer's gun, which had come loose during the struggle between them. Officers are not required to wait to take action to protect their safety until a resisting arrestee has completely freed himself and has obtained a "firm grip" on a weapon, the court commented.

When the opposite is true—that is, the officer, regardless of their actual subjective belief, does not have what the court will view as an objectively reasonable belief that the suspect is threatening them or anyone else, even if the suspect is actually in possession of a firearm, the use of deadly force will be judged improper and may lead to liability. This is illustrated by *Ngo v. Storlie*, No. 06-2771, 495 F.3d 597 (8th Cir. 2007). In that case, a federal appeals court ruled that if the facts were as stated by an undercover officer, shot by a fellow officer after reporting that he had already been shot in the area by a perpetrator, the actions of the shooting officer were not objectively reasonable. A reasonable officer, arriving on the scene after there was a report of an officer shot, would have recognized that the undercover officer did not pose an immediate threat to anyone. While he had a pistol, he dropped it on the ground, and was not pointing it at the officers or reaching for it. He was also not actively resisting arrest or attempting to evade the officers by flight, but was kneeling in the street under a streetlight by himself, and waving his arms above his head trying to attract attention. Further, the shooting officer failed to attempt to give the undercover officer any commands or warnings before firing at him, and the undercover officer did not match the description of the suspect sought, who had shot him.

See also *Ham v. Brice*, No. 05-50657, 203 Fed. Appx. 631 (5th Cir. 2006) (deputy who shot unarmed arrestee fleeing into unpopulated wooded area was not entitled to summary judgment on excessive force claim. The deputy had previously frisked the arrestee, and found no weapons on him before he fled on foot from the scene of his drug arrest); and *Smith v. Cupp*, No. 04-5783, 430 F.3d 766 (6th Cir. 2005) (if deputy sheriff fired final fatal shot at arrestee fleeing in stolen police car after the vehicle passed him, he violated the arrestee's constitutional rights. The arrestee had been taken into custody for the nonviolent offense of making harassing phone calls, and no longer posed an immediate threat to the deputy after driving past him).

In the United States, one can be charged simultaneously under criminal and civil statutes. Often, the outcome of a criminal charge will have an effect upon the accompanying civil charges. Laws are confusing. However, our justice system relies upon "the average citizen" in determining furtherance of a criminal charge via a grand jury indictment. The justice system relies upon average citizens in determining the outcome of a criminal (jury trial) or civil (jury trial). Understanding the applicable laws, cases, policies and procedures regarding the use of force is a monumental task (we are attempting to bring light to issues in understanding lawful use of force and have written an entire text book). So, consider the following:

The State of New Jersey, Department of Law and Public Safety, Division of Criminal Justice Model Grand Jury Instructions on Police Use-of-Force for use according to the Supplemental Law Enforcement Directive Amending Attorney General Law Enforcement Directive 2006-5, dated July 28, 2015: To review this information, go to:http://www.njisj.org/wp-content/uploads/2015/07/AG-Directive_Deadly-Force-Investigations.pdf

[Discuss the applicable law based on the case specific facts]

Your task is to apply this law to the officer's conduct. If you find that the arrest was lawful, then the officer's use of force is justified. If you find that the arrest was unlawful, and that the officer's belief in the lawfulness of the arrest was erroneous and such error was due to ignorance of or mistake as to the law, the officer's use of force was not justified.

gst/Shutterstock.com

Wow, imagine being on the jury having to decide if a police officer violated any of the statutes listed above. Witnesses will present testimony (New Jersey has specific jury instructions regarding the testimony of witnesses; *State v. Henderson* 195 N.J. 521, 2008), arguments presented, evidence presented, and all of the proceedings must be digested by you (the juror).

How does a citizen, who has never faced a deadly threat, apply everything presented during the trial to a perspective of a "reasonable officer"?

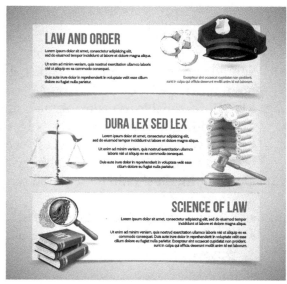

Macrovector/Shutterstock.com

CONCLUSION

Why so much case law? When does qualified immunity apply? When is summary judgment appropriate? When has the law enforcement officer or agency crossed the line from lawful into unlawful? The list of questions is as long as the list of possible responses. Case law evolves. Procedures and policies, therefore, change. Adapting to the most recent rulings and directives from courts and other judicial sources is required for all agencies. In this chapter, we looked at terms, cases, and jury instructions. Easy to make a decision in a split second as a police officer? Easy to make a decision based upon understanding laws, instructions, testimony, evidence, arguments, and then interpreting everything presented into a fair finding of fact?

James Daniels/Shutterstock.com

Discussion Points

1. Should law enforcement officers be held to a different standard than is required now, under the Graham decision?
    - Is it reasonable to make mistakes as a police officer? How about a mistake in shooting or causing the death of a suspect?
    - Do you think police officers receive enough training to handle violent encounters? How about dealing with mentally ill persons?
2. Do you think it should be required for police officers to use nondeadly force in all situations?
    - Should police officers be required to "run" instead of using deadly force?
    - Is there an alternative to using a Taser or pepper spray to control violent suspects?

This form must be completed and turned in for credit. No copies or other format will be accepted.

Student Name ______________________ Date ______________

Course Section ______________________ Chapter ______________

What is the Federal Tort Claims Act; what is a Bivens action; name two of the three remedies for Tort actions and describe them; to use force what must the police articulate:

Student Name _____ Date _____

Course Section _____ Chapter _____

What is the difference between simple and gross negligence; which Title U.S. Code and Subsection are used primarily for Federal civil rights prosecutions criminal; which Title U.S. Code and subsection are used primarily for civil rights lawsuits, explain what factors must be proven in a criminal liability prosecution and what must be proven in a civil liability prosecution.

_____

_____

_____

_____

_____

_____

_____

_____

_____

_____

_____

_____

_____

USE OF FORCE IN CORRECTIONS

It is said that no one truly knows a nation until one has been inside its jails. A nation should not be judged by how it treats its highest citizens, but its lowest ones.

—Nelson Mandela

Key Terms

Eighth Amendment, Excessive Force, Pretrial Detainee, Post-Conviction Detainee, *Johnson v. Glick*, *Hudson v. McMillian*, *Kingsley v. Hendrickson*, Title 42 Section 1983

Learning Objectives

After exploring Chapter 5, the student will be able to:

1. Explain the difference between the constraints of the 4th Amendment and the 8th Amendment.
2. Describe the difference between a pretrial detainee and post-conviction detainee
3. List the reasoning for remedies under Title 42 Section 1983
4. Detail the outcome of *Johnson v. Glick* and the policy implications
5. Explain how *Hudson v. McMillian* changed the scope of the use of force in corrections
6. Describe how *Kingsley v. Hendrickson* impacted the civil rights of those detained in correctional facilities

FORCE AGAINST PRISONERS

Although the use of force by law enforcement is generally viewed under the rule of three—reasonable, necessary, and minimal. Adding to the guiding principle is the use of force triangle—ability, opportunity, and jeopardy. However, we must consider the constitutional rights applicable in differing settings. Federally—the 4th Amendment—the reasonableness standard. States—the 14th Amendment—the due process standard. So, how do

Sirikunkrittaphuk/Shutterstock.com

the courts view postconviction (prisoners who have been sentenced) and use of force? The obvious answer (or so it would seem) would be under the 8th Amendment—the cruel and unusual punishment standard. It would take the Supreme Court of the United States (SCOTUS) an incredible amount of time to come to that conclusion.

Johnson v. Glick, 481 F.2d 1028 Decided June 29, 1973

This appeal concerns an order of the District Court for the Southern District of New York dismissing a complaint under the Civil Rights Act, 42 U.S.C. Sec. 1983 (§ 1983), 28 U.S.C. § 1343(3), for failure to state a claim on which relief can be granted. The complaint was brought against the Warden of the Manhattan House of Detention for Men and a correction officer, described in the complaint only as Officer John, Badge No. 1765, but now identified as John Fuller, by plaintiff Australia Johnson, who had been held in the House of Detention prior to and during his trial in the state courts on felony charges. It alleged that, while plaintiff was being checked back into the House of Detention, Officer Fuller reprimanded Johnson and other men for a claimed failure to follow instructions; that when Johnson endeavored to explain that they were doing only what another officer had told them to do, Officer Fuller rushed into the holding cell, grabbed him by the collar, and struck him twice on the head with something enclosed in the officer's fist; that during this incident the officer threatened him, saying "I'll kill you, old man, I'll break you in half"; that Fuller then harassed Johnson by detaining him in the holding cell for 2 hours before returning him to his cell; that when Johnson requested medical attention, Fuller, who was called upon by another officer to escort Johnson to the jail doctor, instead held him for another 2 hours in another cell before permitting him to see the doctor; and that despite the "pain pills" given him by the doctor, Johnson has since "been having terrible pains in his head."

Recognizing that there were numerous decisions in other circuits that would seem to uphold the validity of the complaint as against the officer, as well as one to the contrary, Judge Knapp nevertheless dismissed the complaint, saying "So far as I am aware no decision in this circuit requires such a conclusion, and it is one at which I would arrive only under constraint." Although we realize that upholding this complaint may well lead to considerable further expansion of actions by state prisoners under 42 U.S.C. § 1983, so long as they may bring their civil rights complaints directly to federal courts without first presenting them to state courts we think the ruling was in error so far as the officer was concerned.

We assume that brutal police conduct violates a right guaranteed by the due process clause of the 14th Amendment. *Rosenberg v. Martin*, 478 F.2d 520, 526 (2 Cir. 1973).

The great weight of authority in favor of the assumption thus stated in Rosenberg has not been accompanied by an equivalent amount of analysis. Many of the opinions, including our own in Martinez and Inmates, rely on a passing reference to the "cruel and unusual punishment" clause of the 8th Amendment. The most extensive judicial treatment of the subject, Judge Aldisert's opinion in *Howell v. Cataldi*, supra, 464 F.2d at 280–282, likewise relies on that clause.

<u>*A case like this, however, does not lie comfortably within the 8th Amendment.*</u>
The text:

Excessive bail shall not be required, nor excessive fines imposed, nor cruel and unusual punishments inflicted suggests action taken, usually by a court, in carrying out a legislative authorization or command. The language, as is well known, is practically a verbatim copy of the tenth clause of the English Bill of Rights, 1 Wm. & Mary, 2d sess., Chapter 2 (1688), which, in turn, embodied a corresponding section

Ozgur Guvenc/Shutterstock.com

of the Declaration of Rights that was a cornerstone of the settlement of the Glorious Revolution. Although George Mason, who drafted the similar clause in the Virginia Declaration of Rights, which was the more immediate progenitor of the 8th Amendment, may have been mistaken in thinking that the provision was aimed merely at torturous rather than at excessive punishments, there can be no disagreement that what sparked the English provision was the conduct of judges under James II. The background of our own Bill of Rights, however, makes clear that the 8th Amendment was intended to apply not only to the acts of judges but as a restraint on legislative action as well.

We do not suggest, however, that the cruel and unusual punishment clause must necessarily be read as limited to acts of legislatures in authorizing sentences or of judges imposing them. It can fairly be deemed to be applicable to the manner in which an otherwise constitutional sentence, as the death penalty was then thought to be, is carried out by an executioner, see Louisiana ex rel. *Francis v. Resweber*, 329 U.S. 459, 67 S. Ct. 374, 91 L.Ed. 422 (1947), or to cover conditions of confinement which may make intolerable an otherwise constitutional term of imprisonment, see *Holt v. Sarver*, 442 F.2d 304 (8 Cir. 1971). On a parity of reasoning, we find no difficulty in considering the cruel and unusual punishment clause to be applicable to such systems of prison discipline as solitary confinement, see *Wright v. McMann*, 387 F.2d 519 (2 Cir. 1967) or corporal punishment, see *Jackson v. Bishop*, 404 F.2d 571 (8 Cir. 1968). The thread common to all these cases is that "punishment" has been deliberately administered for a penal or disciplinary purpose, with the apparent authorization of high prison officials charged by the state with responsibility for care, control, and discipline of prisoners. In contrast, although a spontaneous attack by a guard is "cruel" and, we hope, "unusual," it does not fit any ordinary concept of "punishment."

This is particularly clear in a case like the present where the plaintiff had not yet been found liable to "punishment" of any sort. We have considerable doubt that the cruel and unusual punishment clause is properly applicable at all until after conviction and sentence. See *Anderson v. Nosser*, 456 F.2d 2d 835 (5 Cir.) (en banc), cert. denied, 409 U.S. 848, 93 S. Ct. 53, 34 L.Ed.2d 89 (1972) modifying 438 F.2d 183 (5 Cir. 1971); *Hamilton v. Love*, 328 F. Supp. 1182, 1191 (E.D. Ark. 1971); but see *Rhem v. McGrath*, 326 F. Supp. 681, 690 (S.D.N.Y. 1971). Yet it would be absurd to hold that a pretrial detainee has less constitutional protection against acts of prison guards than one who has been convicted.

The solution lies in the proposition that, both before and after sentence, constitutional protection against police brutality is not limited to conduct violating the specific command of the 8th Amendment or, as in *Monroe v. Pape*, 365 U.S. 167, 81 S. Ct. 473, 5 L.Ed.2d 492 (1961), of the Fourth. *Rochin v. California*, 342 U.S. 165, 72 S. Ct. 205, 96 L.Ed. 183 (1952), must stand for the proposition that, quite apart from any "specific" of the Bill of Rights, application of undue force by law enforcement officers deprives a suspect of liberty without due process of law. If Rochin suffered such a violation of his constitu-

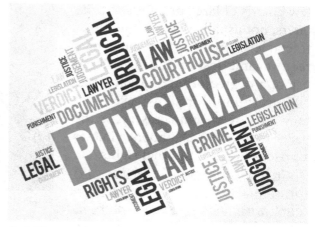

dizain/Shutterstock.com

tional rights by the police as to be entitled to invalidation of a conviction obtained as a consequence, he also was the victim of a violation sufficient to sustain an action under the Civil Rights Act. The same principle should extend to acts of brutality by correctional officers, although the notion of what constitutes brutality may not necessarily be the same. This, apparently, was the view taken by the Seventh Circuit in *Collum v. Butler*, supra, 421 F.2d at 1259–1260, by the Fifth in *Tolbert v. Bragan*, supra, 451 F.2d 1020, and by the Ninth in *Wiltsie v. California Department of Corrections*, supra, 406 F.2d at 517. See also *Jenkins v. Averett*, supra, 424 F.2d at 1232, *Fitzke v. Shappell*, supra, 468 F.2d at 107 and most of the courts faced with challenges to the conditions of pretrial detention have primarily based their analysis directly on the due process clause.

While the Rochin test, "conduct that shocks the conscience," 342 U.S. at 172, 72 S. Ct. 205, is not one that can be applied by a computer, it at least points the way. Certainly the constitutional protection is nowhere nearly so extensive as that afforded by the common law tort action for battery, which makes actionable any intentional and unpermitted contact with the plaintiff's person or anything attached to it and practically identified with it, see Prosser, Torts § 9 (4th ed. 1971); still less is it as extensive as that afforded by the common law tort action for assault, redressing "Any act of such a nature as to excite an apprehension of battery," id. § 10 at 38. Although "the least touching of another in anger is a battery," *Cole v. Turner*, 6 Mod. 149, 87 Eng.Rep. 907, 90 Eng.Rep. 958 (K.B. 1704) (Holt, C. J.), it is not a violation of a constitutional right actionable under 42 U.S.C. § 1983. The management by a few guards of large numbers of prisoners, not usually the most gentle or tractable of men and women, may require and justify the occasional use of a degree of intentional force. Not every push or shove, even if it may later seem unnecessary in the peace of a judge's chambers, violates a prisoner's constitutional rights.

Everett Historical/Shutterstock.com

In determining whether the constitutional line has been crossed, a court must look to such factors as the need for the application of force, the relationship between the need and the amount of force that was used, the extent of injury inflicted, and whether force was applied in a good faith effort to maintain or restore discipline or maliciously and sadistically for the very purpose of causing harm. Taking this view, and reading the complaint with the generosity required in pro se civil rights actions, _Haines v. Kerner_, 404 U.S. 519, 520–521, 92 S. Ct. 594, 30 L.Ed.2d 652 (1972), we think it stated a claim against Officer Fuller.

On the other hand, even on a charitable reading, we see no basis for sustaining the complaint against the warden. The rule in this circuit is that when monetary damages are sought under § 1983, the general doctrine of respondeat superior does not suffice and a showing of some personal responsibility of the defendant is required. Thus in _Martinez v. Mancusi_, supra, 443 F.2d at 924, we conditioned a conclusion of liability of the warden on a finding that he was personally "responsible for what the guards did." Again, in _Wright v. McMann_, supra, 460 F.2d at 134–135, in upholding a damage award as against Warden McMann, we stressed that "there is every reason to believe that he was aware of segregation cell conditions," and that "responsibility for permitting such conditions to exist was ultimately, in any event, squarely his" are in accord.

Here the complaint alleged only that Warden Glick was in charge of all the correctional officers employed at the House of Detention. It did not allege that the warden had authorized the officer's conduct, see _Martinez v. Mancusi_, supra, 443 F.2d at 924, or even that there had been a history of previous episodes requiring the warden to take therapeutic action, cf. *Wright v. McMann*, supra, 460 F.2d at 134–135; it alleged a single spontaneous incident, unforeseen, and unforeseeable by higher authority. While appellant's counsel urged that we permit him to develop further facts that might implicate the warden, the better course is to affirm the dismissal of the complaint against the warden without prejudice to an application for leave to amend if a factual basis for this should appear. We request that counsel assigned by the judge to take this appeal shall continue to act for Johnson in the district court.

Reversed with respect to Officer Fuller; affirmed with respect to Warden Glick. No costs.

In 1986, the Supreme Court decided *Whitley v. Albers*, 475 U.S. 312 (1986) an excessive force case by convicted prisoners against guards in a prison riot. The Court held that to establish that the use of force was excessive, convicts must show that it constituted an "unnecessary and wanton infliction of pain," under the 8th Amendment's cruel and unusual punishment clause. The Court held that in order to meet this standard, the prisoner must focus on the following factor in *Johnson v. Glick*, <u>and prove force was used "*maliciously and sadistically for the very purpose of causing harm.*"</u> <u>The Court also noted that the other Glick factors may be used to help infer wantonness</u>, and stated:

[E]qually relevant are such factors as the extent of the threat to the safety of staff and inmates, as reasonably perceived by the responsible officials on the basis of the facts known to them, and any efforts made to temper the severity of a forceful response.

Whitley explicitly addressed and rejected the application of the less stringent deliberate indifference standard, which is used in the context of inmate claims of insufficient medical care. The Court stated that, in excessive force situations, "<u>a deliberate indifference standard does not adequately capture the importance of [competing] obligations, or convey the appropriate hesitancy to critique in hindsight decisions necessarily made in haste, under pressure, and frequently without the luxury of a second chance.</u>"

Skyward Kick Productions/Shutterstock.com

HUDSON v. McMILLIAN ET AL.

CERTIORARI TO THE UNITED STATES COURT OF APPEALS FOR THE FIFTH CIRCUIT

No. 90-6531. Argued November 13, 1991-Decided February 25, 1992

Petitioner Hudson, a Louisiana prison inmate, testified that minor bruises, facial swelling, loosened teeth, and a cracked dental plate he had suffered resulted from a beating by respondent prison guards McMillian and Woods while he was handcuffed and shackled following an argument with McMillian, and that respondent Mezo, a supervisor on duty, watched the beating but merely told the officers "not to have too much fun." The Magistrate trying Hudson's District Court suit under 42 U.S.C. § 1983 found that the officers used force when there was no need to do so and that Mezo expressly condoned their actions, ruled that respondents had violated the 8th Amendment's prohibition on cruel and unusual punishments, and awarded Hudson damages. The Court of Appeals reversed, holding inter alia, that inmates alleging use of excessive force in violation of the Amendment must prove "significant injury" and that Hudson could not prevail because his injuries were "minor" and required no medical attention.

Held: <u>The use of excessive physical force against a prisoner may constitute cruel and unusual punishment even though the inmate does not suffer serious injury</u>. (Pp. 5–12).

a. Whenever prison officials stand accused of using excessive physical force constituting "the unnecessary and wanton infliction of pain" violative of the Cruel and Unusual Punishments Clause, the core judicial inquiry is that set out in Whitley v. Albers, 475 U.S. 312, 320–321: whether force was applied in a good-faith effort to maintain or restore discipline, or maliciously and sadistically to cause harm. Extending Whitley's application of the "unnecessary and wanton infliction of pain" standard to all allegations of force, whether the prison disturbance is a riot or a lesser disruption, works no innovation. See, for example, Johnson v. Glick, 481 F.2d 1028, cert. denied, 414 U.S. 1033. (Pp. 5–7).

b. Since, under the <u>Whitley approach, the extent of injury suffered by an inmate is one of the factors to be considered in determining whether the use of force</u>

is wanton and unnecessary, 475 U.S., at 321, the absence of serious injury is relevant to, but does not end, the 8th Amendment inquiry. There is no merit to respondents' assertion that a significant injury requirement is mandated by what this Court termed, in Wilson v. Seiter, 501 U.S. 294, 298, the "objective component" of 8th Amendment analysis: whether the alleged wrongdoing is objectively "harmful enough" to establish a constitutional violation, id., at 303. That component is contextual and responsive to "contemporary standards of decency." Estelle v. Gamble, 429 U.S. 97, 103. In the excessive force context, such standards always are violated when prison officials maliciously and sadistically use force to cause harm, see Whitley, 475 U.S., at 327, whether or not significant injury is evident. Moreover, although the Amendment does not reach de minimis uses of physical force, provided that such use is not of a sort repugnant to the conscience of mankind, ibid., the blows directed at Hudson are not de minimis, and the extent of his injuries thus provides no basis for dismissal of his § 1983 claim. (Pp. 7–10).

c.   The dissent's theory that Wilson requires an inmate who alleges excessive force to show significant injury in addition to the unnecessary and wanton infliction of pain misapplies Wilson and ignores the body of this Court's 8th Amendment jurisprudence. Wilson did not involve an allegation of excessive force and, with respect to the "objective component" of an 8th Amendment claim, suggested no departure from Estelle and its progeny. The dissent's argument that excessive force claims and conditions-of-confinement claims are no different in kind is likewise unfounded. To deny the difference between punching a prisoner in the face and serving him unappetizing food is to ignore the concepts of dignity, civilized standards, humanity, and decency that animate the 8th Amendment. See Estelle, supra, at 102.
(Pp. 10 and 11).

d.   This Court takes no position on respondents' legal argument that their conduct was isolated, unauthorized, and against prison policy and therefore beyond the scope of "punishment" prohibited by the 8th Amendment. That argument is inapposite on the record, since the Court of Appeals left intact the Magistrate's determination that the violence at issue was not an isolated assault, and ignores the Magistrate's finding that supervisor Mezo expressly condoned the use of force. Moreover, to the extent that respondents rely on the unauthorized nature of their acts, they make a claim not addressed by the Court of Appeals, not presented by the question on which this Court granted certiorari, and, accordingly, not before this Court. Pp. 11 and 12. 929 F.2d 1014, reversed.

JUSTICE O'CONNOR delivered the opinion of the Court. This case requires us to decide whether the use of excessive physical force against a prisoner may constitute cruel and unusual punishment when the inmate does not suffer serious injury. We answer that question in the affirmative.

At the time of the incident that is the subject of this suit, petitioner Keith Hudson was an inmate at the state penitentiary in Angola, Louisiana. Respondents Jack McMillian, Marvin Woods, and Arthur Mezo served as corrections security officers at the Angola facility. During the early morning hours of October 30, 1983, Hudson and McMillian argued. Assisted by Woods, McMillian then placed Hudson in handcuffs and shackles, took the prisoner out of his cell, and walked him toward the penitentiary's "administrative lockdown" area. Hudson testified that, on the way there, McMillian punched Hudson in the mouth, eyes, chest, and stomach while Woods held the inmate in place and kicked and punched him from behind. He further testified that Mezo, the supervisor on duty, watched the beating but merely told the officers "not to have too much fun." App. 23. As a result of this episode, Hudson suffered minor bruises and swelling of his face, mouth, and lip. The blows also loosened Hudson's teeth and cracked his partial dental plate, rendering it unusable for several months.

Hudson sued the three corrections officers in Federal District Court under Rev. Stat. § 1979, 42 U.S.C. § 1983, alleging a violation of the 8th Amendment's prohibition on cruel and unusual punishments and seeking compensatory damages. The parties consented to disposition of the case before a Magistrate, who found that McMillian and Woods used force when there was no need to do so and that Mezo expressly condoned their actions. App. 26. The Magistrate awarded Hudson damages of $800. Id., at 29.

The Court of Appeals for the Fifth Circuit reversed. 929 F.2d 1014 (1990). It held that inmates alleging use of excessive force in violation of the 8th Amendment must prove: (1) significant injury; (2) resulting "directly and only from the use of force that was clearly excessive to the need"; (3) the excessiveness of which was objectively unreasonable; and (4) that the action constituted an unnecessary and wanton infliction of pain. Id., at 1015. The court determined that respondents' use of force was objectively unreasonable because no force was required. Furthermore, "[t]he conduct of McMillian and Woods qualified as clearly excessive and occasioned unnecessary and wanton infliction of pain." Ibid. However, Hudson could not prevail on his 8th Amendment claim because his injuries were "minor" and required no medical attention. Ibid.

We granted certiorari, 499 U.S. 958 (1991), to determine whether the "significant injury" requirement applied by the Court of Appeals accords with the Constitution's dictate that cruel and unusual punishment shall not be inflicted.

In *Whitley v. Albers*, 475 U.S. 312 (1986), the principal question before us was what legal standard should govern the 8th Amendment claim of an inmate shot by a guard during a prison riot. We based our answer on the settled rule that "the unnecessary and wanton infliction of pain . . . constitutes cruel and unusual punishment forbidden by the Eighth Amendment." Id., at 319 (quoting *Ingraham v. Wright*, 430 U.S. 651, 670 (1977)) (internal quotation marks omitted).

What is necessary to establish an "unnecessary and wanton infliction of pain," we said, varies according to the nature of the alleged constitutional violation. 475 U.S., at 320. For example, the appropriate inquiry when an inmate alleges that prison officials failed to attend to serious medical needs is whether the officials exhibited "deliberate indifference."

See *Estelle v. Gamble*, 429 U.S. 97, 104 (1976). This standard is appropriate because the State's responsibility to provide inmates with medical care ordinarily does not conflict with competing administrative concerns. Whitley, supra, at 320.

By contrast, officials confronted with a prison disturbance must balance the threat unrest poses to inmates, prison workers, administrators, and visitors against the harm inmates may suffer if guards use force. Despite the weight of these competing concerns, corrections officials must make their decisions "in haste, under pressure, and frequently without the luxury of a second chance." 475 U.S., at 320. We accordingly concluded in Whitley that application of the deliberate indifference standard is inappropriate when authorities use force to put down a prison disturbance. Instead, "the question whether the measure taken inflicted unnecessary and wanton pain and suffering ultimately turns on 'whether force was applied in a good faith effort to maintain or restore discipline or maliciously and sadistically for the very purpose of causing harm.'"

Benjamin Haas/Shutterstock.com

Id., at 320–321 (quoting *Johnson v. Glick*, 481 F.2d 1028, 1033 (CA2), cert. denied sub nom. *John v. Johnson*, 414 U.S. 1033 (1973)).

Many of the concerns underlying our holding in Whitley arise whenever guards use force to keep order. Whether the prison disturbance is a riot or a lesser disruption, corrections officers must balance the need "to maintain or restore discipline" through force against the risk of injury to inmates. Both situations may require prison officials to act quickly and decisively. Likewise, both implicate the principle that "[p]rison administrators . . . should be accorded wide-ranging deference in the adoption and execution of policies and practices that in their judgment are needed to preserve internal order and discipline and to maintain institutional security." 475 U.S., at 321–322 (quoting *Bell v. Wolfish*, 441 U.S. 520, 547 (1979)). In recognition of these similarities, we hold that whenever prison officials stand accused of using excessive physical force in violation of the Cruel and Unusual Punishments Clause, the core judicial inquiry is that set out in Whitley: whether force was applied in a good-faith effort to maintain or restore discipline, or maliciously and sadistically to cause harm.

Extending Whitley's application of the "unnecessary and wanton infliction of pain" standard to all allegations of excessive force works no innovation. This Court derived the Whitley test from one articulated by Judge Friendly in *Johnson v. Glick*, supra, a case arising out of a prisoner's claim to have been beaten and harassed by a guard. Moreover, many Courts of Appeals already apply the Whitley standard to allegations of excessive force outside of the riot situation. See *Corselli v. Coughlin*, 842 F.2d 23, 26 (CA2 1988); *Miller v. Leathers*, 913 F.2d 1085, 1087 (CA4 1990) (en banc), cert. denied, 498 U.S. 1109 (1991); *Haynes v. Marshall*, 887 F.2d 700, 703 (CA6 1989); *Stenzel v. Ellis*, 916 F.2d 423, 427 (CA8 1990); *Brown v. Smith*, 813 F.2d 1187, 1188 (CA11 1987). But see *Unwin v. Campbell*, 863 F.2d 124, 130 (CA1 1988) (rejecting application of Whitley standard absent "an actual disturbance").

Under the Whitley approach, the extent of injury suffered by an inmate is one factor that may suggest "whether the use of force could plausibly have been thought necessary" in a particular situation, "or instead evinced such wantonness with respect to the unjustified infliction of harm as is tantamount to a knowing willingness that it occur." 475 U.S., at 321. In determining whether the use of force was wanton and unnecessary, it may also be proper to evaluate the need for application of force, the relationship between that need and the amount of force used, the threat "reasonably perceived by the responsible officials," and "any efforts made to temper the severity of a forceful response." Ibid. The absence of serious injury is therefore relevant to the 8th Amendment inquiry, but does not end it.

Respondents nonetheless assert that a significant injury requirement of the sort imposed by the Fifth Circuit is mandated by what we have termed the "objective component" of 8th Amendment analysis. See *Wilson v. Seiter*, 501 U.S. 294, 298 (1991). Wilson extended the deliberate indifference standard applied to 8th Amendment claims involving medical care to claims about conditions of confinement. In taking this step, we suggested that the subjective aspect of an 8th Amendment claim (with which the Court was concerned) can be distinguished from the objective facet of the same claim. Thus, courts considering a prisoner's claim must ask both if "the officials act[ed] with a sufficiently culpable state of mind" and if the alleged wrongdoing was objectively "harmful enough" to establish a constitutional violation. Id., at 298, 303.

With respect to the objective component of an 8th Amendment violation, Wilson announced no new rule. Instead, that decision suggested a relationship between the requirements applicable to different types of 8th Amendment claims. What is necessary to show sufficient harm for purposes of the Cruel and Unusual Punishments Clause depends upon the claim at issue, for two reasons. First, "[t]he general requirement that an Eighth Amendment claimant allege and prove the unnecessary and wanton infliction of pain should . . . be applied with due regard for differences in the kind of conduct against which an Eighth Amendment objection is lodged." Whitley, supra, at 320. Second, the 8th Amendment's pro-

ermess/Shutterstock.com

hibition of cruel and unusual punishments "draw[s] its meaning from the evolving standards of decency that mark the progress of a maturing society," and so admits of few absolute limitations. *Rhodes v. Chapman*, 452 U.S. 337, 346 (1981) (quoting *Trop v. Dulles*, 356 U.S. 86, 101 (1958) (plurality opinion)).

The objective component of an 8th Amendment claim is therefore contextual and responsive to "contemporary standards of decency." Estelle, supra, at 103. For instance, extreme deprivations are required to make out a conditions-of-confinement claim. Because routine discomfort is "part of the penalty that criminal offenders pay for their offenses against society," Rhodes, supra, at 347, "only those deprivations denying 'the minimal civilized measure of life's necessities' are sufficiently grave to form the basis of an Eighth Amendment violation." Wilson, supra, at 298 (quoting Rhodes, supra, at 347) (citation omitted). A similar analysis applies to medical needs. Because society does not expect that prisoners will have unqualified access to health care, deliberate indifference to medical needs amounts to an 8th Amendment violation only if those needs are "serious." See *Estelle v. Gamble*, 429 U.S., at 103–104.

In the excessive force context, society's expectations are different. <u>When prison officials maliciously and sadistically use force to cause harm, contemporary standards of decency always are violated</u>. See Whitley, supra, at 327. This is true whether or not significant injury is evident. Otherwise, the 8th Amendment would permit any physical punishment, no matter how diabolic or inhuman, inflicting less than some arbitrary quantity of injury. Such a result would have been as unacceptable to the drafters of the 8th Amendment as it is today. See Estelle, supra, at 102 (proscribing torture and barbarous punishment was "the primary concern of the drafters" of the 8th Amendment); *Wilkerson v. Utah*, 99 U.S. 130, 136

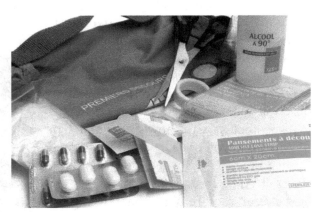
Gilles Paire/Shutterstock.com

(1879) ("[I]t is safe to affirm that punishments of torture . . . and all others in the same line of unnecessary cruelty, are forbidden by [the Eighth Amendment]").

That is not to say that every malevolent touch by a prison guard gives rise to a federal cause of action. See *Johnson v. Glick*, 481 F. 2d, at 1033 ("Not every push or shove, even if it may later seem unnecessary in the peace of a judge's chambers, violates a prisoner's constitutional rights"). The 8th Amendment's prohibition of "cruel and unusual" punishments necessarily excludes from constitutional recognition de minimis uses of physical force, provided that the use of force is not of a sort "repugnant to the conscience of mankind." Whitley, 475 U.S., at 327 (quoting Estelle, supra, at 106) (internal quotation marks omitted).

In this case, the Fifth Circuit found Hudson's claim untenable because his injuries were "minor." 929 F. 2d, at 1015. Yet the blows directed at Hudson, which caused bruises, swelling, loosened teeth, and a cracked dental plate, are not de minimis for

8th Amendment purposes. The extent of Hudson's injuries thus provides no basis for dismissal of his § 1983 claim.

The dissent's theory that Wilson requires an inmate who alleges excessive use of force to show serious injury in addition to the unnecessary and wanton infliction of pain misapplies Wilson and ignores the body of our 8th Amendment jurisprudence. As we have already suggested, the question before the Court in Wilson was "[w]hether a prisoner claiming that conditions of confinement constitute cruel and unusual punishment must show a culpable state of mind on the part of prison officials, and, if so, what state of mind is required." Wilson, supra, at 296. Wilson presented neither an allegation of excessive force nor any issue relating to what was dubbed the "objective component" of an 8th Amendment claim.

Wilson did touch on these matters in the course of summarizing our prior holdings, beginning with *Estelle v. Gamble*, supra. Estelle, we noted, first applied the Cruel and Unusual Punishments Clause to deprivations that were not specifically part of the prisoner's sentence. Wilson, supra, at 297. As might be expected from this primacy, Estelle stated the principle underlying the cases discussed in Wilson: Punishments "incompatible with the evolving standards of decency that mark the progress of a maturing society" or "involv[ing] the unnecessary and wanton infliction of pain" are "repugnant to the Eighth Amendment." Estelle, supra, at 102–103 (internal quotation marks omitted). This is the same rule the dissent would reject. With respect to the objective component of an 8th Amendment claim, however, Wilson suggested no departure from Estelle and its progeny.

The dissent's argument that claims based on excessive force and claims based on conditions of confinement are no different in kind, post, at 24–25, and n. 4, is likewise unfounded. Far from rejecting Whitley's insight that the unnecessary and wanton infliction of pain standard must be applied with regard for the nature of the alleged 8th Amendment violation, the Wilson Court adopted it. See Wilson, 501 U.S., at 302–303. How could it be otherwise when the constitutional touchstone is whether punishment is cruel and unusual? To deny, as the dissent does, the difference between punching a prisoner in the face and serving him unappetizing food is to ignore the "concepts of dignity, civilized standards, humanity, and decency" that animate the 8th Amendment. Estelle, supra, at 102 (quoting *Jackson v. Bishop*, 404 F.2d 571, 579 (CA8 1968))

Respondents argue that, aside from the significant injury test applied by the Fifth Circuit, their conduct cannot constitute an 8th Amendment violation because it was "isolated and unauthorized." Brief for Respondents 28. The beating of Hudson, they contend, arose from "a personal dispute between correctional security officers and a prisoner," and was against prison policy. Ibid. Respondents invoke the reasoning of courts that have held the use of force by prison officers under such circumstances beyond the scope of "punishment" prohibited by the 8th Amendment. See *Johnson v. Glick*, supra, at 1032 ("[A]lthough a spontaneous attack by a guard is 'cruel' and, we hope, 'unusual,' it does not fit any ordinary concept of 'punishment'"); *George v. Evans*, 633 F.2d 413, 416 (CA5 1980) ("[A] single, unauthorized assault by a guard does not constitute cruel and unusual punishment . . . ").But see *Duckworth v. Franzen*, 780 F.2d 645, 652 (CA7 1985) ("If a guard decided to supplement a prisoner's official punishment by beating him, this would be punishment . . . "), cert. denied, 479 U.S. 816 (1986).

We take no position on respondents' legal argument because we find it inapposite on this record. The Court of Appeals left intact the Magistrate's determination that the violence at issue in this case was "not an isolated assault." App. 27, n. 1. Indeed, there was testimony that McMillian and Woods beat another prisoner shortly after they finished with Hudson. Ibid. To the extent that respondents rely on the unauthorized nature of their acts, they make a claim not addressed by the Fifth Circuit, not presented by the question on which we granted certiorari, and, accordingly, not before this Court. Moreover, respondents ignore the Magistrate's finding that Lieutenant Mezo, acting as a supervisor, "expressly condoned the use of force in this instance." App.26.

The judgment of the Court of Appeals is Reversed.

Kingsley v. Hendrickson, 576 U.S. ___ (2015)

An important case about excessive force, in the plaintiff's favor. <u>The precise question in the case is the legal standard for excessive force in the context of pretrial detention.</u> But the Court's reasoning appears to extend significantly further and may undermine established standards for excessive force in the much broader context of prison detention.

After being arrested and taken to pretrial detention, Michael Kingsley refused to remove a piece of paper covering a light fixture in his cell. Jail officers then removed Kingsley from his cell and made him lie down on a hard surface. While the details of what happened next are partly disputed, Kingsley alleges that he did not significantly resist and that officers slammed his head into the hard surface. The officers also used a Taser on Kingsley for several seconds, even though he was handcuffed and lying face down.

The legal question before the Court has to do with the legal standard for finding unconstitutionally excessive force during pretrial detention. When people are held in prisons after trial and conviction, the 8th Amendment provides the appropriate standard and demands a showing of subjective "deliberate indifference" on the part of officers. The reason for that standard is that the 8th Amendment prohibits certain types of "punishment," and the Court has thought that punishment cannot be entirely inadvertent. However, *the 8th Amendment doesn't govern pretrial detention. Instead, cases like Kingsley's are governed by the Due Process Clauses.*

So, should something like the subjective requirement applicable in 8th Amendment prison cases also apply in connection with pretrial due process claims of excessive force? Or, instead, should objective unreasonableness—regardless of the officers' subjective state of mind—be sufficient to create a due process violation?

SCOTUS, in this case, held that the appropriate standard is objective, not subjective. In elaborating this result, the Court made clear that the resulting standard is not easily met. The appropriate analysis focuses on *"the perspective of a reasonable officer on the scene, including what the officer knew at the time, not with the 20/20 vision of hindsight." And the objective inquiry must also take full consideration of the jail's need for "internal order and discipline."*

The Court listed a range of nonexhaustive considerations relevant to the objective inquiry, including: *"the relationship between the need for the use of force and the amount of force used; the extent of the plaintiff's injury; any effort made by the officer to temper or to limit the amount of force; the severity of the security problem at issue; the threat reasonably perceived by the officer; and whether the plaintiff was actively resisting."*

In justifying this outcome, the Court reaffirmed its own precedent that "the Due Process Clause protects a pretrial detainee from the use of excessive force that amounts to punishment." The Court then explained that, "in the absence of an expressed intent to punish, a pretrial detainee can nevertheless prevail by showing that the actions are not 'rationally related to a legitimate non-punitive governmental purpose' or that the actions 'appear excessive in relation to that purpose." Therefore, the Court continued, *"a pretrial detainee can prevail by providing only objective evidence that the challenged governmental action is not rationally related to a legitimate governmental objective or that it is excessive in relation to that purpose."*

We acknowledge that our view that an objective standard is appropriate in the context of excessive force claims brought by pretrial detainees pursuant to the 14th Amendment may raise questions about the use of a subjective standard in the context of excessive force claims brought by convicted prisoners. We are not confronted with such a claim, however, so we need not address that issue today.

The Court noted that many jury instructions and jail policies already assume the objective approach, without creating any obvious problem. The Court also noted that "the use of an objective standard adequately protects an officer who acts in good faith," particularly given the availability of qualified immunity.

Kingsley won't be remembered as the Court's last or most influential case on excessive force, but it should be remembered as an important one. Rather than decide the case based on mechanical doctrinal reasoning, the majority thought about why the doctrinal categories existed—and expressed openness to changing those catego-ries. In time, the case might look like a pivotal moment when the Court began the project of adopting objective unreasonableness standards more broadly, including—perhaps—in the 8th Amendment context.

In a footnote in *Graham v. Connor*, the U.S. Supreme Court stated, "due process clause protects a pretrial detainee from the use of excessive force that amounts to pun-ishment. After conviction, the Eighth

M-SUR/Shutterstock.com

Amendment serves as the primary source of substantive protection . . . in cases . . . where the deliberate use of force is challenged as excessive and unjustified. Any protection that substantive due process affords convicted prisoners against excessive force is, we have held, at least redundant, of that provided by the Eighth Amendment."

INDIVIDUAL LIABILITY

The flip side of the issue presented in *Hudson v. McMillian* is that officers can sometimes inflict significant injury indeed on a prisoner, as long as the force used is justified under the circumstances by a good faith attempt to maintain or restore order. In *Muhammad v. McCarrell*, No. 07-2235, 2008 U.S. App. Lexis 16682 (8th Cir.), for example, a federal appeals court upheld a jury verdict for defendant corrections officers in a lawsuit brought by a prisoner allegedly injured by them when they used force to extract him from his cell. The plaintiff prisoner in this case admitted that he had a weapon in his pocket at the time of the incident. The evidence showed that he had been belligerent and uncooperative, and that he had created a disturbance in his cellblock, taunted an officer, and that pepper spray and a 15 OC Stinger grenade used against the prisoner, as well as tear gas, had little effect and failed to subdue him. The officers then shot a 37MM Ferret OC powder round, designed to break through a barricade, at the cell wall, but he still allegedly refused to comply. They then dispensed a 28b Stinger 37MM 60 Cal. rubber-ball round into the cell, and again failed to subdue the prisoner. Another Ferret OC powder round fired into the cell then went through a mattress that the prisoner used to barricade his cell door, and hit him in the groin area, finally subduing him, but inflicting significant injuries in the process. The force used was justified by the prisoner's own actions.

Similarly, in *Johnson v. Hamilton*, No. 05-1453, 452 F.3d 967 (8th Cir. 2006), a federal appeals court found that no reasonable jury could find that correctional employees used excessive force against an inmate during the incident that led to injuries, including a fractured finger, when he continued to assault the officers even after he was restrained, and was subsequently criminally convicted for his actions.

In contrast, in *Johnson v. Blaukat*, No. 05-3866, 453 F.3d 1108 (8th Cir. 2006), the court ruled that two correctional officers were not entitled to summary judgment in a female prisoner's excessive force lawsuit when there were factual issues about whether they used unnecessary force and pepper spray against her at a time when she was allegedly not actively resisting them. The prisoner had previously been involved in a disturbance along with other prisoners, but had returned to her cell, and claimed that she did nothing at the time that the officers entered her cell other than step in front of one of them to speak to him. She was subsequently allegedly tackled to the floor, and an attempt to handcuff her was made, during which a number of officers allegedly piled on top of her. While she says she attempted to explain that her hand was stuck, an officer allegedly placed an Orcutt Police Nunchaku (OPN) around her neck and choked her, twisting the device until it broke. She also claimed that her head was slammed down on the floor, that her hair was pulled, and that an officer sprayed mace on her face and eyes. It was disputed whether she had stopped resisting at the time, or whether, as the officers claimed, she had "lunged" at them. If the officers used force in a defensive manner, as they claimed, their actions might have been justified, but if they were instead "motivated by anger" and unnecessary, they would have violated the prisoner's rights.

Estate of *Moreland v. Dieter*, No. 03-3734, 395 F.3d 747 (7th Cir. 2005), cert. denied, sub nom., Estate of *Moreland v. Speybroeck*, 545 U.S. 1115 (2005), a federal appeals court upheld a jury's award of $29 million in compensatory and $27.5 million in punitive damages against two deputy sheriffs for causing a pretrial detainee's death through use of excessive force. The facts recited in the court's opinion are a clear illustration of what is meant by the unnecessary use of force to inflict pain.

The prisoner had been arrested in the early morning hours for driving under the influence of alcohol, and allegedly behaved "erratically" during the arrest, doing things like hitting himself in the face. After 2 hours at the police department, he was transferred to the county jail. While he was still "obviously" intoxicated, he entered the jail on his own power and was placed in a "drunk tank" with two other detainees. He immediately provoked a confrontation by directing racial slurs at one of the other detainees in the tank. Sergeant Paul Moffa, the shift supervisor on duty

hafakot/Shutterstock.com

that night, responded to the disturbance and entered the tank with another officer. Moffa grabbed Moreland by the neck or shoulders, threw him to the floor, removed a canister of OC-10 pepper spray 1 from his waist, and sprayed Moreland's face from a distance of roughly four or five inches. Coleman took cover underneath a blanket as pepper spray filled the air, but he heard a struggle between Moreland and Moffa and at one point heard what he said was "the sound of a basket-ball bouncing off concrete." The other inmate in the drunk tank said it sounded like "a melon popping, like dropping a watermelon." They surmised this was the sound of Moreland's head hitting the concrete floor.

The officers handcuffed Moreland behind his back and dragged him out of the drunk tank to a nearby elevator. They set him down on the floor in front of the elevator and prepared to take him to the shower on the fourth floor to wash off the pepper spray. Two other officers, Albright and Holvoet, accompanied Moreland in the elevator to the fourth floor. Moffa, who had been hit by pepper spray ricocheting off Moreland, stayed behind on the first floor. Moreland thrashed about as he was taken upstairs; Albright and Holvoet tried to restrain him by pinning him to the elevator floor.

When the elevator doors opened at the fourth floor cell block, Dieter was waiting to meet them. Holvoet told Dieter that Moreland was the guy "who got Moffa sprayed." Albright testified that he thought this comment was a signal from Moffa to Dieter, his close friend, that Moreland had some "payback" coming. Sawdon arrived on the fourth floor shortly after Moreland and the others.

Dieter lifted Moreland up and hauled him over to the shower. Witnesses testified that Dieter pushed Moreland into the shower with such force that Moreland hit his head against the far wall. Albright testified that Dieter held Moreland from behind and accelerated toward the shower until the two men smashed into the far wall, crushing Moreland between the wall and Dieter's own body. Dieter or another officer turned on the hot water, which exacerbates the pain of pepper spray. In response to Moreland's cries from inside the shower (the defendants maintained he was belligerent, but other officers and witnesses testified that he was crying out for help), Sawdon said to the other officers, "Hey, guys, do you want to see something funny?" He then threw a five-gallon bucket of cold water over Moreland. Other officers gathered outside the shower, watching and laughing as Moreland, still handcuffed, lay with his head in a shallow puddle of water, spit, and mucus, trying to wash the pepper spray off his face.

Dieter and Sawdon then dragged Moreland from the shower and strapped him into a "restraint chair." Designed to control or impair an aggressive inmate who may endanger an officer or another inmate, the "Pro-Straint Restraining Chair" enables officers to shackle and tie down an inmate while keeping him in a seated, upright position. Moreland remained handcuffed while in the restraint chair. According to several inmates who observed what happened from inside their cells, Moreland sat in the restraint chair for several minutes, cursing and yelling at the defendants and asking them why they were doing this to him. According to the inmates, Sawdon kept telling Moreland to shut up. Then Sawdon went into the guard tower at the center of the floor and came out with an OC-10 canister. He approached Moreland and discharged the canister in his face while he was still strapped in the chair. Officers who arrived on the fourth floor shortly thereafter reported noticing the unmistakable residual odor of an OC-10 blast. Some witnesses also reported hearing the sounds of Moreland being beaten during this time.

Dieter and Sawdon then removed Moreland from the restraint chair and forcibly put him back into the shower again. Sometime later the defendants put Moreland back in the restraint chair and moved him into a nearby "attorney's room," out of view of the other inmates. Connie Spicer, the jail's medication aide, arrived on the fourth floor around this time and examined Moreland, whom she described as slouched back in the restraint chair, moaning, and unresponsive. She saw that Moreland had a cut above his left eyebrow that had bled profusely. Dieter and Sawdon told her that Moreland had slipped and fallen. She placed a bandage over the cut. Spicer told the officers that Moreland should be taken to the hospital; however, she testified that Moffa, Dieter, and Sawdon did not want to do this because their shift was ending and transferring Moreland to the hospital would require them to remain at work. Spicer believed (incorrectly, it seems) that she did not have the authority to order the officers to transport Moreland to the hospital. Moreland remained in the restraint chair in the attorney's room, and at 7 a.m. the night shift personnel, including the defendants, left the jail.

Two-day shift officers, Wilson and Johnson, found Moreland unconscious in the attorney's room shortly after 7 a.m. They noticed a large lump on the back of his head, injuries to the front of his face, and a bandage over the cut above his left eye. Wilson took Moreland, still unconscious, to the first floor, changed his clothing, and placed him back in the drunk tank. Spicer saw Moreland in the tank around 9:40 a.m., coughing and unresponsive. At 11:00 a.m., when she checked on him again, Moreland had not moved. The next time she checked Moreland was blue, cold, and lifeless. Moreland was pronounced dead at approximately 1:23 p.m. The coroner and other forensic experts testified that the cause of Moreland's death was an acute subdural hematoma that could only have occurred during the period of time Moreland was confined in the St. Joseph County Jail.

Moreland's estate and parents sued numerous parties, most of whom either settled or were voluntarily dismissed. Sheriff Speybroeck was sued in his official and individual capacities; the district court granted his motion for summary judgment. A trial was held on the claims against Moffa, Dieter, and Sawdon. The jury found Dieter and Sawdon liable, but could not reach agreement on Moffa and a mistrial was declared as to him. The jury returned damages

TypoArt BS/Shutterstock.com

verdicts as follows: $29 million in compensatory damages; $15 million in punitive damages against Dieter and $12.5 million against Sawdon. The case against Moffa was retried, resulting in a verdict in his favor. Dieter and Sawdon appealed the judgment against them, and the plaintiffs cross-appealed the grant of summary judgment to Speybroeck.

McReynolds v. Ala. Dept. of Youth Services, No. 2:04-cv-850, 2008 U.S. Dist. Lexis 35070 (M.D. Ala.), ruling that correctional officers were not entitled to qualified immunity in a lawsuit claiming that three of them beat a detainee at a juvenile detention facility with nightsticks about his head and face after he refused orders to remove his clothes. A fourth officer allegedly watched and failed to intervene. The beating was allegedly severe enough that the detainee required eleven stitches and a doctor at the hospital believed that he might have bled to death without medical attention. The court found that there was evidence from which a reasonable fact finder could find that the force employed was used in a malicious and sadistic manner, rather than in a good faith effort to maintain or restore discipline.

Payne v. Parnell, No. 05-20687, 246 Fed Appx. 884, 2007 U.S. App. Lexis 21227 (Unpub. 5th Cir.), in which the court ruled that a correctional officer who allegedly used a cattle prod against an inmate who was merely working at his prison job was not entitled to summary judgment. If it was true that the prisoner was not causing any disruption or violating any prison rule, a reasonable jury could find that there was no need to use any level of force.

McBride v. Hilton, No. 06-30146, 223 Fed. Appx. 303, 2007 U.S. App. Lexis 2505 (Unpub. 5th Cir.), finding that a deputy used reasonable force against inmate in light of prisoner's history of violence and his violent response to requests to step outside, including his scuffle with deputies.

Johnson v. Moody, No. 06-12422, 206 Fed. Appx. 880, 2006 U.S. App. Lexis 26988 (Unpub. 11th Cir.), in which the court found that an Alabama prisoner who sued correctional officer who allegedly injured his finger by kicking a metal tray door failed to show that he suffered a serious injury or that the officer acted maliciously or sadistically, barring a federal civil rights claim. The officer argued that the incident was an accident, and that it occurred because the prisoner refused to remove his hand from a slot in the door through which food was passed.

Corpus v. Bennett, No. 04-2603, 430 F.3d 917 (8th Cir. 2005), a case in which the trial court was found to have properly reduced jury's award of $75,000 in "nominal" damages to $1 in pretrial detainee's lawsuit, when jury specifically found that jailer used excessive force against the detainee but did not cause any substantial injury. (This appears to be contrary to the standard in Hudson. Not really addressed until Wilkins.)

Atwell v. Hart County, Kentucky, No. 03-6421, 122 Fed. Appx. 215, 2005 U.S. App. Lexis 1771 (Unpub. 6th Cir. 2005), in which jail personnel were found not to have used excessive force in using pepper spray to subdue a detainee suffering from paranoid schizophrenia, acute psychosis, impulse-control disorder, and "polysubstance abuse" who actively resisted his transfer to a hospital to receive treatment.

Cain v. Ambriz, No. 04-40632, 114 Fed. Appx. 600, 2004 U.S. App. Lexis 2075 (Unpub. 5th Cir. 2004), a case in which a prisoner admitted that he refused to comply with an officer's requests. Under these circumstances, the officer's pushing against the prisoner's face with his hand for the purpose of forcing him into his cell was not an excessive use of force.

Wooten v. Law, No. 04-1159, 118 Fed. Appx. 66, 2004 U.S. App. Lexis 24221 (Unpub. 7th Cir. 2004), in which the court ruled that a prisoner's federal civil rights lawsuit against prison guards, claiming that they used excessive force against him, was barred by his prior disciplinary conviction of assault and resisting the guards arising out of the same incident. An award of damages in the prisoner's lawsuit, which was based on the assertion that he had not physically resisted the guards, would necessarily call into question his disciplinary conviction, which had not been set aside, so his lawsuit was barred under the rule stated in *Heck v. Humphrey*, 512 U.S. 477 (1994).

Farmer v. Brennan, 511 U.S.825 (1994), An official's deliberate indifference to a substantial risk of serious harm to an individual in custody violates the 8th Amendment to the Constitution.

Wilkins v. Gaddy, 559 U.S. ___ (2010) affirms the Hudson decision

In *Hudson v. McMillian*, 503 U.S. 1, 4 (1992), this Court held that "the use of excessive physical force against a prisoner may constitute cruel and unusual punishment [even] when the inmate does not suffer serious injury." In this case, the District Court dismissed a prisoner's excessive force claim based entirely on its determination that his injuries were "de minimis." Because the District Court's approach, affirmed on appeal, is at odds with <u>Hudson's direction to decide excessive force claims based on the nature of the force rather than the extent of the injury</u>.

In requiring what amounts to a showing of significant injury in order to state an excessive force claim, the Fourth Circuit has strayed from the clear holding of this Court in Hudson. Like Wilkins, the prisoner in Hudson filed suit under § 1983 alleging that corrections officers had used excessive force in violation of the 8th Amendment. Evidence indicated that the officers had punched Hudson in the mouth, eyes, chest, and stomach without justification, resulting in

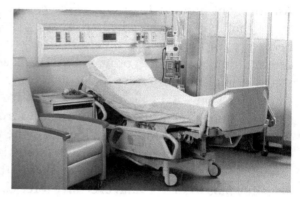

Monkey Business Images/Shutterstock.com

"minor bruises and swelling of his face, mouth, and lip," as well as, loosened teeth and a cracked partial dental plate. 503 U.S., at 4. A Magistrate Judge entered judgment in Hudson's favor, but the Court of Appeals for the Fifth Circuit reversed, holding that an inmate must prove "a significant injury" in order to state an excessive force claim. *Hudson v. McMillian*, 929 F. 2d 1014, 1015 (1990) (per curiam). According to the Court of Appeals, Hudson's injuries, which had not required medical attention, were too "minor" to warrant relief. Ibid.

Reversing the Court of Appeals, the U.S. Supreme Court rejected the notion that "significant injury" is a threshold requirement for stating an excessive force claim. The "core judicial inquiry," was not whether a certain quantum of injury was sustained, but rather "whether force was applied in a good-faith effort to maintain or restore discipline, or maliciously and sadistically to cause harm." 503 U.S., at 7; see also *Whitley v. Albers*, 475 U.S. 312, 319–321 (1986). "When prison officials maliciously and sadistically use force to cause harm," the Court recognized, "contemporary standards of decency always are violated ... whether or not significant injury is evident. Otherwise, the Eighth Amendment would permit any physical punishment, no matter how diabolic or inhuman, inflicting less than some arbitrary quantity of injury." Hudson, 503 U.S., at 9; see also id., at 13–14 (Blackmun, J., concurring in judgment) ("The Court puts to rest a seriously misguided view that pain inflicted by an excessive use of force is actionable under the Eighth Amendment only when coupled with 'significant injury,' e.g., injury that requires medical attention or leaves permanent marks").

This is not to say that the "absence of serious injury" is irrelevant to the 8th Amendment inquiry. Id., at 7. "[T]he extent of injury suffered by an inmate is one factor that may suggest 'whether the use of force could plausibly have been thought necessary' in a particular situation." Ibid. (quoting Whitley, 475 U.S., at 321). The extent of injury may also provide some indication of the amount of force applied. As stated in Hudson, not "every malevolent touch by a prison guard gives rise to a federal cause of action." 503 U.S., at 9. "The Eighth Amendment's prohibition of 'cruel and unusual' punishments necessarily excludes from constitutional recognition de minimis uses of physical force, provided that the use of force is not of a sort repugnant to the conscience of mankind." Ibid. (some internal quotation marks omitted). An inmate who complains of a "push or shove" that causes no discernible injury almost certainly fails to state a valid excessive force claim. Ibid. (quoting *Johnson v. Glick*, 481 F. 2d 1028, 1033 (CA2 1973)).

An inmate who is gratuitously beaten by guards does not lose his ability to pursue an excessive force claim merely because he has the good fortune to escape without serious injury. Accordingly, the Court concluded in Hudson that the supposedly "minor" nature of the injuries "provide[d] no basis for dismissal of [Hudson's] §1983 claim" because "the blows directed at Hudson, which caused bruises, swelling, loosened teeth, and a cracked dental plate, are not de minimis for Eighth Amendment purposes." 503 U.S., at 10.

The allegations made by Wilkins in this case are quite similar to the facts in Hudson, and the District Court's analysis closely resembles the approach Hudson disavowed. Wilkins alleged that he was punched, kicked, kneed, choked, and body slammed "maliciously and sadistically" and "[w]ithout any provocation." Dismissing Wilkins' action, the District Court did not hold that this purported assault, which allegedly left Wilkins with a bruised heel, back pain, and other injuries requiring medical treatment, involved de minimis force. Instead, the court concluded that Wilkins had failed to state a claim because "he simply has not alleged that he suffered anything more than de minimus [sic] injury." No. 3:08–cv–00138 (WD NC, Apr. 16, 2008), at 2.

The notion of "de minimis force" is one that is interpreted broadly. In general, the courts expressly understand the use of force in a corrections setting, for those who have been convicted, is summed up by this quote from *Johnson v. Glick*, 1973, 481 F.2d 1028, 1033; "The management by a few guards of large numbers of prisoners, not usually the most gentle or tractable of men and women, may require and justify the occasional use of a degree of intentional force. Not every push or shove, even if it may later seem unnecessary in the peace of a judge's chambers, violates a prisoner's constitutional rights."

Meredith v. State of Arizona, No. 74-1315. 523 F.2d 481 (1975)

In this case, we can follow the reasoning and case law which constitutes action under § 1983.

Meredith is incarcerated in a state prison in Arizona. He has a medical history of emphysema. In the early morning of September 28, 1973, he asked to be excused from breakfast because he was suffering from an emphysema attack. Permission was denied, and he started to walk to the mess hall. When he was about 500 feet from the hall, his condition worsened. He asked correctional officer Miller the source of the order that he must attend breakfast despite his illness, and Miller answered that the warden had given the order and that he, Miller, intended to enforce it. Meredith complained about his difficulty in breathing, and Miller struck him in the solar plexus. According to the complaint, Miller's blow rendered him "totally handicapped." Thereupon, Miller ordered a junior officer to take Meredith to the isolation building and lock him up. Lieutenant Hall was nearby and ordered Miller to stop harassing Meredith and directed another officer to put Meredith in a wheelchair and take him to the hospital for emergency treatment, which was done. He was given 4 hours of oxygen therapy "to counteract the damage that had been done."

The incident was investigated by Associate Warden Burd, who concluded that the warden had issued no order requiring Meredith to attend meals while suffering from an attack of emphysema, that Miller had acted without authority in directing Meredith to attend breakfast on September 28, and that Meredith was not guilty of any infraction. Meredith sued Miller, Hall, Burd, Warden Cardwell, prison physician Deputy, and the State of Arizona.

Does the complaint, as liberally construed (*Haines v. Kerner*, 1972, 404 U.S. 519, 92 S. Ct. 594, 30 L.Ed.2d 652), state facts bringing Meredith within 42 U.S.C. § 1983, which gives him an action against one who, under the color of state law and without due process deprives him of his constitutional right to "liberty," guaranteed by the 14th Amendment?[1] We think that it does.

First, there is no doubt that Miller was acting in the course of his official duties. What he did was done "under color" of state law. *Gregory v. Thompson*, 9 Cir., 1974, 500 F.2d 59, 62. *See also Williams v. United States*, 1951, 341 U.S. 97, 99, 71 S. Ct. 576, 95 L.Ed. 774.

Second, it is now too late to argue that one who is subjected to an assault and battery by a person acting under color of state law can never have a claim for relief under § 1983. In *Gregory v. Thompson, supra*, 500 F.2d at 62, <u>we squarely held that the right violated by an assault and battery is "the right to be secure in one's person, and is grounded in the due process clause of the Fourteenth Amendment." It is an aspect of the right to liberty.</u>

The only arguable question is whether the particular assault and battery here alleged is such as to fall within § 1983. Heretofore, we have not tried to lay down guidelines as to what assaults and batteries committed by persons acting under color of state law fall within § 1983, and what assaults and batteries do not. Here we deal with a complaint by a prisoner against his custodians, involving the use of force in a setting in which force is sometimes both appropriate and unavoidable. We doubt that, even in that setting, it is possible to lay down a rule for all cases, and we shall not attempt to do so.

We find ourselves in general agreement with the views of Judge Friendly, speaking for the Second Circuit in *Johnson v. Glick*, 1973, 481 F.2d 1028, 1033:

Certainly, the constitutional protection is nowhere nearly so extensive as that afforded by the common law tort action for battery, which makes actionable any intentional and unpermitted contact with the plaintiff's person or anything attached to it and practically identified with it, see Prosser, Torts § 9 (4th ed. 1971); still less is it as extensive as that afforded by the common law tort action for assault, redressing any act of such a nature as to excite an apprehension of battery, id. § 10, at 38 [footnote omitted]. Although the least touching of another in anger is a battery, [citation omitted],

---

1   42 U.S.C. § 1983 specifically provides that: Every person who, under color of any statute, ordinance, regulation, custom, or usage, of any State or Territory, subjects, or causes to be subjected, any citizen of the United States or other person within the jurisdiction thereof to the deprivation of any rights, privileges, or immunities secured by the Constitution and laws, shall be liable to the party injured in an action at law, suit in equity, or other proper proceeding for redress.

it is not a violation of a constitutional right actionable under 42 U.S.C. § 1983. The management by a few guards of large numbers of prisoners, not usually the most gentle or tractable of men and women, may require and justify the occasional use of a degree of intentional force. Not every push or shove, even if it may later seem unnecessary in the peace of a judge's chambers, violates a prisoner's constitutional rights. In determining whether the constitutional line has been crossed, a court must look to such factors as the need for the application of force, the relationship between the need and the amount of force that was used, the extent of injury inflicted, and whether force was applied in a good faith effort to maintain or restore discipline or maliciously and sadistically for the very purpose of causing harm. [Emphasis added]

The foregoing language is predicated on the proposition that the Supreme Court's holding in *Rochin v. California*, 1952, 342 U.S. 165, 72 S. Ct. 205, 96 L.Ed. 183, "points the way." Rochin found a violation of the 14th Amendment, albeit for assault and battery occurring in a different context, in conduct that "shocks the conscience" (342 U.S. at 172, 72 S. Ct. 205), conduct which involves force that is "brutal" and "offensive to human dignity" (342 U.S. at 174, 72 S. Ct. 205). *See Johnson, supra*, 481 F.2d at 1033 and fn. 6.

None of our decisions requires that we adopt a position less restrictive, if that be the proper word, than that taken in *Johnson v. Glick*, quoted *supra*. In *Gregory v. Thompson, supra*, a justice of the peace left his desk in his courtroom in order to throw the plaintiff (aged 65) out, forced the plaintiff out through the door, then threw him to the floor, jumped on him and began to beat him. 500 F.2d at 61. *Allison v. Wilson*, 9 Cir., 1970, 434 F.2d 646, held that the plaintiff prisoner stated a claim under § 1983 by alleging that he had been "physically abused" by two prison guards on two separate occasions (434 F.2d at 647), and that alleging that one guard, "after saying 'I will show you some new rules,' slammed a steel door shut, hitting Allison on the back, is a sufficient allegation of intentional misconduct." (Id. at 647–48). *Brown v. Brown*, 9 Cir., 1966, 368 F.2d 992, *cert. den.*, 1966, 385 U.S. 868, 87 S. Ct. 133, 17 L.Ed.2d 95, held sufficient a complaint in which the plaintiff alleged that he had been kicked and beaten by state officers in an effort to compel his confession of involvement in criminal activities, *Dodd v. Spokane County*, 9 Cir., 1968, 393 F.2d 330, held that a complaint stated a civil rights claim when the plaintiff prisoner alleged that he was beaten by six guards as "punishment" for refusing to testify falsely in a criminal trial. *Wiltsie v. Calif. Dept. of Corrections*, 9 Cir., 1968, 406 F.2d 515, held that a civil rights claim was stated by a prisoner who alleged that six guards had beaten him with fists and billy clubs on his head and that he might suffer permanent disability as a result. Finally, the allegation that a plaintiff prisoner had been "beat, kicked, knocked, stomped, thrashed, teargassed and cursed" by his custodians was held to state a § 1983 claim in *Allison v. Calif. Adult Authority*, 9 Cir., 1969, 419 F.2d 822.

None of these cases held that the constitutional protection of the 14th Amendment due process clause is synonymous with that afforded by the common law against the torts of assault and battery. And one can only surmise what analytical principles were applied. *Cf. Johnson v. Glick, supra,* 481 F.2d at 1033, conjecturing that the reasoning of this circuit in *Wiltsie v. California Department of Corrections, supra,* was the same as that of the Fifth Circuit in *Tolbert v. Bragan,* 1971, 451 F.2d 1020, and the Seventh Circuit in *Collum v. Butler,* 421 F.2d 1257.

We conclude that, when construed liberally as *Haines v. Kerner, supra,* requires, the complaint does state a claim under § 1983 as construed in *Johnson v. Glick, supra.* It alleges an unprovoked assault and battery by a guard upon a prisoner known by the guard to be suffering from an attack of emphysema, by striking him in the solar plexus, hard enough that the "attack rendered the patient plaintiff totally handicapped." We think that as described in the complaint, Miller's conduct can be fairly characterized as intentional, unjustified, brutal, and offensive to human dignity. Under *Johnson v. Glick, supra,* conduct that can be so described violates the victim's constitutional right to due process. We need not decide whether conduct that is less reprehensible would also violate that right. Whether Meredith can prove his allegations is another matter upon which we express no opinion.

The dismissal of Meredith's claims against the state of Arizona and prison physician Deputy must be affirmed. Meredith may not sue the State as such, and he has not plausibly alleged any facts supporting a claim against Dr. Deputy.

Meredith's claims against Warden Cardwell, Associate Warden Burd, and Correctional Officer (Lieutenant) Hall, if he has any, must be based on the doctrine of *respondeat superior*.[2] He states no facts indicating that any of them personally did anything that violated any of Meredith's rights. Whether the doctrine is available in this action is a question of state law. (See *Hesselgesser v. Reilly,* 9 Cir., 1971, 440 F.2d 901, 902–03.) In reevaluating the pleadings on remand, the district court will have an opportunity to consider whether *respondeat superior* is applicable under Arizona law[3]; if it should decide that *respondeat superior* is

---

2   It is not clear whether Lieutenant Hall was Miller's superior. Plaintiff's complaint reveals that Hall countermanded Miller's instruction that plaintiff be taken to the isolation building and locked up. On remand the district court will have an opportunity to inquire into this issue.

3   See, for example, 12 Ariz.Rev.Stat. § 38–463 (West 1974); *Dogarin v. Connor,* 1967, 6 Ariz.App. 473, 433 P.2d 653, 656–57, 658. Liability for punitive damages under the doctrine of *respondeat superior* lies only if the superior "has directed, participated in, acquiesced or ratified [the acts of the offending subordinate]." *Boies v. Cole,* 1965, 99 Ariz. 198, 205, 407 P.2d 917, 922; *Dogarin v. Connor, supra,* 433 P.2d at 659–60.

momente/Shutterstock.com

applicable, it will permit amendment to the complaint to state the facts, if any, upon which Meredith claims that vicarious liability of Lieutenant Hall, Associate Warden Burd, and Warden Cardwell is based.

It was not error to set aside the defendants' default in filing an answer.

The judgment in favor of the state of Arizona and of defendant Deputy is affirmed. The judgments in favor of defendants Miller, Hall, Burd, and Cardwell are reversed and the case is remanded for further proceedings.

OTHER FACTORS TO CONSIDER IN THE USE OF FORCE IN CORRECTIONS

Institutional Factors

1. Institutional Environment: An unnatural environment which contributes to the emotional stress of the incarcerated.
2. Substandard Facilities: Facilities that lack heating, lighting, ventilation, and/or poor maintenance.
3. Overcrowding: The jail population is at an all-time high and is expected to escalate.
4. Idleness and Lack of Programs: Individuals require something to do.

Inmate Population Factors

1. Antisocial Inmates: Sociopaths, societal misfits, and other deviants are included in the jail population.
2. Mentally Ill Inmates: Some mentally ill inmates are psychopaths, and can also be included in the general population.
3. Racial/Ethnic Minorities: Racial and ethnic identity lead to the formation of groups which compete for power and control.
4. Prison Gangs: Typically formed along racial lines, first formed for self-protection, now are branching toward traditional organized crime.
5. Revolutionary Organizations: Members of these groups are organized to spread their influence inside jail and consider themselves to be "political prisoners."
6. Fear: With the varied mix of people inside jail, conflict is sure to happen. Some violence is result of inmates attempting to protect themselves from other inmates.
7. Collective Behavior: When inmates become frustrated, it is easier for agitators to convince others to pursue violent or aggressive acts.

Administrative Factors

1. Frequent Turnover of Management: Changes in management cause inconsistency of programs.
2. Frequent Turnover of Staff: Inexperienced staff cannot be expected to deal with problems, especially crisis situations as well as experienced staff.
3. Staff Recruitment and Hiring: Pay is low and stress is high, which does not increase appeal to becoming a corrections officer.
4. Inadequate Training: Sometimes correctional staff enter service with little or no training.
5. Breeches of Security: Personnel become lax in security procedures.

Noninstitutional Causes

1. Public Apathy: With little or no support from the community, morale will suffer.
2. Punitive Attitude: Staff can reflect a punitive attitude toward the inmates, increasing tension.

3. Social Unrest: The inmate population can reflect the outside community.
4. Inadequate Funding: Without funding to adequately provide for the inmate population, tensions can increase.
5. Inequities in the Criminal Justice System: The disparity of sentencing can also increase tensions.

The U.S. Court of Appeals for the Fifth District adopted a standard for excessive force claims. In order for a plaintiff to prevail on excessive force claims, the court held that he or she must prove that:

1. A significant injury, which:
2. Resulted directly and only from the use of force that was clearly excessive to the need, the excessiveness of which was:
3. Objectively unreasonable, and:
4. The action constituted an unnecessary and wanton infliction of pain.

The court must ask whether the force was "applied in good faith effort to maintain or restore discipline or maliciously and sadistically for the very purpose of causing harm." If the last element is missing, there is no liability, the court stated, regardless of "how significant the injury, how far in excess of the need, and how unreasonable" the force used.

Therefore, <u>unlike in policing, the underlying intent of the correctional officer does play a large role in the finding of excessive force</u>. In other words, the motivation for the force will be evaluated. Whether the force was used to maintain or gain control or to harm will be considered.

To review

The U.S. Supreme Court has ruled that the 8th Amendment's ban on cruel and unusual punishment is obligatory on the states through the 14th Amendment, *Robinson v. California*, 370 U.S. 660, 82 S. Ct. 1417, 8 L.Ed.2d 758 (1972).

Cruel and unusual punishment prohibition of the 8th Amendment applies to county jails as institutions.

"Convicted prisoners are protected by the Eight Amendment to the US Constitution which prohibits the imposition of cruel and unusual punishment. Like most constitutional declarations, the exact meaning of 'cruel and unusual punishment' is somewhat elusive. Consequently, we look to the broad principle underlying the constitutional terms."

"The basic concept underlying the Eighth Amendment is nothing less than the dignity of man... The words of the amendment are not precise ... Their scope is not static. The amendment must draw its meaning from the evolving standards of decency that mark the progress of a maturing society." The amendment prohibits penalties that transgress today's "broad and idealistic concept of dignity, civilized standards, humanity, and decency." *Campbell v. Cauthron*, 623 F.2d 503 (8th Cir. 1980), *Hutto v. Finney*, 437 U.S. 678, 685 (1978); *Trop v. Dulles*, 356 U.S. 86 (1958).

An important distinction exists within the 8th Amendment between pretrial detainees and posttrial convicted misdemeanants and felons. Since the due process clause prohibits punishment prior to conviction, the constitutional issue rests on determination of whether the conditions of confinement are punitive in nature. This deals, in part, with the intention of detention facility officials; however, courts have held that, even in the absence of expressed punitive intent, "if a restriction or condition is not reasonably related to a legitimate goal—be it arbitrary or purposeless—a court permissibly may infer that a purpose of the constitutionally be inflicted upon detainees." *Bell v. Wolfish*, 441 U.S. 520 (1979); *Campbell v. Cauthron*, supra.

Gwoeii/Shutterstock.com

The 8th Amendment proscribes the "unnecessary and wanton infliction of pain." *Gregg v. Georgia*, 428 U.S. 153, 173 (1976).

The 8th Amendment proscribes more than physically barbarous punishments. Its prohibition extends to penal measures which are incompatible with "the evolving standards of decency that mark the progress of a maturing society." *Trop v. Dulles*, 356 U.S. 86, 101 (1958). Confinement itself, under certain conditions, may violate the amendment's prohibition of cruel and unusual punishment.

The 8th Amendment proscription of cruel and unusual punishment "is not limited to specific acts directed at selected individuals, but is equally pertinent to general conditions of confinement that may prevail at a prison," *Gates v. Collier*, 501 F.2d 1291, (5th Cir. 1974).

Summary

Although the courts have given corrections a bit more "latitude" in the use of force, the guiding principles are not far from those governing law enforcement. Reasonableness, when used as the basis for action, will always be a defensible position for both officer and administrator. The courts have made a distinction between pretrial detainee and postconviction detainee. Policies reflecting the current constitutional interpretations and implementing current landmark cases will provide the best method to avert unlawful force.

Discussion Points

1. Why is the use of force viewed differently in a correctional setting than in policing?
   - Do prisoners, whether convicted or awaiting trial, have less rights than those of citizens on the street?
   - Is there enough oversight in corrections on the use of force?
2. Should body cameras be required for correctional officers?
   - If body cameras should be required, when should the cameras be activated?
   - Should the video from the body cameras become public domain?

This form must be completed and turned in for credit. No copies or other format will be accepted.

Student Name _____ Date _____

Course Section _____ Chapter _____

To be submitted to instructor. This page will only be accepted. No copies or other forms allowed.

Describe some differences between the court's view on use of force in corrections as opposed to use of force in policing:

_____

_____

_____

_____

_____

_____

_____

_____

_____

_____

_____

_____

_____

_____

CHAPTER 6

USE-OF-FORCE REPORTING

*"Figures often beguile me, particularly
when I am arranging them myself."*

—Mark Twain

Key Terms

Descriptive Statistics, Open Public Records
Act, Use-of-Force Report, Compliance
Hold, Physical Force, Mechanical Force,
Deadly Force

Learning Objectives

After exploring Chapter 6, the student will be able to:

1. Explain the fundamental significance of using data to support conclusions.
2. Explain the purpose for transparency as applied to the Open Public Records Act (OPRA).
3. List five exemptions to the OPRA.
4. Describe and list the data variables located on the use-of-force report.
5. Explain the components of physical, mechanical, and deadly force.
6. List five types of officer force categorized on the use-of-force report.

"There are three kinds of lies: lies, damn lies, and statistics." The quote is linked to Samuel Clemens (Mark Twain) and British Prime Minister Benjamin Disraeli, of the nineteenth century. The outlook portrayed echoes through time. One must question the motivation and reasoning of the researcher(s) when drawing conclusions from statistical analyses. Along with scrutiny, consumers of research must understand research methodology and the ultimate "significance" of a particular study.

Numbers are powerful. Numbers unleash control for policy, media, and decisionmaking for the citizen who's paying attention. Whether it's *Consumer Reports* or your local baseball team's box score; numbers affect judgment. We, as consumers of information, must recognize what the numbers are telling us.

Everett Historical/Shutterstock.com

To that end, the authors of this chapter took a 3-year sample (2013–2015) of use-of-force reports from of a Mid-Atlantic U.S. county, to demonstrate fundamental statistical reporting using descriptive statistics. What are descriptive statistics? Descriptive statistics describe the main features of the study that are frequently broken down into probability processes to blanket the study onto the population being examined. In this study, the authors gathered historical data collected by the government.

But first, how did the authors acquire government information? In New Jersey, as in the other states, there is an abundance of public material accessible to the community. The Open Public Records Act (OPRA) has shaped the guidelines for the release of public records. Here's a little about OPRA and how it affects the governmental employees and the citizens seeking data.

THE NEW JERSEY OPRA AND EXEMPTIONS

The New Jersey OPRA was established by State Legislature on January 8, 2002. OPRA decreed several modifications in the law regarding the public's right to retrieve government records. The law became operative on July 7, 2002. NJ OPRA law increased resident's privileges for access to government records (State of New Jersey, 2015).

The regulation dictates that any governmental employee's written product, what they record (within guidelines), and the resultant files that are generated are deemed a public record (accessible to the general populace). However, there are 24 exceptions or exemptions to the law. It is to be understood that any and all records are retrievable by the public unless it falls under the prescribed exceptions.

The exemptions are outlined as follows: (1) inter-agency of intra-agency advisory, consultative or deliberative material, (2) legislative records, (3) medical examiner records and death investigations, (4) criminal investigations, (5) victim's records, (6) trade secrets, and propriety, commercial and financial information, (7) any attorney/client privileges, (8) administrative technological information involving computer security, (9) emergency and security information for buildings and facilities, (10) security measures and surveillance techniques, (11) information, if disclosed would give an advantage to government contract bidders, (12) information generated by public employees concerning sexual harassment, grievances, and collective bargaining negotiations, (13) communication between public agencies and their insurance carrier, (14) information kept confidential pursuant to a court order, (15) certificates of honorable discharge from the U.S. military, (16) personal identifying information, (17) certain records of higher education institutions, (18) biotechnology trade secrets, (19) personal information of victim's and convicts, (20) ongoing investigations that are detrimental to the public interest, (21) public defender records, (22) other exemptions contained in other state, federal statutes, executive orders, rules of Court, the New Jersey Constitution, or Judicial case law, (23) personnel and pension records, and (24) privacy interests that the government has a duty to not disclose that if exposed would violate a person's right to privacy. The aforementioned exceptions were the original deflection from "all records" being inaccessible to the public; however, in 2002, Governor Jim McGreevey created an Executive Order to limit public access to some records that are maintained by the Office of the Governor.

HOW DOES OPRA AFFECT THE POLICE AND LOCAL GOVERNMENT?

As applied to police operations, generally police officers have the understanding that most of their official work is discoverable and accountable under New Jersey Rules of Court (Pound, 1952; Wefing, 1997). Thus, creating a sense of liability in every action taken during the course of duty. The knowledge of public access to records needs to be realized in the new, fresh age of policing; immersed with constant video, audio surveillance, private citizen smartphone documentation, and the imminent current trend to employ body cameras on patrol officers. With the onset of new and emerging ways in which generated information and its mandatory archiving, the police department must be conscious of the outcome of storing large amount of data as it applies to OPRA. Additionally, how the massive amount of information creates an administrative gridlock and how it increases the public demand for accountability in contemporary law enforcement. Such concerns should not only be observed in the legal venue of prosecuting suspects and the professional accountability of public servants, but also in the budgetary limits that concern storage, staff, and analysis of data.

Certainly, many of the exemptions pertain to police departments and their operations (death investigations, criminal investigations, personal identifiers, personnel issues, privacy, etc.). The list goes further within the stated OPRA exemptions. The prominent issues concerning the police department, or any other municipal/county/ state governed agency are the requests for information that must be analyzed, redacted, accepted, declined, and acted upon, whether the request is valid or not. OPRA requests take administrative time and consume resources of local and state governments.

In addition, police departments and its members must be mindful that the interpretations of what is an "exemption" have changed with recent case law. Most prominently is the decision in Bergen County, New Jersey regarding the transparency of internal affairs records in October of 2014. Judge Peter Doyne, JSC, Bergen County, ruled the names of police officers who are subject to an internal affairs complaint, as well as, the names of complainants, cannot be guarded from the public under the state Open Public Records Law (Baxter, 2014).

In the decision, the New Jersey State Superior Court in Bergen County found that the Bergen County Sheriff's Office incorrectly redacted the information in records provided to John Paff (the head of a local open government advocacy group). In addition to the ruling about the internal affairs records, the judge further concluded that the State Attorney General guidelines had no bearing on the public records law, as argued by the county (Baxter, 2015).

The consequences of the arrival of added technological data that are now part of municipal government records and the relaxing of OPRA law in New Jersey necessitates that municipal employees must be more vigilant than ever concerning use of public computers, data, recording systems, and general documentation of information generated while at work. Separately, regarding complaints against police officers and municipal employees, workers must be aware that this information is public record and ruled unrestricted to the general populace. Understanding these rules of the profession is essential to police organizational cohesiveness and accomplishment.

Billion Photos/Shutterstock.com

One of the records available to the public via an OPRA request, and commonly requested, is the *use-of-force report*, which is mandated and governed by the New Jersey State Attorney General Office. One might ask, "What's a *Use of Force Report* and what will it tell me?" Let's dissect the report so we can understand more about what it reveals.

THE USE-OF-FORCE REPORT

Use-of-force reports are specifically designed to provide detailed information of police-citizen encounters when the police use force. Even if the force is not deemed legal, the use-of-force report form must accompany a general police report. The use-of-force report covers several details of the encounter, including but not limited to race; gender, age, time of day, type of incident, type of force, injuries or deaths, and so on. Therefore, it is important to look at the actual form to understand the strengths and weaknesses of this data-gathering tool.

Incident Information

Use-of-force reports generally start with *Incident Information*. Incident information includes basic necessary material (dates, times, locations, incident numbers, police agency) to begin categorization of the incident. Most importantly, incident information reveals the "type" of incident. The choices of "Type of Incident" include: crime in progress, domestic, other dispute, suspicious person, traffic stop, and the ominous "Other" selection.

Piotr Wawrzyniuk/Shutterstock.com

Crimes in Progress

"Crimes in Progress" ranges from property crimes, such as burglary, shoplifting, and theft. Also, crimes against persons identified as: assault, sexual assault, robbery, and homicide. It is a broad collection of offenses, any of which compel police response through different processes. These crimes are mostly instances where police officers are called for help, but also can be self-initiated by the officer when, by coincidence, they observe the crime in front of them.

Domestic

"Domestic" refers to any incident falling under the umbrella of domestic violence. Domestic violence laws protect people from violence in the home, which can prevail unrestrained for decades, if not reported. These incidents are usually volatile, emotionally charged encounters. Police officers are mandated to make arrests when arriving on domestic violence scenes where visible scenes of injury are present on the victim or when certain crimes have occurred. Mandatory arrest causes much resentment. It is a very emotional time for all involved. Governmental officials make decisions, grounded by law, that affect relationships developed by others. Whether the relationship is brutally wrong, or an argument escalated into a one-time physical fight, police respond and perform their duty to protect others from violence and fear in the home. The domestic violence event is usually volatile, especially when the victim does not want their abuser arrested. Domestic violence is an important law enforcement issue for victims and law enforcement officers, because of the prevailing danger during these occurrences for all involved.

Other Disputes

"Other Disputes" can be arguments between household members that do not constitute domestic violence, such as family disputes between juveniles. Additionally, other clashes between people fall into this category, such as neighbor disputes, customer disputes with businesses, and any other argument not fueled by intimate relationships outlined in the Domestic Violence Act.

Suspicious Person

"Suspicious Persons" are calls from citizens describing a person who is "out of place," specifically because of their behavior. For example, a person who is not familiar to a specific neighborhood is walking around and knocking on front doors, asking if someone is home who doesn't live there (a rudimentary daytime burglar ruse). When the homeowner answers the door and says they don't know anybody by that name, the practiced burglar

TungCheung/Shutterstock.com

says, "Oh, I must have the wrong address." The burglar was hopeful no one answered, because they do not want a confrontation. They want to break into an unoccupied home to steal things that can be turned into cash to fuel a drug habit, fulfill a gambling debt, or satisfy whatever need, through a criminal act.

Suspicious persons also include reports of loud noises; people in unexpected areas at strange hours, and any other peculiar circumstances that citizens report to the police to investigate.

Traffic Stop

The traffic stop is one of the most contentious topics in law enforcement because of the usual discretion police officers have to enforce traffic. Mainly, the traffic stop is a self-initiated law enforcement activity, which draws upon officer motivation and intention. There are many claims of racial bias and discrimination in the application of traffic laws or criminal law for that matter. Additionally, traffic violations are mostly minor intrusions of the law (except for driving while intoxicated, speeding, reckless driving,

Anne Kitzman/Shutterstock.com

etc.), perpetuating upheaval at times, when use-of-force situations escalate from noncompliance, or feelings of discrimination. Police officers have discretion when enforcing breaches in the traffic code, they can essentially choose if they want to issue a summons or not for most violations. Discretion allows officers the latitude to operate within the boundaries of "the letter of the law" and the "spirit of the law." The "letter of the law" is strict to the principles of law, equal in its applications. The "spirit of the law" incorporates the "social consensus" and invites the use of common sense. For example, a police officer stops an 89-year-old woman because her registration has been expired for 2 years. Upon conducting the traffic stop, the officer recognizes the driver is suffering from some type of dementia or loss of mental faculty. The officer is not required to enforce the traffic code but rather, provide assistance in obtaining proper help for the afflicted person. Such circumstances illustrate why police should not be required to enforce every violation observed during the course of a shift.

The traffic stop is, perhaps, the most common police citizen contact, where the officer observes and confronts the public on a violation of the law. Persons who would normally not encounter police can be part of the populous of the motoring public. These interactions are roadside and unfamiliar to both the officer and the person being stopped; neither knows what to expect. Police officers routinely stop cars and develop instincts that help them process the stop. Whether the officer call dispatchers for initial driver information, a supervisor for guidance, or other officers for back up, the seasoned officer becomes an expert for these contacts.

The traffic stop invites the unknown. The officer does not know whom they are approaching. The motorist may not know why they are stopped, or they don't want the officer to uncover something they are trying to conceal. Such human interaction is unpredictable and can swiftly turn confrontational for both officer and citizen, spiraling into a "use-of-force" episode. Important to understand are the legal foundations required for an officer to lawfully effectuate a motor vehicle stop.

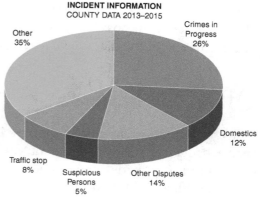

INCIDENT INFORMATION
COUNTY DATA 2013–2015

Courtesy of Jeffrey Schwartz/Michael Virga.

Other

The loathsome "Other" preoccupies us. As will be seen in the data, the "Other" category is popular. Whether the officer reporting is lazy, or the report itself needs improvement, or the complexity of police work is overwhelming; the "Other" can be a trendy occurrence in use-of-force reporting. It appears a bit counterproductive to use the "Other" category. The "Use-of-Force Report" is generally uniform across the nation. It is clear that confronting people who are suffering from a variety of mental illnesses is not represented on these reports. Certainly, these instances can be addressed in the "Other" category, which is probably the case. Ultimately, the "Other"

Types of incidents							
	Crimes in progress	**Domestics**	**Other disputes**	**Suspicious persons**	**Traffic stop**	**Other**	**Total**
Total	303	140	160	59	89	400	1,151
	26%	12%	14%	5%	8%	35%	100%

leaves for open invitations of speculation or even miscalculation. The elimination of the "Other" is impossible; however, if it dominates data points, the selection and discrimination of the data must be reviewed.

Officer Information

Officer information is a simple concept; it's basically the pedigree report on the officer (name, badge, rank, duty assignment, years of service, sex, race, age, injured, uniformed, or on duty). It provides knowledge of the general officer's background for statistical analyses. Officer information delivers a reference for officer experience and capacity.

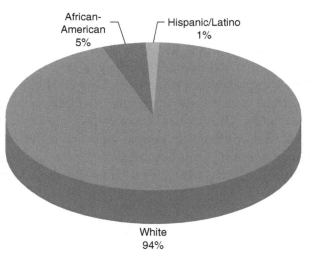

OFFICER INFORMATION
COUNTY DATA 2013–2015

African-American 5%

Hispanic/Latino 1%

White 94%

Courtesy of Jeffrey Schwartz/Michael Virga.

Officer information					
	White	**African American**	**Hispanic/ Latino**	**Asian**	**Total**
Total	1,804	93	27	0	1,924
	94%	5%	1%	0%	100%

Subject Information

Subject information supplies similar identifying information as observed in the officer category (sex, race, age, injured, etc.). Also, subject information provided fields of data for arrests, if the subject was under the influence, charges placed against the individual, and if any other "unusual condition" existed. Subject information applies identifiers to the individual, but then splits into the "Subjects Actions" and the "Officers Use of Force Towards the Subject." Here lies the confrontation. After sifting through the minutiae of officer/subject features, the actual use of force is disclosed.

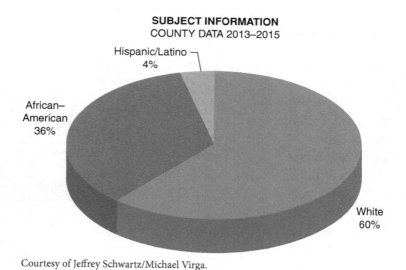

SUBJECT INFORMATION
COUNTY DATA 2013–2015

Hispanic/Latino 4%

African–American 36%

White 60%

Courtesy of Jeffrey Schwartz/Michael Virga.

Subject information						
	White	**African American**	**Hispanic/ Latino**	**Asian**	**Other**	**Total**
Total	579	344	39	2	2	966
	60%	36%	4%	0%	0.2%	100%

Subject Actions

Subject actions are the behavior by the individual who is confronted by police, triggering the use of force by an officer. The categories include the following:

- Resisted police officer control
- Physical threat or attack on an officer or another
- Threatened or attacked officer or another with a blunt object
- Threatened or attacked officer or another with a knife/cutting object
- Threatened or attacked officer or another with a motor vehicle
- Threatened or attacked another with a firearm
- Fired at another officer, or other (specify)

It is important to note these actions are not mutually exclusive and often occur simultaneously with other defiant behaviors toward police.

The categories are broad. For example, "resisted police officer control" can mean refusing to allow your arms to be placed behind the back for handcuffing. It can also be a foot pursuit, where the officer must tackle an offender to the ground to stop them from fleeing and effect an arrest. The range of each category will vary. The actions by the subject have the "other" category as well, which includes a vast assortment of possibility. The options of "Subject actions" are generally descriptive enough to explain the type of resistance employed by the individual.

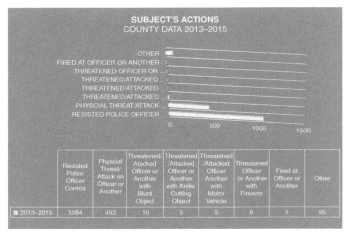

Courtesy of Jeffrey Schwartz/Michael Virga.

	Resisted Police Officer Control	Physcial Threat/ Attack on Officer or Another	Threatened/ Atacked Officer or Another with Blunt Object	Threatened /Attacked Officer or Another with Knife/ Cutting Object	Threatened /Attacked Officer Another with Motor Vehicle	Threatened Officer or Another with Firearm	Fired at Officer or Another	Other
2013–2015	1084	493	16	5	5	6	1	95

Officer Use-of-Force Toward the Subject

When an officer uses force to achieve a lawful, law enforcement objective, most of the time it is during an arrest situation. However, when trying to control someone who is suffering from a mental illness (dementia, bipolar disorder, schizophrenia), the officer will not always necessarily place the subject under arrest. In New Jersey, when officers are confronted by people making threats of suicide (harming themselves) or are believed to be a danger to others, they are required to take steps to have that person evaluated by a mental health official. Such encounters are not always the result of a criminal act; citizens or family who are concerned for the well-being of a person can initiate this process. Often, these situations evolve into police officers using force to complete their duty. Unfortunately, here reasoning and sensitivity training will not change the outcome most of the time. Normally, the family/concerned person calls the police when the situation has become volatile. Sometimes, the person with the mental health issue has stopped taking their intervention medication for weeks, prior to the family/concerned person calling the police. Sometimes, the person with the mental health issue is acting out and uncontrollable by those who are familiar, known, and normally received well. Now, the police are asked to step in and calm the situation in which those who usually can, have been unsuccessful. Therefore, the likelihood of use of force is high by the responding police. Simply, if the people who know the person can't calm them down, why do we expect the stranger in a police uniform to do so? Even with advanced training in handling persons with mental health issues, the use of most intervention techniques has long passed. It might be all the police are able to do is subdue the person to allow them to have the treatment that is needed. Family might not understand and become concerned that the police are trying to harm the person (who the family called the police to help). The situation can get out of hand rather quickly.

It is very difficult to know when to talk and when to act in confronting a person with mental health issues. While it is necessary to understand the person has an issue; safety for the person, the officer(s), and the family become the priority. It may appear counterintuitive that the very people called to help are now fighting with the person afflicted with a mental health issue. However, (at times) it is impossible to do anything other than control the person with the mental health issue. There are times that force must be used and is the only option available. Talking and having the understanding a mental health issue exists (when feasible) should factor into the encounter.

Arrests

Police officers are required to have probable cause to make arrests. Once the officer is lawfully placing someone in custody, the right to use force to make the arrest exists.

Additionally, federally and in every state there is a provision whereby no one can resist arrest (even if unlawful).

Here are the options of force listed on the use-of-force report:

- Compliance hold
- Hands/fists
- Kicks/feet
- Chemical/natural agent
- Strike/use of baton or other object
- Canine
- Firearms discharge (some indicate "intentional" and "accidental" along with number of shots fired and number of hits)
- Other (specify)

We have discussed in general terms, force is guided by necessity. When looking at specific forms or tools in the application of force upon another, we must keep certain principles in mind. We know law enforcement officers must make split second decisions in uncertain, tense, dangerous, and rapidly evolving situations. When the decision to use force is made, the officer must act immediately and with certainty. Any less of an effort in a use-of-force situation will result in injury. The question then turns to "why does the officer have to be so brutal"? The alternative is nothing short of a disaster. If the use of force is done based upon actions, the law is decisive; the less likely (in cases not involving deadly force) injury will occur to suspect/officer/bystander. How is that possible (one may be thinking)? If the officer makes a correct decision; based upon their training and experience, then the following was already considered:

BortN66/Shutterstock.com

1. Minimum—am I choosing the most minimal use of force applicable to stop the actions of the suspect in this situation? Will I endanger others? Will I endanger

myself or the suspect unnecessarily? Am I confident in my ability to carry out this use of force decisively?

2. Necessary—is it absolutely necessary to use force? If so, what force is appropriate to stop the actions of the suspect? Will I endanger others? Will I endanger myself or the suspect when there might be another option? Am I certain, based upon my training/experience/totality of the circumstances, that this use of force is needed?

3. Reasonable—am I choosing the right tool/method or way of using force in this situation to stop the actions of the suspect? Will I endanger others? Will I endanger myself or the suspect unnecessarily? Am I confident in my ability to carry out this use of force decisively? Would another officer, with my training and experience; with the same facts known to me at this time, do the same thing as I choose to do?

Law enforcement officers are tasked with making split second decisions, most of the time, captured on video. Does the video show the viewer everything that transpired? Does the video accurately portray the facts known to the officer at the time? According to the landmark case of *Graham v. Connor*, hindsight is not allowed to enter the arena in the calculus of reasonableness. However, are the guidelines from Graham actually transitioned into real life scenarios? People have taken to the streets in protests based upon a few seconds of a video, most particularly with a white officer (who make up nearly 75% of all policing) using force against an African American (who make up a disproportionate amount of those arrested, convicted, or incarcerated). We have discussed some of the socioeconomic issues that lead to such statistical disparities.

Michael Warwick/Shutterstock.com

Discuss the following scenario:

Consider the following scenario in which you are the police officer: (here you will be a white male police officer for this scenario).

You are on patrol in a marked police vehicle. You are sent a radio call from dispatch about an armed robbery that has just occurred. A black male, approximately early 20s in age, medium build, red short sleeve shirt, jean pants, dark sneakers threatened to shoot the victim (suspect displayed a dark-colored handgun) if the victim would not give the suspect money just withdrawn from an ATM on the street. You are provided the location and description of the suspect. You are only two city blocks from the location. Dispatch radios information in the direction of flight of the suspect (suspect running from the scene). The direction the suspect is running will place the suspect directly in front of you as you turn down the next street corner. Therefore, you stop your patrol vehicle and exit at the street corner (you are in full uniform). You peer around a building at the street corner. You observe a black male, approximately early 20s in age, medium build, red short sleeve shirt, jean pants, dark sneakers running from the location of the crime toward where you have now exited your patrol vehicle. You wait for the black male to get within about 15 feet of the street corner. You observe no vehicles or pedestrians in the immediate area.

What do you do?

1. Do you tackle the person (who matches the description of the armed robber and who is running from the area of the crime and running in the exact location dispatch advised the suspect who committed the armed robbery was running) toward your location?
2. Do you wait for the person to come near you, so you can pepper spray them and take them to the ground to handcuff them?
3. Do you jump from around the street corner, gun drawn, and order the person running toward you to stop/get on the ground with their hands up?

4. Do you shoot the person running toward you? (remember, a person can produce a firearm and shoot twice in less time than you—even if you have your firearm pointed toward the person)
5. Do you use any other form of force and attempt to stop the running person?

Scenario continued:

I will only choose one of the many options you have as the police officer in the scenario. We will move around the street corner, attempt to find cover (a place where we might not be shot so easily if behind), point our firearm at the person and order the person to stop. We will order the person to show us his hands and to keep his hands up/away from his body. Sound good? Okay, now what does the running person do in this scenario? Let us discuss some of the options the running person has:

1. Comply with your commands to stop, put his hands up and away from his body. The person then complies with your commands to kneel down (keeping his hands away from his body) and turn away from facing you when instructed.
2. The person continues to run and attempts to run across the street, away from you.
3. The person continues toward you. The person is now walking. However, the person will not raise their hands or stop walking toward you.
4. The person stands in place and accuses you of racism. Further, the person yells for you to shoot him (since you want to kill him because he is African American and you are a white officer).
5. The person stops running, starts to walk backward and places one of his hands behind his back.
6. The person places his hand in an area you are unable to observe in any of the earlier situations, except number one.

What do you do?

I will choose only one of the many options the person who you are trying to stop has in this scenario.

The person chooses to comply with your commands and stops running. The person keeps their hands away from their body and raises their hands. The person continues to follow instructions—you ask the person to slowly turn a full circle with their hands up and fingers spread (in this way you might observe any telltale signs they are armed, also, if they were carrying an improvised explosive device [IED] they would not be able to conceal a trigger switch or actuator button if their hands are up and their fingers are spread). Once they have completed a full circle and a half, they listen to commands to kneel on the ground, keeping their hands up and away from their body. They then followed commands for them to go to a prone position (keeping their hands extended and away from their body). They listen to commands and place their extended arms to their side—keeping the palms of their hands up and arms extended away from their body. Another officer now appears and provides tactical cover (meaning the other officer is in a position to shoot (or react with the proper use of force) toward the person and you are not in the way—should the person make movements to their body or create a threat. You approach the prone person, who remains compliant. You handcuff the prone person with extremely low amount of force necessary as they comply with the handcuffing procedure.

LifetimeStock/Shutterstock.com

One outcome from one response in an incredible complex event. In a perfect world (well, in a perfect world there would not have been a robbery), the suspect complies. If the suspect complies, does there appear to be a need to use force? However, all too often, a varying degree of responses normally includes some form of noncompliance. So, with noncompliance, does the likelihood in the use of force increase? In the aforementioned scenario, could noncompliance lead to the use of deadly force? If so, under what circumstances would the officer be justified? Under what circumstances would the officer not be justified? If nonlethal force was used, when is it excessive? In fact, could the person who is now an armed robbery suspect has absolutely done not one thing unlawful and is in the wrong place, at the wrong time?

Just one example of the complex decisions, a law enforcement officer must make in a split second. If the officer is wrong, someone (including the officer) could be killed or severely injured.

What do we expect from the police? Is putting oneself in danger unnecessarily in the job description of police officer? For lawful interactions, lawful use of force, the police are reactive in response. Why? The officer must first make observations. Then, draw rational inferences and using the totality of circumstances make a decision. How much time does an officer have to make an assessment and then act?

A point of discussion: does the suspect want to get away more than the police officer wants to catch him or her? Does the suspect follow a long list of rules and regulations? Does the suspect have to explain their actions and articulate why they chose to do something? Does the suspect always provide the action and the police the reaction? If so, who is always at the advantage?

Consider the two following terms: training and experience

Two words which convey the ability of an officer to form a basis in determining reasonableness of actions. We could devote the entire chapter to describing training and experience (in meaning and in practice). Interpretations of training and experience by prosecutors can make the difference between charging an officer and supporting an officer. Interpretations of training and experience by jurors can make a difference in an indictment, no bill, not guilty verdict or a finding of guilt. Interpretations of training and experience by police administration can make a difference in condemning or supporting an officer. The list can be substantial with examples of how training and experience influence nearly all inputs within the criminal justice process.

So, why do most police officers fail to obtain or attain additional/advanced training? For example, most police agencies require officers to shoot a qualification course of fire with their duty handguns about twice a year. Unless the agency is large or has an incredibly large budget, there is no easy place to practice shooting. There is usually no "free" access to ammunition, one of the requirements in order to practice shooting. There is usually no "time" for an officer to practice shooting. Meaning, if a police officer did want to practice shooting, the following are the difficulties or issues they can face:

Training

Knowledge, competencies
professional development
teaching of vocational or prac
practical skills provides the b
• On-the-job training tak
• Off-the-job training aw

Ivelin Radkov/Shutterstock.com

1. Where to go shooting. The officer would have to purchase a membership to a gun range.
2. Ammunition. The officer would have to purchase practice ammunition to use at the range they just paid to join.
3. Time off. The officer would need to use their time off to go to the shooting range, which they paid for, with the ammunition they paid for. Spending more time away from family, obligations, and alike.
4. Targets. The officer would need to purchase targets to shoot at for the practice at the expensive range, shooting their expensive ammunition, while on the brief time they have off from the job.
5. Practice properly. The officer may need an experienced instructor or at least a range safety officer to safely practice shooting.
6. Perception and matters of record. The officer by joining a gun range, purchasing ammunition, targets, and taking the time to go practice shooting; has now opened themselves up to scrutiny, as well as, potential liability.
You may be saying, wait, that makes no sense. The officer should be commended for going out of their way to practice. Well, perception and matter of record now are realities for this officer. Can that officer be labeled a "gun nut," "overzealous," "training so he can shoot people first and ask questions later"? If the gun range has video, can the practice sessions be discoverable evidence? What if the officer only practiced "head shots"? What if the officer shoots at only black silhouetted targets, is that officer racist? What if the officer shoots very well, but when in a real situation the officer is not accurate? Questions can be endless. At the end of the day, does the officer have more potential liability?
7. Cleaning the firearm. The officer must clean and take the time to make sure the firearm functions properly after time at the range. The process can take up to an hour for some firearms. More time away from family, obligations, and alike.

So, if officers do not take the time to improve or even simply practice skills with firearms, how much time and effort is spent on practicing with control holds/take down tactics? Problems associated with practice in this area can be even more daunting. Briefly: what type of training is taking place, is it in accordance with police rules/regulations, is it in accordance with current case law and use of force guidelines, do

NEstudio/Shutterstock.com

civilian mixed martial arts (MMA) or other types of physical combat align with the Attorney General's Guidelines in use of force, is the training done with using the most minimal amount of force that is necessary to control a person resisting arrest. The problems are many with liability, perception, and matters of record in unarmed use-of-force practice too. We live in a litigious society. Further, a society that is filled with social media. No one can go unnoticed.

Therefore, when a police officer takes the initiative to acquire additional training, someone knows about it. However, an officer that does nothing to further their training, can also set themselves in a position for liability.

Now, let us look at the most common use of force—compliance holds. Police officers receive minimal training in the skill set they will use most often:

Compliance Holds

Compliance holds can be pulling arms behind backs for handcuffing, wristlocks, or any other physical hold used to gain compliance from an arrestee. It is the most common reported use of force by the police, and also the most minimal use of force. Generally, this type of force is used when subjects are not obeying commands, passively resisting by pulling arms away, and so on. It's not easy to handcuff someone who doesn't want to be handcuffed. It can be as marginal as not giving the officer access to your arms, which may escalate the use of force, as the subject begins to resist physically, and so on. An important note: although one may envision countless hours of training, numerous practice sessions to allow an officer to understand physical force, training with experts in compliance holds, or other such training, does not normally occur. The "average" police officer receives minimal training in compliance holds. Actual "hands on" time engaged in training with combative or noncompliant persons in minimal. So, can there be an over reliance on or

1000 Words/Shutterstock.com

dangerous situation created when an officer fails to gain control using compliance holds and must escalate the use of force to gain control? After all, it is not the officer's fault the suspect is resisting or is it? Now, the situation continues to escalate and lethal force is not the only option. Did the officer, by not having a skill set in compliance holds, create a lethal force situation? We can have a discussion about the liability of obtaining additional training in the area of compliance holds. If an officer pays for additional training, takes the time to do the training; what are some issues that can be thought of?

Hands/Fists and Kicks/Feet

Hands/fists and Kicks/feet are reserved for actual strikes. Punching, kicking, knee strikes, open-palm strikes, and closed fists are all physical uses of force falling into this category. The force is greater, more violent, and a step above the compliance holds. Where does an officer learn how to apply strikes to a suspect? What approved techniques are there in a particular state or in a particular agency? When strikes are used, the resulting video might look really violent. However, should the police enter into a boxing match with the suspect? Should the police engage in MMA fighting with the suspect? Should the police strike a suspect in the head or choke suspects? If so, when, where, and how did the police officer learn an approved technique to do so? Police in New Jersey consider *Compliance holds, Hands/fists, and Kicks/feet* as *physical force*.

Agencies can categorize tools or use-of-force options "higher" or "lower" within their own department policies than other police agencies within the same state (common in most states). The best example lies right here, with pepper spray (oleoresin capsicum-OC). To begin, pepper spray or OC, is an inflammatory agent. In the approved form of OC, only a propellant and pepper are used. No chemicals or other agents are added to the mixture contained in an approved OC delivery system. OC has an expiration date, comes in many delivery systems and is not considered a chemical agent. Foam, cone mist, stream, and gel are some of the most prevalent forms of delivery systems for OC. Percentage of OC is important. OC, refers to the industrial extraction process that takes out the oily residue of the hot peppers. It's that oily residue that's incorporated into an aerosol spray to form pepper spray. The higher the concentrate of pepper oil in the mixture within the OC delivery system, the longer decontamination will be for someone exposed to the OC. OC is comprised of several different capsaicinoids. There are five major capsaicinoids responsible for providing the pungency (hotness of a pepper). Capsaicin is the strongest of the five. Therefore, it is the percentage of the total capsaicinoids, not the OC percentage that is most important. Most law enforcement pepper sprays range from 0.18% to 1.33% major capsaicinoids.

Scoville heat units (SHUs) are another method used to measure the pungency of pepper sprays. The habanero is one of the hottest chili pepper, measuring 325,000 SHU. Most law enforcement pepper sprays measure 2,000,000 SHU, which is over six times hotter than a habanero.

The cost common SHU rating among law enforcement pepper spray is 2.5 million. While there are some manufactures that produce pepper spray with over 5 million SHU, most agencies opt for the norm (5 million SHU can cause skin to actually burn). Typically, with a 5% or 10% mixture, the recovery time for someone directly exposed to the pepper spray should be between 20 and 30 minutes, any agency approving OC for use will have a procedure to provide a decontamination process for someone directly exposed to the OC. Some agencies go to great lengths for decontamination, requiring officers who directly expose a suspect to bring that suspect to a hospital.

Chemical/Natural Agent

Chemical/natural agent refers to both chemical and natural agents. Chemical agents used by police include chloroacetophenone (CN), more universally recognized as "mace." It is a pulmonary irritant and more toxic and powerful than "tear gas," chlorobenzylidene malononitrile (CS), both developed during World War I. These chemical agents started as the principal crowd control substances for police during rioting, however, the more natural substance, "OC spray," has been regularly used in modern day American policing. CN and CS are lachrymation instruments (a chemical compound irritating eyes, triggering pain, and short-term loss of eyesight), with the possibility of a toxic/lethal dose. OC is a natural agent and has no lethal dosage.

Vladimir Arndt/Shutterstock.com

Strike/Use of Baton or other Object

Strike/use of baton or other object involves use-of-force scenarios where expandable batons, PR-24's, "nightsticks," truncheons, "billy-clubs," and so on are used to strike an uncooperative subject. The most common modern version of this tool is the expandable baton, located collapsed on an officer's duty belt and less cumbersome than the other earlier models. The types of mechanical tools are regulated state to state. The use of a baton is considered using mechanical force. Training time in the use of batons has drastically been reduced in police academies throughout the nation. The traditional mechanical force tool in law enforcement was the PR-24 (side-handled baton). Fashioned after the tonfa (an Okinawan martial art weapon), the PR-24 was the standard in use and training. The PR-24 has a baton portion 24 inches long, hence, the 24 in the name of the tool. Numerous hours of training, 24 (by happenstance) hours was the normal amount of time allocated to learning skills to be effective with the PR-24 in most police academies. However, learning the skill necessary to be actually effective with the side-handled baton was not easy. Most officers did not retain nor continue to train with the PR-24 tool. The PR-24 was not simple to carry, was not easy to use and mostly was left in an officer's locker or in the patrol car. While an expandable version became available (improved to a tool known as the control device), most officers did not want to use the PR-24 tool. With the advent of technology to create an expandable side-handled baton, came the innovation of an expandable straight baton. The "night stick" or straight baton was something most officers would use. Although hard to carry and mostly left in a patrol car, the straight baton was much easier to use. In fact, when officers who did not train properly with

merion_merion/Shutterstock.com

the side-handled baton would use the side-handled baton, the officers would use the tool in a fashion similar to a straight baton (a two-handed grip and would employ striking tactics meant for a straight baton). So, the expandable baton grew to be the most prevalent striking tool in law enforcement. Training time in the academy decreased in hours. Officers are now more likely to carry the expandable baton on their duty belt.

However, there are problems associated with the use of the expandable baton. Carry position is critical for an officer.

Should an officer be equipped with an expandable baton that is friction lock, most all batons are friction lock, or with an auto-lock baton. An auto-lock baton is not a friction-lock baton. It actually locks into place using a camshaft, ball-bearing locking

Grisha Bruev/Shutterstock.com

mechanism, ensuring the baton will remain locked open while an officer delivers strikes and jabs. Unlike other batons, the shafts also rotate, enhancing weapon retention. The Monadnock auto-lock baton closes without striking it to the ground or compromising your position. A simple press of a button sends the shafts back into the handle, without having to bend over and repetitively strike the baton on a hard surface.

The typical friction lock baton must be struck directly against a hard surface to collapse.

Canine

Canine is the use of a trained patrol dog to apprehend a subject, usually resulting in a bite of some sort. There is case law guiding all use-of-force scenarios, but the use of the *Canine* requires special attention, as seen in the U.S. Supreme Court, and also in the extensive training of the officers selected to handle the dogs. In terms of categorizing use of force, the use of *chemical/natural agents*, *batons or objects*, and *canines* are considered *mechanical force*.

Firearm

Firearm use against a subject is a simple concept to grasp, one of extreme violence, exposing the subject to *deadly force*. Police carry handguns, shotguns, assault rifles, and so on. Any of these firearms used against subject fall into this category and constitutes *deadly force*. As discussed, there are limited situations where officers can resort to the use of deadly force as explained in *Graham v. Connor* and *Tennessee v. Garner*.

Use-of-force incidents inevitably lead to injuries, sometimes even death.

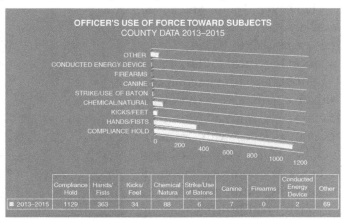

	Compliance Hold	Hands/Fists	Kicks/Feet	Chemical/Natural	Strike/Use of Batons	Canine	Firearms	Conducted Energy Device	Other
2013-2015	1129	363	34	88	6	7	0	2	69

Courtesy of Jeffrey Schwartz/Michael Virga.

Through the course of the 3 years represented by this data, no deaths occurred (Officers or Subjects). When these encounters turn violent, the result can typically end with medical attention on the scene or even a trip to the hospital. In this study, of the 1,151 incidents where the police used any type of force, only 178 (15.46%) subjects were injured and 78 (6.78%) police officers. The number of injuries can be for a variety of reasons, one might be attributed that the police are tasked and trained to use the minimal amount of force possibly to accomplish a law enforcement objective (as can be seen in this study with number of compliance holds reported during the time frame).

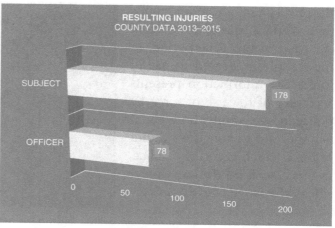

Courtesy of Jeffrey Schwartz/Michael Virga.

The data presented here is considered "raw". When collecting information for analysis, this is the launching point. The numbers display what occurred in this area, with these people, in this specific time frame. It has not been tested against other data or correlated to draw conclusions of significance (Significance testing explores to see if random chance explains the result through p-values).

CONCLUSION

In this chapter, we surveyed the collection of data and its importance for reporting and accountability. Additionally, we looked at transparency of local governments and the accessibility of information for normal, everyday citizens. By examining the law, we can see information that can be obtained and also the information that is restricted. Through an Open Records request (OPRA), we investigated the details of the *use of force report*, and the variety of information located in the document. Also, we represented the raw data in tables and graphs to provide a snapshot of what occurred in this time period, in this county, in regard to use of force. The information presents a picture of the use of force by police in one county; however, it is important to note the amount of force which is used by police, in this case, is on the less violent side of the range of use of force.

Militarist/Shutterstock.com

USE OF FORCE

Attorney General's Use of Force Policy

Issued April 1985 Revised June 2000

http://www.nj.gov/lps/dcj/agguide/useofforce2001.pdf

See Model Use-of-Force Report and Use-of-Force Policy from the New Jersey Attorney General at http://www.nj.gov/oag/dcj/agguide/useofforce2001.pdf

bikeriderlondon/Shutterstock.com

Discussion Points

1. If government must maintain transparency and open governmental records for view by the public, why is it necessary to exempt some forms of documentation?
   - Should documents be assessed on a "case-by-case" basis or should there be "bright-line" rules concerning the release of certain documents?

- In your opinion, do you believe more documents should be allowed for release or would you prefer more restrictions on the release of government records?

2. Police officers can resort to physical, mechanical, and deadly force to accomplish law enforcement objectives. Why is it important to collect detailed data of police use of force?

   - Do you think information gathered from use of force reporting guide decision-making, policy, and police procedure?
   - How can the use-of-force report be used to inform the public about standard documented incidents of the police using force?

References

Baxter, C. (2014). Names of police subject to internal affairs complaints are public records, judge rules. *NJ Advance Media for NJ.com*. Retrieved from http://www.nj.com/news/index.ssf/2014/10/names_of_police_subject_to_internal_affairs_complaints_are_public_records_judge_rules.html

Open Public Records Act. (2015). *Government Records Council, State of New Jersey*. Retrieved May 5, 2015.

Pound, R. (1952). Procedure under rules of Court in New Jersey. *Harvard Law Review*, 66(1), 28–46.

Use of Force Policy. (2001). *New Jersey Attorney General's Office, State of New Jersey*. Retrieved from http://www.nj.gov/oag/dcj/agguide/useofforce2001.pdf

Wefing, J. B. (1997). New Jersey Supreme Court 1948–1998: Fifty years of independence and activism. *Rutgers LJ, 29*, 701.

Student Name _____ Date _____

Course Section _____ Chapter _____

Using some recent examples, discuss how the media plays a role in the perception of the police in use of force, include the use or non-use of body cameras, surveillance, cell phone video, do citizens have a right to video the police, do citizens get in the way, etc. Are citizens challenging the police in situations exacerbating the situation? Or, are police overzealous in the use of force when challenged? Explain.

_____

_____

_____

_____

_____

_____

_____

_____

_____

_____

_____

_____

_____

_____

_____

CHAPTER 7

CONSENT DECREES

The ability of the police to perform their duties is dependent upon public approval of police existence, actions, behavior, and the ability of the police to secure and maintain public respect.

—Sir Robert Peele in Peelian Principle #2

blvdone/Shutterstock.com

Key Terms

Consent Decree, 1994 Violent Crime Control and Law Enforcement Act, Racial Profiling, Span of Control, Early Warning Systems, Body-Worn Cameras, and Behavioral Health Training

Learning Objectives

After exploring Chapter 7, the student will be able to:

1. List 4 Consent Decrees and the major changes implemented regarding police reform to those agencies.
2. Explain the fundamental modification to police oversight in the United States enacted by the 1994 Violent Crime Control and Law Enforcement Act.
3. Describe Racial Profiling and the remedies imposed upon the New Jersey State Police (NJSP) to correct bias-based policing tactics.
4. Explain the importance of police supervision and "span of control."
5. Explain how recommendations in current consent decrees date back to original police procedures developed in the 19th century.
6. Describe "Early Warning Systems" for police personnel and its main features involving police supervision.

Consent Decrees spawn from the 1994 Violent Crime Control and Law Enforcement Act. This act bestows the U.S. Department of Justice Civil Rights Division power, to scrutinize state and local law enforcement agencies deemed to have unconstitutional procedures or participate in unconstitutional patterns of law enforcement behavior. The act was ratified in the aftermath of the 1992 Los Angeles riots (Fagan & Geller, 2010). The riots soared from the prolonged theme of police brutality against U.S. minorities in the nation's history.

The law focuses on general, organizational practices, rather than singular objections to an acute incident involving obvious police misconduct. When a consent decree is administered, it is considered for broad repairs to police agencies operating contrary to the U.S. Constitution, many which are brought to center because of fiercely debated, nationally broadcasted incidents, as is the case in Ferguson, Missouri 2014 or Baltimore, Maryland 2015.

Importantly, the right to bring suit under this law lies solely with the U.S. Justice Department at the Federal government level. The regulation furnishes the Department of Justice with the weight to impose civil litigations against local governments in order to compel them to embrace modifications to past practices of policing and improve upon future policing plans (policeforum.org).

Predominantly, consent decrees are dispensed when police departments engage in some type of systemic discriminatory behavior involving use of force, unlawful stops and searches, and biased-based policing. One notable example, is the consent decree filed against the NJSP for the racial profiling of African Americans during traffic stops on the New Jersey Turnpike and the Garden State Parkway in the late 1990s (Fagan & Geller, 2010).

Consent decrees, generally, originate from the federal level. However, the ongoing case in Oakland, California from 2003, initiated by a class action-type suit from the common public, broke the trend. In this instance, over one hundred citizens petitioned for the federal government to -intervene with the Oakland Police Department (OPD) over injustices involving the use of force. The government answered with a consent decree.

Consent Decrees and/or *Memorandum of Agreements* regularly take years to be settled, as reforms are mandated, forcing the agency to cure a faulty or biased past law enforcement practice. Often the reforms take time to be implemented across organizational lines. When consent decrees are employed, federal inspectors are sent to oversee the changes and their application. The selection of the "Federal Monitor" is significant to the process. Monitors must have practical familiarity of the problems and corrections needed for the police department and policing in general. The Federal Monitor must be able to arbitrate and resolve problems. The monitors work to accomplish efficient, operational conclusions so agencies can repair deficiencies in policies and procedures.

Through this chapter, we explore portions of three separate federal consent decrees imposed upon law enforcement agencies since 1994, signed by President Bill Clinton in the reverberation of the Los Angeles riots. The three consent decrees discussed are with the NJSP concerning motor vehicle stops and racial profiling, the OPD and use of force, and most recently Albuquerque, New Mexico regarding "rogue" units in Special Weapons and Tactics (SWAT) and the handling of the mentally ill citizens.

THE NJSP: DOCUMENTED CARS STOPS/RACIAL PROFILING

The NJSP is one of the most distinguished law enforcement agencies in the United States of America. They are highly trained; well equipped, and scrutinized by the public they serve, as they should be. The instantaneous examination and perpetual analysis, forces this agency to be fluid to change and improve, by the nature of the citizenry. The NJSP is professional and competent; a beacon for local law enforcement in New Jersey. The NJSP often blaze the path for county and local law enforcement in New Jersey and nationally.

Natalia Bratslavsky/Shutterstock.com

In the late 1990s, after the Violent Crime Control and Law Enforcement Act was passed, the NJSP was brought under inquiry for "systemic" racial profiling. In 1998, Troopers on the New Jersey State Turnpike shot four unarmed minority males in a van.

According to Fagan and Geller (2010), calculations confirmed, via logistic regression, minority motorists are more likely to be searched by police than white drivers, regardless of the race of the police officer. Through an inspection by the Federal government, and agreement with the NJSP, a consent decree was constructed to address past practices in motor vehicle stops. The following is an excerpt of the actual agreement and the results affecting police policy.

Excerpt from NJSP Consent Decree

Policy Requirements

Except in the "suspect-specific" ("be on the lookout" or "BOLO") situation described below, state troopers shall continue to be prohibited from considering in any fashion and to any degree the race or national or ethnic origin of civilian drivers or passengers in deciding which vehicles to subject to any motor vehicle stop and in deciding upon the scope or substance of any enforcement action or procedure in connection with or during the course of a motor vehicle stop. Where state troopers are seeking to detain, apprehend, or otherwise be on the lookout for one or more specific suspects who have been identified or described in part by race or national or ethnic origin, state troopers may rely in part on race or national or ethnic origin in determining whether reasonable suspicion exists that a given individual is the person being sought.

The State Police has adopted a protocol captioned "F-55 (Motor Vehicle Stops)," dated December 14, 1999, which establishes criteria to be followed by state troopers in selecting which vehicles to stop for violation of state motor vehicle laws. This protocol includes the nondiscrimination requirements set forth in and has been approved by the United States in so far as the protocol identifies practices and procedures required by the Decree. The State shall implement this protocol as soon as practicable. The State shall monitor and evaluate the implementation of the motor vehicle stop criteria and shall revise the criteria as may be necessary or appropriate to ensure compliance. Prior to the implementation of any revised criteria, the State shall obtain approval from the United States and the Independent Monitor.

In order to help ensure that state troopers use their authority to conduct consensual motor vehicle searches in a nondiscriminatory manner, the State Police shall continue to require: that state troopers may request consent to search a motor vehicle only where troopers can articulate a reasonable suspicion that a search would reveal evidence of a crime; that every consent search of a vehicle be based on written consent of the driver or other person authorized to give consent which precedes the search; that the scope of a consent search be limited to the scope of the consent that is given by the driver or other person authorized to give consent; that the driver or other person authorized to give consent has the right to be present during a consent search at a location consistent with the safety of both the state trooper and the motor vehicle occupants, which right can only be waived after the driver or other person authorized to give consent is advised of such right; that the driver or other person authorized to give consent who has granted written consent may orally withdraw that consent at any time during the search without giving a reason; and that state troopers immediately must stop a consent search of a vehicle if and when consent is withdrawn (except that a search may continue if permitted on some nonconsensual basis).

Incident Documentation and Review

Motor Vehicle Stop Data

The State has adopted protocols for Motor Vehicle Stops, Activity Reporting Systems, Patrol Procedures, Radio Procedures, MVR equipment, Consent Searches, and a Motor Vehicle Stop Search Reports and Property Reports that require state troopers utilizing vehicles, both marked and unmarked, for patrols on roadways to accurately record in written reports, logs, radio communications, radio recordings and/or video recordings, the following information concerning all motor vehicle stops:

1. Name and identification number of trooper(s) who initiated the stop
2. Name and identification number of trooper(s) who actively participated in the stop
3. Date, time, and location of the stop
4. Time at which the stop commenced and at which it ended
5. License number/state of stopped vehicle
5A. Description of stopped vehicle
6. The gender and race/ethnicity of the driver, and the driver's date of birth if known
7. The gender and race/ethnicity of any passenger who was requested to exit the vehicle, frisked, searched, requested to consent to a vehicle search, or arrested
8. Whether the driver was issued a summons or warning and the category of violation (i.e., moving violation or nonmoving violation)
8A. Specific violations cited or warned
9. The reason for the stop (i.e., moving violation or nonmoving violation, other [probablecause/BOLO])
10. Whether the vehicle occupant(s) were requested to exit the vehicle
11. Whether the vehicle occupant(s) were frisked

12. Whether consent to search the vehicle was requested and whether consent was granted
    a. The basis for requesting consent to search the vehicle
13. Whether a drug-detection canine was deployed and whether an alert occurred
    a. A description of the circumstances that prompted the deployment of a drug-detection canine
14. Whether a nonconsensual search of the vehicle was conducted
    a. The circumstances that prompted a nonconsensual search of the vehicle
15. Whether any contraband or other property was seized
    a. A description of the type and quantity of any contraband or other property seized
16. Whether the vehicle occupant(s) were arrested, and if so, the specific charges
17. Whether the vehicle occupant(s) were subjected to deadly, physical, mechanical, or chemical force
    a. A description of the circumstances that prompted the use of force; and a description of any injuries to state troopers and vehicle occupants as a result of the use of force
18. The trooper's race and gender
19. The trooper's specific assignment at the time of the stop (on duty only) including squad.
    b. The protocols have been approved by the United States insofar as the protocols identify practices and procedures required by this Decree. The State shall implement these protocols as soon as practicable.
    c. The State shall prepare or revise such forms, reports, and logs as may be required to implement this to eliminate duplication and reduce paperwork.
    d. As experience and the availability of new technology may warrant, the State Police may revise the protocols adopted pursuant to this paragraph by adopting protocols establishing the new reporting procedures and by amending (to the extent necessary) the forms, reports, and logs adopted to implement this paragraph.
    e. Prior to implementation, of any revised protocols and forms, reports, and logs adopted pursuant to subparagraph (d) of this paragraph, the State shall obtain approval of the United States and the Independent Monitor. The United States and the Independent Monitor shall be deemed to have provided such approval unless they advise the State of any objection to a revised protocol within 30 days of receiving same. The approval requirement of this

subparagraph extends to protocols, forms, reports, and logs only insofar as they implement practices and procedures required by this Decree.

20. **Communication Center Call-In's for Motor Vehicle Stops.** The primary purpose of the communications center is to monitor officer safety. State troopers utilizing vehicles, both marked and unmarked, for patrols on roadways shall continue to document all motor vehicle stops, by calling in or otherwise notifying the communications center of each motor vehicle stop. All motor vehicle stop information that is transmitted to the communications center by state troopers pursuant to protocols shall be recorded by the center by means of the center's Computer Aided Dispatch (CAD) system or other appropriate means.

   a. The initial call shall be made at the beginning of the stop before the trooper approaches the stopped vehicle, unless the circumstances make prior notice unsafe or impractical, in which event the state trooper shall notify the communications center as soon as practicable. The State Police shall continue to require that, in calling in or otherwise notifying the communications center of a motor vehicle stop, state troopers shall provide the communications center with a description of the stopped vehicle and its occupants (including the number of occupants, their apparent race/ethnicity, and their apparent gender). Troopers also shall inform the communications center of the reason for the stop, namely, moving violation, nonmoving violation, or other.

   b. State troopers shall notify the communications center prior to conducting a consent search or nonconsensual search of a motor vehicle, unless the circumstances make prior notice unsafe or impractical.

   c. At the conclusion of the stop, before the trooper leaves the scene, the trooper shall notify the communications center that the stop has been concluded, notify the center whether any summons or written warning was issued or custodial arrest was made, communicate any information that is required to be provided by the protocols that was not previously provided, and correct any information previously provided that was inaccurate. If circumstances make it unsafe or impractical to notify the communications center of this information immediately at the conclusion of the stop, the information shall be provided to the communications center as soon as practicable.

   d. The communications center shall inform the trooper of an incident number assigned to each motor vehicle stop that involved a motor vehicle procedure (i.e., occupant requested to exit vehicle, occupant frisked, request for consent search, search, drug dog deployed, seizure, arrest or use of force), and troopers shall utilize that incident number to cross reference other documents prepared regarding that stop. Likewise, all motor vehicle stop information recorded by the communication center about a particular motor vehicle stop shall be identified by the unique incident number assigned to that motor vehicle stop.

21. **Consent Searches of Motor Vehicles.** The State Police shall continue to require that whenever a state trooper wishes to conduct or conducts a consensual search of a motor vehicle in connection with a motor vehicle stop, the trooper must complete a "consent to search" form and report. The "consent to search" form shall contain information which must be presented to the driver or other person authorized to give consent before a consent search may be commenced. This form shall be prepared in English and Spanish. The "consent to search" report shall contain additional information which must be documented for State Police records.

   a. The State Police shall require that all "consent to search" forms include the following information:

   1. The date and location of the stop.

   2. The name and identification number of the trooper making the request for consent to search.

   3. The names and identification numbers of any additional troopers who actively participatein the discussion with the driver or passenger(s) concerning the request for consent to search.

   4. A statement informing the driver or other person authorized to give consent of the right to refuse to grant consent to search, and that if the driver or other person authorized to give consent grants consent, the driver or other person authorized to give consent at any time for any reason may withdraw consent to search.

   5. A statement informing the driver or other person authorized to give consent of the right to be present during the search at a location consistent with the safety of both the state trooper and the motor vehicle occupant(s) which right may be knowingly waived

   6. Check-off boxes to indicate whether consent has been granted, and if consent is granted, the driver or other person authorized to give consent shall check the appropriate box and sign and date the form.

   7. If the driver or other person authorized to give consent refuses consent, the trooper or the driver or other person authorized to give consent shall so note on the form and the driver or other person authorized to give consent shall not be required to sign the form.

b. A state trooper who requests permission to conduct a consent search shall document in a written report the following information regardless of whether the request for permission to conduct a search was granted or denied:

1. The name of the driver or other person authorized to give consent to whom the request for consent is directed, and that person's gender, race/ethnicity, and, if known, date of birth.
2. The names and identification numbers of all troopers who actively participate in the search.
3. The circumstances which constituted the reasonable suspicion giving rise to the request for consent.
4. If consent initially is granted and then is withdrawn, the fact that this occurred, and whether the search continued based on probable cause or other nonconsensual ground, or was terminated as a result of the withdrawal of consent.
5. A description of the type and quantity of any contraband or other property seized.
6. Whether the discussion concerning the request for consent to search and/or any ensuing consent search were recorded using MVR equipment.

c. The trooper shall sign and date the form and the report after each is fully completed.

The changes to the documentation of motor vehicle stops were radical in the 1990s to the turn of the century. Documentations of these incidents were, by no means, as archived as the NJSP consent decree produced; however, they are quite commonplace today in the State of New Jersey. The consent decree of 1998 -reverberated throughout the State of New Jersey, altering policies and pro-

Tashatuvango/Shutterstock.com

cedures through municipal police agencies throughout the state, including the entire nation if they were paying attention. "Paying attention," is a common theme for local law enforcement, as consent decrees begin to be levied by the U.S. government against law enforcement agencies across the nation, police executives begin to look around and absorb "best practices" as imposed upon other agencies by the Department of Justice.

OPD: INVESTIGATING COMPLAINTS, EARLY WARNING SYSTEMS AND SPAN OF CONTROL

The *Allen et al. v. the City of Oakland* case exposed the "Riders" to the people of the United States and pressed for policing reform. The self-proclaimed "Riders" were four policemen working nights in Oakland's most crime-ridden zones. The "Riders" developed into the foulest police disgrace in the history of the OPD, and in general, American policing. Charges and civil rights violations asserted as the "Riders" engineered bogus evidence, planted contraband and repeatedly used brutal force against the public in common practice.

The "Riders" case developed from a fledgling police academy graduate, who was assigned to the area where these officers continually violated the civil rights of Oakland residents. It only took about two weeks. Two weeks for this green officer to drop his badge on his supervisor's desk, leaving only with the repulsion of what he witnessed. Stemming from this green officer's objections, convictions were reversed and future cases were terminated for the possibility of questionable testimony from these officers, as their credibility had been shattered (Monmaney, 2000, *LATimes*). The OPD entered into a consent decree with the federal government in 2003. At the time of the publication of this text, the department has still not fulfilled the requirements mandated.

EARLY WARNING SYSTEMS AND INVESTIGATING CITIZEN COMPLAINTS

More importantly, the "Riders" case and the Oakland consent decree created a "early warning system." Early warning systems are supervisory devices aimed for detecting law enforcement officers who exhibit inadequate behaviors; and confronting them to remedy the problem before it is exacerbated or too late. Early warning systems form an avenue for police supervision to review subordinate actions (Walker, Alpert, & Kenney, 2000). Several "flag" and benchmarks are imbedded in these systems to highlight police behavior, which should be addressed by supervisors. Particularly, early warning systems are general, central documentation centers, where officers are praised for remarkable work and disciplined for unsatisfactory performances. The early warning systems are intended to cut police misconduct with a structure grounded on accountability with the added forum for documenting model performance. All related to the officer's and public's demand for a sense of duty in law enforcement personnel.

kropic1/Shutterstock.com

"Early warning systems" are revolutionary to the traditional vanguard strategy of managing police personnel. Conventional police management relied upon a catalogue of police rules and regulations for reactionary discipline (Westley, 1970). The large volume of rules and regulations inundate the officers and are often used subjectively by front-line supervisors and command staff to enforce discipline in reaction to a complaint.

The OPD "Riders" case highlights the importance of taking citizen and anonymous complaints, just as an agency praises officers with exemplary behavior. That is, creating an avenue for formal documentation of disciplinary action, with a procedure to correct the problem. Remedies can be additional training, reassignment, or other actions to correct the employee's behavior.

In addition, the "Riders" case shaped "early warning systems" to contest the façade of past police management tactics of not addressing inexcusable police behaviors. Early warning systems rely upon a series of factors, mostly with an emphasis on front-line supervision.

Reporting

In the aftermath, the first part of memorializing a police-citizen contact is the police report. The police report is a fluid, malleable document. That is, the report ranges from a basic incident report with identifying, time-stamping information, with officer narrative to additional supplementary forms based upon the incident (victim notification, use of force reports, arrest reports, domestic violence checklists, crash reports, supplemental officer reports, and additional ancillary forms that are -incident-driven). The front-line supervisor, typically a patrol sergeant, reviews the work to certify the report is in compliance with law and departmental regulation. If the supervisor was not on the scene, the review of the police report is a crucial point for assessing officer performance and behavior. Ultimately, the reporting phase falls upon the individual officer as the report review bleeds into the supervisory role.

Supervision

The front-line supervisor captures a significant point in every group or establishment because of the personal impact they have upon the behavior of the people who actually provide the service in the realm of law enforcement. Front-line supervisors occupy this role with anemphasis of teamwork and production (Iannone & Iannone, 2001). With that, the police supervisor is responsible for confirming compliance with police procedure and also safeguarding the

Dmitry Kalinovsky/Shutterstock.com

rights of the public. Serving the best interests of the -citizenry is accomplished by being in the field and leading responses to fresh incidents, and also reviewing the work of subordinates. The front-line supervisor needs to be a "Swiss-Army Knife," or a master of all trades. In addition to maintaining relationships with police personnel and the public, the front-line supervisor must be a planner, a teacher, quality-controller, administrator, decision-maker, and ultimately, a leader. The front-line supervisor has is a large task; however, it is essential to managing acceptable ground-level police operations.

Span of Control

"Span of control" suggests the number of subordinates who can be effectively managed by one supervisor. The "magic" number is not fixed. It is dependent upon type of work, geographical boundaries, environmental and political forces, response times, consistency of operation, and administrative capacities (Iannone & Iannone, 2001). In terms of the OPD consent decree, the federal government requires the following in this excerpt.

SUPERVISORY SPAN OF CONTROL AND UNITY OF COMMAND

Within 260 days from the effective date of this agreement (*Allen v. City* of Oakland) the Chief of Police shall, based upon contemporary police standards and best practices, develop and implement policies to address the following standards and provisions:

A. Approval of Field-Arrest by Supervisor

OPD shall develop standards for field supervisors that encourage or mandate close and frequent supervisory contacts with subordinates on calls for service. The policies developed in this Section shall require supervisors to respond to the scene of (at least) the following categories of arrest, unless community unrest or other conditions at the scene make this impractical:

a. Felonies;
b. Narcotics-related possessory offenses;
c. Where there is an investigated use of force;
d. Stipulated offenses under the California Penal Code

The responding supervisor shall review the arrest documentation to determine whether probable cause for the arrest, or reasonable suspicion for the stop, is articulated, to ensure that available witnesses are identified, to approve or disapprove the arrest in the field, and to log the contact.

B. Unity of Command

With rare exceptions (justified on a case-by-case-basis), each member or employee of the Department shall have a single, clearly identified supervisor or manager.

In general, sergeants should work the same schedule and have the same days off as the individuals they supervise.

C. Span of Control for Supervisors

Within 90 days from the effective date of this agreement, OPD shall develop and implement a policy to ensure appropriate supervision of its Area Command Teams. The policy shall provide that:

1. Under normal conditions, OPD shall assign one primary sergeant to each area Command Field Team, and, in general, (with certain exceptions) that supervisor's span of control shall not exceed (8) members.
2. During day-to-day operations, in the absence of the primary supervisor (e.g. due to sickness, vacation, compensatory time off, schools, and other leaves), the Watch Commander shall determine, based upon Departmental policy and operational needs, whether or not to backfill for the absence of the sergeant on leave.
3. If a special operation, (e.g. Beat Feet, Traffic Offenders Program (STOP), etc.) requires more than (8) members, the Area Commander or Watch Commander shall determine the reasonable span of control for the supervisor.
4. If long-term backfill requires the loan or transfer of a supervisor from another unit, the Chief of Police or Deputy Chief of Police shall make the decision.

D. Members' Employees' and Supervisors' Performance Review

1. Every OPD/commander/manager shall meet at least twice per year with each of his/her members, employees and supervisors, to coach them regarding their strengths and weaknesses. These meetings shall be documented. If a member, employee or supervisor exhibits a performance problem, the commander/ manager shall meet with him/her in accordance with the provision of Section … of this Agreement. Commanders/managers shall meet promptly with affected subordinates regarding complaints or commendations received.
2. Supervisors shall meet individually with members and employees at least twice per month for informal performance reviews.
3. Supervisors and commanders/managers shall be responsible for identifying patterns of improper behavior of their subordinates. In particular, Bureau of Field Operations sergeants and lieutenants shall scrutinize arrests and uses of force that have been historically associated with police misconduct, including arrests for very small amounts of drugs, arrests pursuant to searches with no underlying offense leading to the search, (California Penal Code citations).

Failure to identify such patterns and instances of misconduct when the supervisors or commanders/managers knew or reasonable should have known the misconduct shall constitute grounds for discipline.

E. OPD/DA Liasion Commander

Within 60 days from the effective date of this Agreement, OPD shall establish a Management- Level Liaison (MLL) to the courts, the District Attorney's Office, and the Public Defender's Office. This unit or person shall ensure that cases which are lost or dropped due to bad reports, defective search warrants, granted "Motions to Suppress" contradictory evidence or testimony, or any other indication of performance problems or misconduct, are tracked. The OPD MLL shall be required to meet and cooperate with the Federal Monitor. The DA's and PD's Offices may attend meetings as they deem appropriate.

F. Command Staff Rotation

The Chief of Police is committed to the regular rotation of Departmental command staff as consistent with best practices in law enforcement agency management, based upon the Department's immediate needs and best interests, including:

1. Special skills needed for an assignment;
2. Career development; and
3. Increasing Departmental efficiency and effectiveness

The OPD consent decree outlines a variety of measures for police forces to become compliant with "best practices" in law enforcement. It delineates the amount or intensity of oversight required to supervise street-level policing. Additionally, the decree forms the foundation for police rules, concerning assessments and follow-ups with general performance. The decree addresses the span of control in supervisor to subordinate ratio and also intricately defines documentation procedures. On the command level, the decree orders for the creation of a position to be in contact with the courts (prosecutors, public defenders, court clerks, etc.) to track defective cases varying from unlawful arrests/searches to defective warrants.

Separately, the OPD consent decree spells out a Command Staff rotation. The reasoning in the order is for commanders to be assigned upon special skills, rotated for career development, or to improve departmental efficiency and effectiveness. It creates a "cross-training" for police commanders to dilute divisiveness from fidelities of a certain assignment (Patrol, Investigations, Community Policing, SWAT, K-9, School Resources, etc.).

THE NEW ORLEANS POLICE DEPARTMENT AND USE OF FORCE

The New Orleans Police Department (NOPD) is afflicted with a troubled history in their agency regarding incidents with questionable uses of force. One highlighted episode (Post-Hurricane Katrina), is the notorious police shootings during the aftermath of the storm on the Danziger Bridge. In the confusion after the flooding, police responded to a report that police were being shot at near this particular bridge. Officers, in plainclothes

Gary Paul Lewis/Shutterstock.com

in an unmarked van, drove to the scene and opened fire indiscriminately. Six civilians were shot by the police officers. After several legal proceedings, the officers plead guilty in April, 2016. A 17-year old and a mentally ill man were killed on the bridge along with others injured. An ensuing inquiry determined all of the people on the bridge were unarmed. The incident produced a homicide investigation, and highlighted deficiencies with systemic practices with NOPD regarding use of force.

In 2011, the Federal Government and the NOPD entered into a consent decree due to a federal investigation. Examiners determined that the NOPD had a "pattern and practice of unconstitutional conduct" disrupting several constitutional requirements some listed as:

1. Use of excessive force
2. Unconstitutional stops, searches, and arrests
3. Racial and ethnic profiling

4. Failure to investigate sexual assaults and domestic violence
5. Among others ...

In the NOPD, the U.S. government recognized fractured procedures for assessment, insufficient training, unproductive supervision, and an absence of accountability for officers. Below is an excerpt of the Justice Department's decree as applied to the use of force:

III. USE OF FORCE

NOPD agrees to develop and implement force policies, training, and review mechanisms that ensure that force by NOPD officers is used in accordance with the rights secured or protected by the Constitution and the laws of the United States, and that any unreasonable uses of force are identified and responded to appropriately. NOPD agrees to ensure that officers use nonforce techniques to effect compliance with police orders whenever feasible; use of force only when necessary, and in a manner that avoids unnecessary injury to officers and civilians; and de-escalate the use of force at the earliest possible moment. To achieve these outcomes, NOPD agrees to implement the requirements set below:

A. Use of Force Principles

Use of force by NOPD officers, regardless of the type of force or weapon used, shall abide by the following requirements:

A. Officers shall use advisements, warnings, and verbal persuasion, when possible, before resorting to force;
B. Force shall be de-escalated immediately as resistance decreases;
C. When feasible based on the circumstances, officers will use disengagement; area containment; surveillance; waiting out a subject; summoning reinforcements; and/or calling in specialized units, in order to reduce the need for force and increase officer and civilian safety;
D. Officers shall allow individuals time to submit to arrest before force is used wherever possible;
E. NOPD shall explicitly prohibit neck hold, except where lethal force is authorized;
F. NOPD shall explicitly prohibit head strikes with a hard object, except where lethal force is authorized;
G. NOPD shall explicitly prohibit using force against persons in handcuffs, except as objectively reasonable to prevent imminent bodily harm to the officer or

another person or persons, or, as objectively reasonable, where physical removal is necessary to overcome passive resistance;

H. NOPD shall explicitly prohibit the use of force above unresisted handcuffing to overcome passive resistance, except that physical removal is permitted as necessary and objectively reasonable;

I. Unholstering a firearm and pointing it a person constitutes a use of force, and shall be accordingly be done only as objectively reasonable to accomplish a lawful police objective;

J. Officers shall not use force to attempt to effect compliance with a command that is unlawful. Any use of force by an officer to subdue an individual resisting arrest or detention is unreasonable when the initial arrest or detention of the individual was unlawful;

K. Immediately following a use of force, officers and, upon arrival, a supervisor shall inspect and observe subjects for injury complaints of pain resulting from the use of force, and immediately obtain any necessary medical care. This may require an officer to require emergency first aid until professional medical care providers are on scene.

B. General Use of Force Policy

NOPD agrees to develop and implement an overarching agency-wide use of force policy that complies with applicable law and comports with best practices and current professional standards. The comprehensive use of force policy shall include all force techniques, technologies, and weapons, both lethal and less-lethal that are available to NOPD officers, including standard- issue weapons that are made available to all officers and weapons that are made available to specialized units. The comprehensive use of force policy shall clearly define and describe each use of force option and the circumstances under which force principles articulated above, and shall specify that the unreasonable use of force will subject the officers to discipline, possible criminal prosecution, and/or civil liability.

In addition to a primary agency-wide use of force policy, NOPD agrees to develop and implement policies and protocols for each authorized weapon, including each types of force … No officer shall carry any weapon, or use force, that is not authorized by the Department. NOPD se of force policies shall include training and certification requirements that each officer must meet before being permitted to carry and use the authorized weapons.

The NOPD will "develop and implement an overarching agency-wide use of force policy that complies with applicable law and comports with best practices and current professional standards." This language is verbatim in other federal consent decrees, notably it appears in the agreement between the Justice Department and Albuquerque Police Department (APD) in New Mexico, as we discuss with separate issues later in this chapter. This agreement specifies officer behavior in use of force incident. It takes general use of force policy a step further, addressing issues such as the unholstering/pointing a firearm at a subject and resorting to "disengagement" as a de-escalation tactic. The general theme is for force to be used as the last alternative, when attempting to accomplish a lawful law enforcement objective. The Federal government emphasizes officers to use "persuasion," "warnings," and verbal commands to calm situations and use force as a final option. Additionally important in this decree, is the complete withdrawal of force, once the subject is brought under control and secured by police.

APD: BODY CAMERAS, BEHAVIORAL HEALTH TRAINING AND EARLY INTERVENTION SYSTEMS

In April 2014, the U.S. Justice Department established systemic, organizational, and unlawful repetition of excessive force in the APD. Attention focused on the APD after a sequence of 37 police-involved shootings over a 4-year period, where 23 were lethal (Lovett, 2014). New to the common language of consent decrees regarding use of force, this particular agreement involves training for officers to manage subjects with mental illnesses. Additionally, the consent decree addresses new technological surges for law enforcement with the arrival of and demand for body cameras. In this decree and in departmental policies across the United States, officers are commanded to wear body cameras to chronicle many contacts with the public, if not all. The

Al Mueller/Shutterstock.com

APD earned national notoriety when, James Boyd, homeless and suffering from mental illness, was killed by gunfire from APD officers in the hills of the Sandia Mountains in New Mexico in March 2014.

The following excerpt from the APD consent decree addresses policies for the application of body-warn cameras, managing people suffering mental illnesses, and the administration of early warning systems.

On-Body Recording Systems for Documenting Police Activities

To maintain high-level, quality service; to ensure officer safety and accountability; and to promote constitutional, effective policing, APD is committed to the consistent and effective use of on-body recording systems. Within six months of the Effective Date, APD agrees to revise and update its policies and procedures regarding on-body recording systems to require:

a. Specific and clear guidance when on-body recording systems are used, including who will be assigned to wear the cameras and where on the body the cameras are authorized to be placed;

b. Officers to ensure that their on-body recording systems are working properly during police action;

c. Officers to notify their supervisors when they learn that their on-body recording systems are not functioning;

d. Officers are required to inform arrestees when they are recording, unless doing so would be unsafe, impractical, or impossible;

e. Activation of on-body recording systems before all encounters with individuals who are the subject of a stop based on reasonable suspicion or probable cause, arrest, or vehicle search, as well as police action involving subjects known to have mental illness;

f. Supervisors to review recordings of all officers listed in any misconduct complaints made directly to the supervisor or APD report regarding any incident involving injuries to an officer, uses of force, or foot pursuits;

g. Supervisors to review recordings regularly and to incorporate the knowledge gained from this review into their ongoing evaluation and supervision of officers; and

h. APD to retain and preserve non-evidentiary recordings for at least 60 days and consistent with state disclosure laws, and evidentiary recordings for at least one year, or, if a case remains in investigation or litigation, until the case is resolved.

APD shall submit all new or revised on-body recording system policies and procedures to the Monitor and DOJ for review, comment, and approval prior to publication and implementation. Upon approval by the Monitor and DOJ, policies shall be implemented within two months.

The Parties recognize that training regarding on-body recording systems is necessary and critical. APD shall develop and provide training regarding on-body recording systems for all patrol officers, supervisors, and command staff. APD will develop a training curriculum, with input from the Monitor and DOJ that relies on national guidelines, standards, and best practices.

APD agrees to develop and implement a schedule for testing on-body recording systems to confirm that they are in proper working order. Officers shall be responsible for ensuring that on-body recording systems assigned to them are functioning properly at the beginning and end of each shift according to the guidance of their system's manufacturer and shall report immediately any improperly functioning equipment to a supervisor.

Supervisors shall be responsible for ensuring that officers under their command use on-body recording systems as required by APD policy. Supervisors shall report equipment problems and seek to have equipment repaired as needed. Supervisors shall refer for investigation any officer who intentionally fails to activate his or her on-body recording system before incidents required to be recorded by APD policy.

At least on a monthly basis, APD shall review on-body recording system videos to ensure that the equipment is operating properly and that officers are using the systems appropriately and in accordance with APD policy and to identify areas in which additional training or guidance is needed.

APD policies shall comply with all existing laws and regulations, including those governing evidence collection and retention, public disclosure of information, and consent.

APD shall ensure that on-body recording system videos are properly categorized and accessible. On-body recording system videos shall be classified according to the kind of incident or event captured in the footage.

Officers who wear on-body recording systems shall be required to articulate on camera or in writing their reasoning if they fail to record an activity that is required by APD policy to be recorded. Intentional or otherwise unjustified failure to activate an on-body recording system when required by APD policy shall subject the officer to discipline.

APD shall ensure that on-body recording systems are only used in conjunction with official law enforcement duties. On-body recording systems shall not be used to record encounters with known undercover officers or confidential informants; when officers are engaged in personal activities; when officers are having conversations with other Department personnel that involve case strategy or tactics; and in any location where individuals have a reasonable expectation of privacy (e.g., restroom or locker room).

APD shall ensure that all on-body recording system recordings are properly stored by the end of each officer's subsequent shift. All images and sounds recorded by on-body recording systems are the exclusive property of APD.

The Parties are committed to the effective use of on-body recording systems and to utilizing best practices. APD currently deploys several different platforms for on-body recording systems that have a range of technological capabilities and cost considerations. The City has engaged outside experts to conduct a study of its on-body recording system program. Given these issues, within one year of the Effective Date, APD shall consult with community stakeholders, officers, the police officer's union, and community residents to gather input on APD's on-body recording system policy and to revise the policy, as necessary, to ensure it complies with applicable law, this Agreement, and best practices.

Body warn cameras are part of the new age of policing. With the inception of consent decrees and orders from federal monitors, many "best practices" have been crafted and applied by polcing agencies across the nation. Body-warn cameras have several purposes, one as an element of oversight over law enforcement to protect citizens from abuse of police power. Additionally, the cameras serve as a defense function for police officers, safeguarding them from false allegations and inaccurate depictions of the law enforcement encounter. Below is an state example of body warn camera policy from the State of New Jersey. It outlines when body cameras must be activated and general rules for their operation, storage/retention requirements, and release for public view.

State of New Jersey Attorney General Law Enforcement Directive No. 2015-1

Law Enforcement Directive Regarding Police Body Warn Cameras (BWCs) and Stored BWC Recordings

Circumstances When Activation by a Uniformed Officer Generally is Required

Except as otherwise expressly provided in section 7 or any other provision in this Directive, a uniformed officer equipped with a BWC shall be required to activate the device in any of the following circumstances as soon as it is safe and practicable to do so:

a) the officer initiates an investigative detention (a Delaware v. Prouse traffic stop, a Terry v. Ohio criminal suspicion stop, or a checkpoint or roadblock stop);

b) the officer is responding to a call for service and is at or near the location to which the officer has been dispatched;

c) the officer is conducting a motorist aid or community caretaking check;

d) the officer is interviewing a witness in the course of investigating a criminal offense;

e) the officer is conducting a custodial interrogation of a suspect, unless the interrogation is otherwise being recorded in accordance with Rule 3:17 (electronic recordation of station house interrogations); the officer is making an arrest;

g) the officer is conducting a protective frisk for weapons;

h) the officer is conducting any kind of search (consensual or otherwise);

i) the officer is engaged in a police response to any type of civil disorder in circumstances where the officer is engaged with or in the presence of civilians and the officer or any other officer on the scene may be required to employ constructive authority or force;

j) the officer uses constructive authority or force, or reasonably believes that constructive authority or force may be used in any encounter or situation not otherwise listed in this subsection based on specific and articulable facts warranting heightened caution that are documented by narration on the recording and/or in any investigation or incident report;

k) the officer is transporting an arrestee to a police station, county jail, or other place of confinement, or a hospital or other medical care or mental health facility; or

l) the officer reasonably believes that any other officer on the scene has undertaken or is engaged in any of the foregoing police actions/activities.

Two or more of the these listed activities are likely to occur during a single encounter or event. For example, a frisk ordinarily occurs after an officer already has initiated an investigative detention i.e., a "stop"), and a custodial interrogation typically occurs after the officer has arrested the person being interrogated. Although these specified activities often will co-occur and overlap, they are presented in this section to ensure complete coverage of the circumstances when a BWC must be activated. The specified activity that occurs first during an unfolding encounter will trigger the obligation to activate a BWC. As explained in section 5.4, once activated based upon the initiation of any of the listed police activities, the BWC generally must remain in operation until the police-

Rob Wilson/Shutterstock.com

civilian encounter is concluded i.e., until the officer is no longer interacting with or in the presence of the civilian), and not just while the officer is engaged in the specified activity that required activation.

<u>Special Activation Rules Governing Deadly-Force Incidents and Other Exigent Circumstances Where Officers Are in Danger</u>

Notwithstanding any other provision of this Directive, when an officer equipped with a BWC is dispatched to or otherwise goes to the scene of an incident knowing or reasonably believing that police deadly force has been or is being employed, or to a scene where an officer has requested emergency assistance (ems., an officer in distress, shots fired, etc.), the officer shall activate the BWC before arriving at the scene when feasible. Notwithstanding any other provision of this Directive, an officer while at the scene of a police deadly-force event orthe on-scene investigation of that event shall not de-activate the BWC unless instructed to do so by the assistant prosecutor or assistant or deputy attorney general supervising the investigation of the deadly force incident pursuant to Attorney General Law Enforcement Directive No.2006-5, or his or her designee. Such instruction may be given telephonically by the assistant prosecutor, assistant or deputy attorney general, or designee supervising the investigation.

<u>Authorization for Access to BWC Recordings Related to Use-of-Force Investigations</u>

The assistant prosecutor or assistant or deputy attorney general overseeing a police use of force investigation pursuant to Attorney General Law Enforcement Directive No. 2006-5, or his or her designee, may in the exercise of sound discretion authorize a civilian or law enforcement witness to be given access to or view a BWC recording of the incident under investigation. To ensure the integrity of investigations of police-involved shootings and other use-of-force incidents and to avoid possible contamination of a witness's personal recollection of events that could undermine his or her credibility as a witness, notwithstanding any other provision of this Directive, no civilian or law enforcement witness, including the principals) of the investigation, shall be given access to or view a BWC recording of the incident, or a BWC recording of the response or on-scene investigation of the incident, without the express prior approval of the assistant prosecutor, assistant or deputy attorney general, or designee.

For full New Jersey Attorney General Guidelines on governing body warn cameras please visit https://nj.gov/oag/newsreleases15/AG-Directive_Body-Cams.pdf

The Albuquerque Police Department, with the Boyd shooting, brought the issue of police using force against citizens who are suffering from mental illness. As more people are diagnosed and suffering from some type of mental disease or behavioral disorder, the police are often the front-line agency confronting these people in public. The federal government recognizes, along with APD, that training is required for officers when handling this population. However, use of force incidents do occur during these incidents and officers must be properly equipped to bring these episodes to successful conclusions. A successful conclusion to the incident can be attained through training and a thoughtful direction of resources. The following is an excerpt from the APD consent decree, outlining crisis intervention.

CRISIS INTERVENTION

To maintain high-level, quality service; to ensure officer safety and accountability; and to promote constitutional, effective policing, APD agrees to minimize the necessity for the use of force against individuals in crisis due to mental illness or a diagnosed behavioral disorder and, where appropriate, assist in facilitating access to community-based treatment, supports, and services to improve outcomes for the individuals. APD agrees to develop, implement, and support more integrated, specialized responses to individuals in mental health crisis through collaborative partnerships with community stakeholders, specialized training, and improved communication and coordination with mental health professionals. To achieve these outcomes, APD agrees to implement the requirements below.

Mental Health Response Advisory Committee

Within six months of the Effective Date, APD and the City shall establish a Mental Health Response Advisory Committee ("Advisory Committee") with subject matter expertise and experience that will assist in identifying and developing solutions and interventions that are designed to lead to improved outcomes for individuals perceived to be or actually suffering from mental illness or experiencing a mental health crisis. The Advisory Committee shall analyze and recommend appropriate changes to policies, procedures, and training methods regarding police contact with individuals with mental illness.

The Advisory Committee shall include representation from APD command staff, crisis intervention certified responders, Crisis Intervention Unit ("CIU"), Crisis Outreach and Support Team ("COAST"), and City-contracted mental health professionals. APD shall also seek representation from the Department of Family and Community Services, the University of New Mexico Psychiatric Department, community mental health professionals, advocacy groups for consumers of mental health services (such as the National Alliance on Mental Illness and Disability Rights New Mexico), mental health service providers, homeless service providers, interested community members designated by the Forensic Intervention Consortium, and other similar groups.

The Advisory Committee shall provide guidance to assist the City in developing and expanding the number of crisis intervention certified responders, CIU, and COAST. The Advisory Committee shall also be responsible for considering new and current response strategies for dealing with chronically homeless individuals or individuals perceived to be or actually suffering from a mental illness, identifying training needs, and providing guidance on effective responses to a behavioral crisis event.

APD, with guidance from the Advisory Committee, shall develop protocols that govern the release and exchange of information about individuals with known mental illness to facilitate necessary and appropriate communication while protecting their confidentiality.

Within nine months of the Effective Date, APD shall provide the Advisory Committee with data collected by crisis intervention certified responders, CIU, and COAST pursuant to this Agreement for the sole purpose of facilitating program guidance. Also within nine months of the Effective Date, the Advisory Committee shall review the behavioral health training curriculum; identify mental health resources that may be available to APD;

network and build more relationships; and provide guidance on scenario-based training involving typical situations that occur when mental illness is a factor.

The Advisory Committee shall seek to enhance coordination with local behavioral health systems, with the goal of connecting chronically homeless individuals and individuals experiencing mental health crisis with available services.

Within 12 months of the Effective Date, and annually thereafter, the Advisory Committee will provide a public report to APD that will be made available on APD's website, which shall include recommendations for improvement, training priorities, changes in policies and procedures, and identifying available mental health resources.

Behavioral Health Training

APD has undertaken an aggressive program to provide behavioral health training to its officers. This Agreement is designed to support and leverage that commitment.

APD agrees to continue providing state-mandated, basic behavioral health training to all cadets in the academy. APD also agrees to provide 40 hours of basic crisis intervention training for field officers to all academy graduates upon their completion of the field training program. APD is also providing 40 hours of basic crisis intervention training for field officers to all current officers, which APD agrees to complete by the end of 2015.

The behavioral health and crisis intervention training provided to all officers will continue to address field assessment and identification, suicide intervention, crisis de-escalation, scenario-based exercises, and community mental health resources. APD training shall include interaction with individuals with a mental illness and coordination with advocacy groups that protect the rights of individuals with disabilities or those who are chronically homeless. Additionally, the behavioral health and crisis intervention training will provide clear guidance as to when an officer may detain an individual solely because of his or her crisis and refer them for further services when needed.

121. APD shall ensure that new telecommunicators receive 20 hours of behavioral health training. This training shall include: telephonic suicide intervention; crisis management and de-escalation; interactions with individuals with mental illness; descriptive information that should be gathered when telecommunicators suspect that a call involves someone with mental illness; the roles and functions of COAST, crisis intervention certified responders, and CIU; the types of calls that should be directed to particular officers or teams; and recording information in the dispatch database about calls in which mental illness may be a factor.

APD shall provide two hours of in-service training to all existing officers and telecommunicators on behavioral health-related topics biannually.

Crisis Intervention Certified Responders and Crisis Intervention Unit

APD shall maintain a sufficient number of crisis intervention certified responders who are specially trained officers across the Department who retain their normal duties and responsibilities and also respond to calls involving those in mental health crisis. APD shall also maintain a Crisis Intervention Unit ("CIU") composed of specially trained detectives housed at the Family Advocacy Center whose primary responsibilities are to respond to mental health crisis calls and maintain contact with mentally ill individuals who have posed a danger to themselves or others in the past or are likely to do so in the future. APD agrees to expand both the number of crisis intervention certified responders and CIU.

The number of crisis intervention certified responders will be driven by the demand for crisis intervention services, with an initial goal of 40% of Field Services officers who volunteer to take on specialized crisis intervention duties in the field. Within one year of the Effective Date, APD shall reassess the number of crisis intervention certified responders, following the staffing assessment and resource study required by Paragraph 204 of this Agreement.

During basic crisis intervention training for field officers provided to new and current officers, training facilitators shall recommend officers with apparent or demonstrated skills and abilities in crisis de-escalation and interacting with individuals with mental illness to serve as crisis intervention certified responders.

Within 18 months of the Effective Date, APD shall require crisis intervention certified responders and CIU to undergo at least eight hours of in-service crisis intervention training biannually.

Within 18 months of the Effective Date, APD will ensure that there is sufficient coverage of crisis intervention certified responders to maximize the availability of specialized responses to incidents and calls for service involving individuals in mental health crisis; and warrant service, tactical deployments, and welfare checks involving individuals with known mental illness.

APD will ensure that crisis intervention certified responders or CIU will take the lead, once on scene and when appropriate, in interacting with individuals in crisis. If a supervisor has assumed responsibility for the scene, the supervisor will seek input of the crisis intervention certified responder or CIU on strategies for resolving the crisis when it is practical to do so.

APD shall collect data on the use of crisis intervention certified responders and CIU. This data will be collected for management purposes only and shall not include personal identifying information of subjects or complainants. APD shall collect the following data:

a. Date, shift, and area command of the incident;

b. Subject's age, race/ethnicity, and gender;

c. Whether the subject was armed and the type of weapon;

d. Whether the subject claims to be a U.S. military veteran;

e. Name and badge number of crisis intervention certified responder or CIU detective on the scene;

f. Whether a supervisor responded to the scene;

g. Techniques or equipment used;

h. Any injuries to officers, subjects, or others;

i. Disposition of the encounter (e.g., arrest, citation, referral); and

j. A brief narrative of the event (if not included in any other document).

APD will utilize incident information from actual encounters to develop case studies and teaching scenarios for roll-call, behavioral health, and crisis intervention training; to recognize and highlight successful individual officer performance; to develop new response strategies for repeat calls for service; to identify training needs for in-service behavioral health or crisis intervention training; to make behavioral health or crisis intervention training curriculum changes; and to identify systemic issues that impede APD's ability to provide an appropriate response to an incident involving an individual experiencing a mental health crisis.

Working in collaboration with the Advisory Committee, the City shall develop and implement a protocol that addresses situations involving barricaded, suicidal subjects who are not posing an imminent risk of harm to anyone except themselves. The protocol will have the goal of protecting the safety of officers and suicidal subjects while providing suicidal subjects with access to mental health services.

Crisis Prevention

APD shall continue to utilize COAST and CIU to follow up with chronically homeless individuals and individuals with a known mental illness who have a history of law enforcement encounters and to proactively work to connect these individuals with mental health service providers.

COAST and CIU shall provide crisis prevention services and disposition and treatment options to chronically homeless individuals and individuals with a known mental illness who are at risk of experiencing a mental health crisis and assist with follow-up calls or visits.

APD shall continue to utilize protocols for when officers should make referrals to and coordinate with COAST and CIU to provide prevention services and disposition and treatment options.

APD shall maintain a sufficient number of trained and qualified mental health professionals in COAST and full-time detectives in CIU to satisfy its obligations under this Agreement. Within three months of completing the staffing assessment and resource study required by Paragraph 204 of this Agreement, APD shall develop a recruitment, selection, and training plan to assign, within 24 months of the study, 12 full-time detectives to the CIU, or the target number of detectives identified by the study, whichever is less.

COAST and CIU shall continue to look for opportunities to coordinate in developing initiatives to improve outreach, service delivery, crisis prevention, and referrals to community health resources.

APD shall collect and analyze data to demonstrate the impact of and inform modifications to crisis prevention services. This data will be collected for management purposes only and shall not include personal identifying information of subjects or complainants. APD shall collect the following data:

a. Number of individuals in the COAST and CIU case loads;
b. Number of individuals receiving crisis prevention services;
c. Date, shift, and area command of incidents or follow up encounters;
d. Subject's age, race/ethnicity, and gender;
e. Whether the subject claims to be a U.S. military veteran;
f. Techniques or equipment used;
g. Any injuries to officers, subjects, or others;
h. Disposition of the encounter (e.g., arrest, citation, referral); and
i. A brief narrative of the event (if not included in any other document).

Early Intervention Systems

Within nine months of the Effective Date, APD shall revise and update its Early Intervention System to enhance its effectiveness as a management tool that promotes supervisory awareness and proactive identification of both potentially problematic as well as commendable behavior among officers. APD supervisors shall be trained to proficiency in the interpretation of

Early Intervention System data and the range of non-punitive corrective action to modify behavior and improve performance; manage risk and liability; and address underlying stressors to promote officer well-being.

APD shall review and adjust, where appropriate, the threshold levels for each Early Identification System indicator to allow for peer-group comparisons between officers with similar assignments and duties.

APD shall implement rolling thresholds so that an officer who has received an intervention of use of force should not be permitted to engage in additional uses of force before again triggering a review.

The Early Intervention System shall be a component of an integrated employee management system and shall include a computerized relational database, which shall be used to collect, maintain, integrate, and retrieve data department-wide and for each officer regarding, at a minimum:

a. Uses of force;
b. Injuries and deaths to persons in custody;
c. Failures to record incidents with on-body recording systems that are required to be recorded under APD policy, whether or not corrective action was taken, and cited violations of the APD's on-body recording policy;
d. All civilian or administrative complaints and their dispositions;
e. All judicial proceedings where an officer is the subject of a protective or restraining order;
f. All vehicle pursuits and traffic collisions involving APD equipment;
g. All instances in which APD is informed by a prosecuting authority that a declination to prosecute any crime occurred, in whole or in part, because the officer failed to activate his or her on-body recording system;
h. All disciplinary action taken against employees;
i. All non-punitive corrective action required of employees;
j. All awards and commendations received by employees, including those received from civilians, as well as special acts performed by employees;
k. Demographic category for each civilian involved in a use of force or search and seizure incident sufficient to assess bias;
l. All criminal proceedings initiated against an officer, as well as all civil or administrative claims filed with, and all civil lawsuits served upon, the City and/or its officers or agents, allegedly resulting from APD operations or the actions of APD personnel; and
m. All offense reports in which an officer is a suspect or offender.

APD shall develop and implement a protocol for using the updated Early Intervention System and information obtained from it. The protocol for using the Early Intervention System shall address data storage, data retrieval, reporting, data analysis, pattern identification, supervisory use, supervisory/departmental intervention, documentation and audits, access to the system, and confidentiality of personally identifiable information. The protocol shall also require unit supervisors to periodically review Early Intervention System data for officers under their command.

APD shall maintain all personally identifying information about an officer included in the Early Intervention System for at least five years following the officer's separation from the agency except where prohibited by law. Information necessary for aggregate statistical analysis will be maintained indefinitely in the Early Intervention System. On an ongoing basis, APD will enter information into the Early Intervention System in a timely, accurate, and complete manner and shall maintain the data in a secure and confidential manner.

APD shall provide in-service training to all employees, including officers, supervisors, and commanders, regarding the updated Early Intervention System protocols within six months of the system improvements to ensure proper understanding and use of the system. APD supervisors shall be trained to use the Early Intervention System as designed and to help improve the performance of officers under their command. Commanders and supervisors shall be trained in evaluating and making appropriate comparisons in order to identify any significant individual or group patterns of behavior.

Following the initial implementation of the updated Early Intervention System, and as experience and the availability of new technology may warrant, the City may add, subtract, or modify thresholds, data tables and fields; modify the list of documents scanned or electronically attached; and add, subtract, or modify standardized reports and queries as appropriate. The Parties shall jointly review all proposals that limit the functions of the Early Intervention System that are required by this Agreement before such proposals are implemented to ensure they continue to comply with the intent of this Agreement.

As discussed in the Albuquerque consent decree, three major current issues are highlighted: the use of body cameras, handling the mentally ill, and early warning systems. The use of body cameras for the recording of policecitizen contacts is front and center in current law enforcement topics and debates. Body cameras are deployed in many police agencies across the United States and many more are researching and accepting bids for companies to deliver these devices for immediate use for documenting police operations. The body camera is a step forward from the traditional "dash" camera, which remains in a fixed position and often loses the ability to record audio as an officer move out of range from the vehicle. The body camera is self-powered, and will record anywhere the officer goes during official police activities. Police departments are drawing up policies for their use and many already have policies regarding

Skyward Kick Productions/Shutterstock.com

when to and when not to record. A huge issue concerning body cameras is logistics. How much of this data can be stored, where will it be stored, how much will it cost to operate and maintain, how long will it be retained? In addition, the inundation of open public records requests for these videos may place huge strains on resources and records personnel. In any event, body cameras are here and will be a focal issue in American policing for the future.

The APD decree addresses issues when police encounter members of society who suffer from mental illnesses. The decree calls for additional training for officers and specialized training in crisis intervention for some to respond to incidents involving this population. The purpose for this change is to ensure proper referrals are being made and social services are called upon when contact is made with afflicted individuals in a police encounter. The decree calls for a database to be constructed, for management purposes only, so the program and crisis interventions can be evaluated and modified based upon the information collected. Important facts include, but are not limited to, details such as:

- Was force used by the police?
- What is the subject's race, gender, or are they a military veteran?
- Was the subject detained, arrested, or referred to another agency?
- Techniques used?
- Was there follow-up contacts
- What are the caseloads of these specially assigned officer?

Such new directives create an added form of responsibility for law enforcement officers. Compliance with the new directives dealing with mentally ill citizens will require extensive training and resources to accomplish these goals set out to be completed by APD through its agreement with the federal -government. It takes previous police policy to require police officers to have advanced training in responding to calls for service involving the mentally ill. The orders listed in the decree are very similar to The Crisis Intervention Team (CIT) known as the "Memphis

Lightspring/Shutterstock.com

Model." CIT is an original first-responder prototype of crisis intervention with community, health care, and advocacy partnerships spearheaded by first-responding police officers (Dupont, Cochran, & Pillsbury, 2007). CIT is crisis intervention training for law enforcement officers, essentially equipping them to assist individuals suffering from mental illness. The CIT goal is to increase the safety of patrol officers and citizens within the community involved with this population (Watson, Morabito, Draine, & Ottati, 2008).

In line with the progression of early warning systems from Oakland to Albuquerque in 2014, the U.S. Department of Justice emphasizes the use of these data collection systems to monitor officer performance and monitor quality control of officer behavior. Early warning systems are data-driven administrative instruments for classifying law enforcement officers with performance issues or engaging in "at-risk" behavior. The early warning system sets up a data driven tool for management to intercede and use police officer accountability to modify officer behavior (Walker, Alpert, & Kenney, 2000). Early warning systems can guide police supervision for monitoring officer behavior (good or bad) and highlight areas where additional training, discipline or even reward officers for behavior that are in congruence with organizational goals.

Since the inception of consent decrees in 1994, the U.S. Federal Government has selected a variety of American police agencies to employ their form of "best practices." Many of these orders are being implemented nation-wide in an effort to reform police departments through training and policy building. The decrees largely fall back to initial police procedures as set forth by Sir Robert Peel in the 19th century, *"The police are the public, and the public are the police, and ... police should use only the minimum degree of physical force which is necessary on any particular occasion for achieving a police objective."* Many of the issues affecting police-citizen contacts (racial profiling, use of force, early warning systems) reflect perceptions of the stakeholders (public, police, and media) of the police role. Efforts in these decrees ultimately strive to build

a katz/Shutterstock.com

public trust and provide transparency. The implementation of these changes to departmental policy, hopefully, can bridge some of the gaps in perception of law enforcement on either side. As police are mandated to employ new tactics (the advance of body cameras and early warning systems), the idea is to bring police procedure in practice and the perception of the public/media in correspondence, so police objectives can be accomplished with public approval.

Discussion Points

1. The 1994 Violent Crime Control and Law Enforcement Act allows the U.S. Justice Department to investigate police agencies for systemic issues in police behavior and procedure. The investigation are not generally initiated by an acute incident, do you believe this to be true.

   - Do you think an acute, nationally broadcasted incident draws attention to a policy agency and forces the federal government to look deeper into its practices?
   - Are consent decrees and their mandates enough to achieve change in a police agency?

2. "Early Warning Systems" are supervision tools for law enforcement agencies. They collect information regarding police officer performance, positive and negative. In your opinion, do you believe these records systems are "cure all" for past front-line supervision issues?
   - Some officers have higher numbers of documented use of force. Do you think there should be controls in place to investigate officers with higher occurrences or do you think these incidents should be judged on a "case-by-case" basis?
   - How do you think "Early Warning Systems" and their use, affect the workplace environment, especially the interactions between officers and their direct supervisor?

References

Consent Decree, Delphine Allen, et al., *Plaintiffs, v. City of Oakland*, et al., Defendants (March 14, 2003). Retrieved from http://web.law.columbia.edu/sites/default/files/microsites/contract-economic-organization/files/Allen%20v.%20City%20of%20Oakland.pdf

Consent Decree, *United States v. The City of Albuquerque* (2014, 14 November) Retrieved from https://www.justice.gov/sites/default/files/crt/legacy/2014/12/19/apd_settlement_ 11-14-14.pdf

Consent Decree, *United States v. City of New Orleans* (2003, 11 January). Retrieved from http://www.nola.gov/getattachment/NOPD/About-Us/NOPD-Consent-Decree/NOPD- Consent-Decree-7-24-12.pdf/

Consent Decree, *United States v. The State of New Jersey* (1999, 31 December) Retrieved from http://www.njpublicsafety.com/jointapp.htm

Dupont, R., Cochran, S., & Pillsbury, S. (2007). *Crisis intervention team core elements*. Unpublished report, University of Memphis.

Fagan, J., & Geller, A. (2010). Profiling and consent: Stops, searches and seizures after Soto. Paper presented at the fifth Annual Conference on Empirical Legal Studies Paper. http://ssrn.com/abstract=1641326

Iannone, N. F., & Iannone, M. D. (2001). *Supervision of police personnel* (6th ed.). Upper Saddle River, NJ: Prentice-Hall.

Lovett, I. (2014, October 31). "Albuquerque agrees to changes on use of force." *The New York Times*. Retrieved from http://www.nytimes.com/2014/11/01/us/albuquerque-police- shootingssettlement.html?_r=0

Monmaney, T. (2000, December 11). "Rampart-Like Scandal Rocks Oakland Justice System, Politics." *The Los Angeles Times*. Retrieved from http://articles.latimes.com/2000/dec/11/ news/mn-64091

Walker, S., Alpert, G. P., & Kenney, D. J. (2000). Early warning systems for police: Concept, history, and issues. *Police Quarterly, 3*(2), 132–152.

Watson, A. C., Morabito, M. S., Draine, J., & Ottati, V. (2008). Improving police response to persons with mental illness: A multi-level conceptualization of CIT. *International Journal of Law and Psychiatry, 31*(4), 359–368.

Student Name _____ Date _____

Course Section _____ Chapter _____

Many of the police consent decrees set by the U.S. Justice Departments have common themes originating from Sir Robert Peel, to the current introduction of body-worn cameras for account-ability. Discuss the collective themes within the consent decrees in this text.

_____

_____

_____

_____

_____

_____

_____

_____

_____

_____

_____

_____

_____

_____

CONCLUDING STATISTICS

Today we make explicit what was implicit in Garner's analysis, and hold that all claims that law enforcement officers have used excessive force—deadly or not—in the course of an arrest, investigatory stop, or other "seizure" of a free citizen should be analyzed under the 4th Amendment and its "reasonableness" standard, rather than under a "substantive due process" approach.

1000 Words/Shutterstock.com

—Chief Justice William Rehnquist in the *Graham v. Connor* opinion

Key Terms

Reliable Data, Officer Involved Shootings (OIS), Deadly Weapon, Active Attack, Armed, Unarmed, and Suspicious Person

Learning Objectives

After exploring Chapter 8, the student will be able to:

1. Discuss statistics and the different ways data can be interpreted.
2. Describe trends in OIS over the last 10 years.
3. Explain what constitutes an armed suspect.
4. Discuss why unarmed suspects might be the subject of deadly force.
5. Understand why police officers can make a legitimate mistake identifying weapons suspects may have.

According to "Deadly Calls and Fatal Encounters Analysis of U. S. law enforcement line of duty deaths when officers responded to dispatched calls for service and conducted enforcement (2010–2014)":

In 2015, the National Law Enforcement Officers Memorial Fund (NLEOMF) entered into a cooperative agreement with the U.S. Department of Justice COPS office to study officer line-of duty deaths.

Researchers from the NLEOMF, specifically from its Officer Safety, Wellness and Research Department, examined five years of research fatality data and accompanying case files in an effort to determine what information was made available to responding officers when handling calls for service that involved an officer death. The review included 684 total cases.

The largest category of **excluded cases was Traffic related**, with 272.

Officers shot while not responding to a call was the second largest category of excluded cases, totaling 134; consisted of instances, where officers were ambushed in unprovoked attacks, performing tactical operations, serving warrants, and conducting follow-up investigative work.

Calls for officers to respond to a **complaint of a domestic dispute or domestic-related incident** represented the largest single group, 20% of cases.

Disturbance calls were the next largest category, representing 18% of the calls identified in the study.

Officer Needs Assistance calls were the third largest category, accounted for 11% of the calls identified in the study; comprised entirely of priority (emergency) responses to assist fellow officers with rapidly-evolving threats or incidents that required additional manpower to handle the situation.

Calls for service involving **Robbery, Burglary, and Suspicious Persons or Vehicles** represented 9%, 9%, and 8%, respectively.

Of the 91 calls for service cases reviewed, 88 officers died as a result of gunfire. One officer was pushed and fell to his death, another officer was stabbed, and one officer was intentionally struck by a vehicle.

Nearly half, or 45%, of the cases reviewed involved subjects reported to be armed or who had made threats. (The percentage here is important to remember when we review data from *The Washington Post*—compiling information on police shootings in 2015 and 2016).

At least 19% of the cases involved officers responding to a call that involved a subject with a reported mental illness. Close to half of those reportedly mentally ill suspects were either known to be armed or had previously made threats. (The percentage here is important when viewing data from *The Washington Post*).

For the period studied, the team identified 41 cases of self-initiated activity that resulted in a line-of-duty death. The most common type of self-initiated activity found in the study was when officers conducted a traffic stop on a vehicle for a routine violation such as speeding or an equipment violation. This form of contact represented 63% of the overall self-initiated activity examined in the study.

Traffic Stops accounted for 26 (63%) of the 41 self-initiated cases that lead to line–of-duty fatalities. Enforcing traffic regulations represent the most common form of contact the public has with law enforcement.

Officers who were killed before initial contact account for eight (31%) of the 26 *Traffic Stop* cases. These cases involved officers who were shot while still in their patrol vehicles, having just exited their vehicles, or while approaching the window of the suspect's vehicle.

The most frequent time an officer was killed was during their contact and interview of the occupant(s)—accounted for 11 cases (42%). The circumstances with these cases vary, ranging from situations where it was one officer and one subject outside of the vehicle, to multiple officers performing a pat down on a driver while the unattended passenger exited the vehicle and shot at officers.

In examining, the 26 *Traffic Stop* cases, it was found that 69% of the officers were shot after contacting the driver or passengers.

Fifty percent, involved a traffic stop on a vehicle that was occupied by only one person. Two occupants were present during 42% of the traffic stop cases, and 8% of the cases involved three or more occupants. Statistically the stop conducted upon a vehicle containing more than just the driver is no more dangerous than the stop of the single occupant vehicle. Half of the 13 *Traffic Stops* involved vehicles with multiple occupants. In those cases, it was nearly equal as to whether the driver or passenger was the suspected shooter in the officer's death. Passengers were responsible for shooting the officer in seven (54%) of the 13 cases.

All of the cases under the suspicious person/vehicle category involved a single officer approaching a parked vehicle or stopping a suspect who was on foot to determine if they were engaged in criminal activity.

Seven of the twelve cases involved the stop of a suspicious person; where the officer engaged a suspicious person who was walking or in one instance on a bicycle, and effected or attempted to conduct a stop of that person.

Unknowns will always pose stressful situations for law enforcement. These "unknown" encounters take form in suspicious persons and vehicles, observations, not knowing if the other person is carrying a weapon, so forth? This circumstance's revert to the *danger* component of the "working personality," first presented by Skolnick. They create anxiety and contribute to the flow of police-citizen contacts.

a katz/Shutterstock.com

2015 YEAR FATALITY DATA

One hundred twenty-three law enforcement officers lost their lives in the line of duty in 2015. Of those 123 cases, 48 died in traffic-related incidents, 41 officers were shot, and 28 died as a result of other circumstances such as heart attacks, falls, or job-related illnesses as a result of the 9/11 rescue and recovery operations. Six were killed in a bomb explosion while conducting counter-terrorism operations abroad.

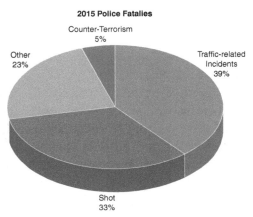

2015 Police Fatalies

Counter-Terrorism
5%

Other
23%

Traffic-related
Incidents
39%

Shot
33%

Courtesy of Jeffrey Schwartz/Michael Virga.

FIREARMS-RELATED FATALITIES

In looking at the 41 officers shot, 39 were intentionally shot by suspects while two officers were inadvertently shot during training. The most common type of activity involved in those fatal encounters was the self-initiated traffic stop. Seven of the 39 officers feloniously shot were killed while conducting traffic stops.

Six officers were shot and killed in ambush-style attacks in a variety of calls for service and circumstances. Of those ambush-style attacks, four appear to have been perpetrated against unsuspecting officers as they were seated in their cars, or engaged in nonenforcement activity.

In eight of the incidents in which officers were shot and killed, domestic violence or domestic-related disputes were the overt or underlying cause of the encounter between law enforcement and the suspect.

Five of these fatal cases stemmed from officers responding to a domestic disturbance call, while one case involved an officer serving a "domestic injunction," another officer was killed

lev radin/Shutterstock.com

as he responded to a domestic-related *Shots Fired* call and a detective was shot while guarding an injured prisoner charged with a domestic-related offense at a hospital.

Five officers were shot and killed while investigating suspicious persons. Four officers were killed while attempting to arrest suspects for a variety of crimes, such as robbery or serving an arrest warrant.

The 123 law enforcement deaths in 2015, which includes federal agents, correctional officers, and territorial and tribal agencies, represented a 1% increase over 2014 and a 9% increase over 2013.

There have also been studies that, contrary to this report's findings, indicated that officers are more likely to be killed or injured while responding to robberies and burglaries compared to domestic violence calls. In a study of 771 law enforcement deaths from 1996–2009, "When Officers Die: Understanding Deadly Domestic Violence Call for Service," *The Police Chief* magazine, by Shannon Meyer, PhD, and Randall H. Carroll, the researchers concluded that there was a myth regarding the greater danger posed by domestic violence calls and their research actually supports a different set of call types being more dangerous.

Analysis of the fatality data by the Department of Justice (DOJ) in 2010 to 2014, shows that domestic-related calls for service resulted in 22% of officer fatalities within the 5-year study period; more than any other type of call.

Summary

Calls related to domestic disputes and domestic-related incidents, represented the highest number of fatal types of calls for service, and were also the underlying cause of several other calls for service that resulted in law enforcement fatalities.

Calls that were classified as disturbances, such as disorderly persons, noise complaints, or nuisance violations were the next largest category of call type in which responding officers were killed, accounting for 18% of the total call type analyzed.

In 45% of all the cases in which officers were responding to a dispatched call for service that ended in a fatality, the officers had been advised the suspect(s) might be armed, or they had made prior threats. This number represents calls from all of the categories.

At least 19% of the suspects in the cases examined were reportedly suffering from a mental illness.

Sixty-three percent of officers who were killed while engaged in self-initiated action were conducting a traffic stop for vehicle enforcement.

The next largest categories of activity were officers stopping suspicious persons or suspicious vehicles representing 17% and 12%, respectively.

Fifty percent of the fatal cases involving traffic stops involved only one occupant in the stopped vehicle.

In 42% of the fatal traffic stop cases, the officers were assaulted while speaking to the occupants of the car.

Totals

From 2011 to 2017, total officers killed on duty, according to the Law Enforcement Officers Memorial Fund research:

Year	Total Fatalities
2011	185
2012	141
2013	120
2014	148
2015	160
2016	159
2017	129

From 2008 to 2017 the totals for deaths, assaults and assaults with injuries in law enforcement:

Year	Deaths*	Assaults**	Assaults with Injuries**
2008	159	61,087	15,554
2009	139	57,268	14,948
2010	171	56,491	14,744
2011	185	55,631	14,798

Year	Deaths*	Assaults**	Assaults with Injuries**
2012	141	53,867	14,678
2013	120	49,851	14,565
2014	148	49,725	13,824
2015	160	51,548	14,453
2016	159	58,627	16,677
2017	129	N/A***	N/A***
Average Per Year	**151**	**49,409**	**13,424**

* *Source:* National Law Enforcement Officers Memorial Fund
** FBI/LEOKA Data
*** LEOKA Report Available Fall 2017
Updated March 15, 2018

- There are more than **900,000** sworn law enforcement officers now serving in the United States, which is the highest figure ever. About **12 percent** of those are female.
- According to the preliminary FBI's *Uniform Crime Report* from January to June 2016-2017, an estimated **442,824** Violent Crimes occurred nationwide, a decrease of **0.8%**.
- Crime fighting has taken its toll. Since the first recorded police death in 1791, there have been over **21,000** law enforcement officers killed in the line of duty. Currently, there are **21,541** names engraved on the walls of the National Law Enforcement Officers Memorial.
- A total of **1,511** law enforcement officers died in the line of duty during the past 10 years, an average of one death every **58** hours or **151** per year. There were **129** law enforcement officers killed in the line of duty in 2017.
- There have been **58,627** assaults against law enforcement officers in 2016, resulting in **16,677** injuries.

- The **1920s** were the deadliest decade in law enforcement history, when a total of **2,480** officers died, or an average of almost **248** each year. The deadliest year in law enforcement history was **1930**, when **310** officers were killed. That figure dropped dramatically in the **1990s**, to an average of **162** per year.
- The deadliest day in law enforcement history was September 11, 2001, when **72** officers were killed while responding to the terrorist attacks on America.
- New York City has lost more officers in the line of duty than any other department, with **833** deaths. Texas has lost **1,731** officers, more than any other state. The state with the fewest deaths is Vermont, with **23**.
- There are **1,135** federal officers listed on the Memorial, as well as **707** correctional officers and **41** military law enforcement officers.
- There are **328** female officers listed on the Memorial; **nine** female officers were killed in 2017.
- During the past ten years, more incidents that resulted in felonious fatalities occurred on **Friday** than any other day of the week. The fewest number of felonious incidents occurred on **Tuesday**.

2018 by NLEOMF
http://www.nleomf.org/facts/enforcement/

Preliminary 2018 Law Enforcement Officer Fatalities
January 1 through October 14, 2018 vs. January 1 through October 14, 2017

	2018	2017	% Change
Total Fatalities	110	109	+1%
Firearms-related	44	39	+13%

Please note: These numbers reflect total officer fatalities comparing January 1 through October 14, 2018 vs. January 1 through October 14, 2017

http://www.nleomf.org/facts/officer-fatalities-data/

Over the Past Decade (2008-2017)

	2008	2009	2010	2011	2012	2013	2014	2015	2016	2017	Total
Aircraft Accident	3	4	2	1	3	1	0	3	1	2	**20**
Auto Crash	45	39	51	44	27	29	33	36	29	31	**364**
Beaten	1	0	2	3	2	0	0	1	1	6	**16**
Bicycle Accident	0	0	1	0	0	0	0	0	0	0	**1**
Boating Accident	0	0	1	0	1	0	0	0	0	2	**4**
Bomb-Related Incident	2	0	0	1	0	1	0	6	0	0	**10**
Drowned	1	0	3	4	1	2	2	1	2	5	**21**
Electrocuted	1	0	0	1	0	1	0	1	0	0	**4**
Fall	0	0	1	4	4	6	0	2	2	0	**19**
Horse-Related Accident	0	0	0	0	1	0	0	0	1	0	**2**

(Continued)

(Continued)

	2008	2009	2010	2011	2012	2013	2014	2015	2016	2017	Total
Job-Related Illness	34	32	30	33	25	27	45	50	28	21	**325**
Motorcycle Crash	9	3	6	5	8	5	6	6	10	5	**63**
Poisoned	1	0	0	0	0	0	0	0	0	0	**1**
Shot	41	50	60	73	50	34	50	43	67	46	**514**
Stabbed	2	0	0	2	5	2	0	0	1	1	**13**
Strangled	0	0	0	1	0	0	2	0	1	0	**4**
Struck by Falling Object	0	0	0	0	0	0	0	0	0	0	**0**
Struck by Train	1	0	0	2	0	0	0	0	0	0	**3**
Struck by Vehicle	18	11	14	10	14	12	10	11	16	10	**126**
Terrorist Attack	0	0	0	1	0	0	0	0	0	0	**1**
TOTAL	159	139	171	185	141	120	148	160	159	129	**1511**

Addition AL Data	2008	2009	2010	2011	2012	2013	2014	2015	2016	2017	Total
Female Officers Killed	15	4	8	12	13	7	7	15	7	9	97
Officers Killed Wearing Body Armor	62%	66%	63%	63%	51%	51%	68%	61%	63%	55%	

Source: https://ucr.fbi.gov/leoka/2017/topic-pages/felonious_topic_page_-2017

Overview

In 2015, 41 law enforcement officers died from injuries incurred in the line of duty during felonious incidents

- Line-of-duty deaths occurred in 21 states and in Puerto Rico.
- By region, 19 officers were feloniously killed in the South, 9 officers in the West, 5 officers in the Midwest, 4 officers in the Northeast, and 4 officers in Puerto Rico.

Of the officers feloniously killed, 24 were employed by city police departments, including 10 who were members of law enforcement agencies in cities with 250,000 or more inhabitants.

Circumstances

- 8 officers died as a result of investigating suspicious persons or circumstances.
- 7 officers were killed as a result of tactical situations (barricaded offender, hostage taking, high-risk entry, etc.).
- 6 officers were fatally injured during traffic pursuits or stops.
- 5 officers died as a result of arrest situations.
- 4 officers were killed in ambush situations.
- 3 officers who died had responded to disturbance calls.
- 3 officers were killed in unprovoked attacks.
- 2 officers were fatally injured while handling, transporting, or maintaining custody of prisoners.
- 2 officers were handling persons with mental illness.
- 1 officer was conducting an investigative activity (surveillance, search, interview, etc.).

Profile of alleged known assailants

In 2015, 37 alleged offenders were identified in connection with the 41 law enforcement officers feloniously killed. Of those offenders, the following characteristics are known:

- The average age of the alleged offenders was 33 years old.
- The average height was 5 feet 11 inches tall, and the average weight was 188 pounds.

- All 37 alleged offenders were male.
- 17 of the alleged offenders were Black/African American, 16 were White, 1 was American Indian/Alaska Native, and race was not reported for 3 offenders.
- 9 of the alleged offenders were under judicial supervision at the time of the incidents.
- 10 of the alleged offenders were under the influence of a controlled substance at the time of the fatal incidents.
- 6 of the alleged offenders were under the influence of alcohol or were intoxicated at the time of the fatal incidents.
- 31 of the alleged offenders had prior criminal arrests.

Overview

- In 2015, the FBI collected assault data from 11,961 law enforcement agencies that employed 507,852 officers. These officers provided service to more than 241.3 million persons, or 75.1 percent of the nation's population.
- Law enforcement agencies reported that 50,212 officers were assaulted while performing their duties in 2015.
- The rate of officer assaults in 2015 was 9.9 per 100 sworn officers.

Circumstances

Of all officers who were assaulted in 2015:

- 32.4 percent were responding to disturbance calls.
- 15.6 percent were attempting other arrests.
- 12.2 percent were handling, transporting, or maintaining custody of prisoners.

In 2016, 66 law enforcement officers died from injuries incurred in the line of duty during felonious incidents.

- Line-of-duty deaths occurred in 29 states and in Puerto Rico.
- By region, 30 officers were feloniously killed in the South, 17 officers in the West, 13 officers in the Midwest, 4 officers in the Northeast, and 2 officers in Puerto Rico.

Of the officers feloniously killed, 41 were employed by city police departments, including 12 who were members of law enforcement agencies in cities with 250,000 or more inhabitants.

Circumstances

- 17 officers were killed in ambush situations.
- 13 officers who died had responded to disturbance calls.
- 9 officers died as a result of investigating suspicious persons or circumstances.
- 9 officers died as a result of arrest situations.
- 6 officers were killed as a result of tactical situations (barricaded offender, hostage taking, high-risk entry, etc.).
- 5 officers were conducting investigative activities (surveillance, search, interview, etc.).
- 4 officers were fatally injured during traffic pursuits/stops.
- 3 officers were killed in unprovoked attacks.

Weapons

- Of the officers killed in 2016, most (62) were killed with firearms. Of these, 37 were killed with handguns.
- 14 officers fired their weapons; 11 officers attempted to fire their weapons.
- 3 officers had their weapons stolen.
- 19 officers were slain with firearms when they were 0-5 feet from the offenders.

Profile of alleged known assailants

In 2016, 59 alleged offenders were identified in connection with the 66 law enforcement officers feloniously killed. Of those offenders, the following characteristics are known:

- The average age of the alleged offenders was 34 years old.
- The average height was 5 feet 10 inches tall, and the average weight was 187 pounds.

- 55 alleged offenders were male. The gender of 4 offenders was not reported.
- 32 of the alleged offenders were White, 15 were Black/African American, 1 was American Indian/Alaska Native, and race was not reported for 11 offenders.
- 14 of the alleged offenders were under judicial supervision at the times of the incidents.
- 14 of the alleged offenders were under the influence of a controlled substance at the times of the fatal incidents.
- 2 of the alleged offenders were under the influence of alcohol or were intoxicated at the times of the fatal incidents.
- 45 of the alleged offenders had prior criminal arrests.

Overview

In 2016, the FBI collected assault data from 12,421 law enforcement agencies that employed 586,446 officers. These officers provided service to more than 268.2 million persons, or 83.0 percent of the nation's population.

- Law enforcement agencies reported that 57,180 officers were assaulted while performing their duties in 2016.
- The rate of officer assaults in 2016 was 9.8 per 100 sworn officers.

Circumstances

Of all officers who were assaulted in 2016:

- 32.2 percent were responding to disturbance calls (family quarrels, bar fights, etc.).
- 15.6 percent were attempting other arrests.
- 12.6 percent were handling, transporting, or maintaining custody of prisoners. (Based on

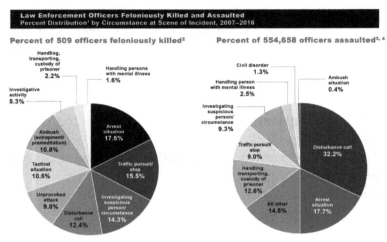

Law Enforcement Officers Feloniously Killed and Assaulted
Percent Distribution[1] by Circumstance at Scene of Incident, 2007–2016

[1] Because of rounding, the percentages may not add to 100.0.

[2] The circumstance category of "All other" does not apply to the data collected for law enforcement officers feloniously killed.

[3] The circumstance categories of "Ambush (entrapment/premeditation)" and "Unprovoked attack" are included in the "Ambush situation" data collected for law enforcement officers assaulted.

[4] The circumstance categories of "Investigative activity" and "Tactical situation" are included in the "All other" data collected for law enforcement officers assaulted.

Source: https://ucr.fbi.gov/leoka/2016/figures-and-maps/figure-4

Overview

In 2017, 46 law enforcement officers died from injuries incurred in the line of duty during felonious incidents.

- Line-of-duty deaths occurred in 25 states and in Puerto Rico.
- By region, 24 officers were feloniously killed in the South, 11 officers in the Midwest, 6 officers in the West, 3 officers in the Northeast, and 2 officers in Puerto Rico. Of the officers feloniously killed, 26 were employed by city police departments, including 8 who were members of law enforcement agencies in cities with 250,000 or more inhabitants.

Circumstances encountered by victim officer upon arrival at the scene of the incident

- 21 officers died as a result of investigative or enforcement activities.
    - 6 were investigating suspicious persons or circumstances.
    - 6 were involved in tactical situations.

- 3 were conducting traffic violation stops.
- 2 were performing investigative activities.
- 1 was investigating a drug-related matter.
- 1 was investigating a motor vehicle crash.
- 1 was conducting a felony traffic stop.
- 1 was interacting with a wanted person.
- 6 officers were involved in pursuits.
  - 4 were involved in foot pursuits.
  - 2 were involved in vehicular pursuits.
- 5 officers were ambushed (entrapment/premeditation).
- 4 officers were involved in arrest situations.
  - 3 were verbally advising offenders during the arrest situations.
  - 1 was attempting to control/handcuff/restrain the offender(s) during the arrest situation.
- 3 officers were involved in unprovoked attacks.
- 2 officers were assisting other law enforcement officers.
  - 1 was deploying or providing equipment such as traffic cones or flares.
  - 1 was assisting another officer with a vehicular pursuit.
- 2 officers responded to crimes in progress.
  - 1 was a robbery in progress.
  - 1 was a report of a shooting or shots being fired.
- 1 officer was on administrative assignment and was performing a prisoner transport.
- 1 officer responded to a disorder/disturbance and encountered a domestic disturbance upon arrival.
- 1 officer encountered or was assisting an emotionally disturbed person.

Profile of alleged known assailants

In 2017, 44 alleged offenders were identified in connection with the 46 law enforcement officers feloniously killed. Of those offenders, the following characteristics are known:

- The average age of the alleged offenders was 36 years old.
- The average height was 5 feet 10 inches tall, and the average weight was 184 pounds.

Table 23

Law Enforcement Officers Feloniously Killed

Circumstance at Scene of Incident, 2006–2015

Circumstance		Total	2006	2007	2008	2009	2010	2011	2012	2013	2014	2015
Number of victim officers	Total	491	48	58	41	48	56	72	49	27	51	41
Disturbance call	Total	58	8	5	1	6	6	10	4	4	11	3
	Disturbance (bar fight, person with firearm, etc.)	37	6	3	1	4	2	5	3	3	10	0
	Domestic disturbance (family quarrel, etc.)	21	2	2	0	2	4	5	1	1	1	3
Arrest situation	Total	92	12	17	9	8	14	10	7	6	4	5
	Burglary in progress/ pursuing burglary suspect	9	0	1	2	1	3	0	1	0	0	1

Circumstance		Total	2006	2007	2008	2009	2010	2011	2012	2013	2014	2015
	Robbery in progress/pursuing robbery suspect	38	6	7	1	3	6	6	3	3	0	3
	Drug-related matter	8	2	1	1	0	1	0	2	0	1	0
	Attempting other arrest	37	4	8	5	4	4	4	1	3	3	1
Civil disorder (mass disobedience, riot, etc.)	Total	0	0	0	0	0	0	0	0	0	0	0
Handling, transporting, custody of prisoner	Total	12	1	1	1	2	1	1	3	0	0	2
Investigating suspicious person/circumstance	Total	70	6	4	7	4	8	12	8	5	8	8
Ambush (entrapment/premeditation)	Total	36	1	9	1	6	2	2	3	1	7	4
Unprovoked attack	Total	56	9	7	5	9	11	6	1	4	1	3

(Continued)

(Continued)

Circumstance		Total	2006	2007	2008	2009	2010	2011	2012	2013	2014	2015
Investigative activity (surveillance, search, interview, etc.)	Total	**22**	0	1	2	0	2	4	6	1	5	1
Handling person with mental illness	Total	**9**	1	0	0	0	0	0	3	0	3	2
Traffic pursuit/stop	Total	**83**	8	11	8	8	9	14	9	2	8	6
	Felony vehicle stop	**29**	0	5	5	2	3	7	5	0	1	1
	Traffic violation stop	**54**	8	6	3	6	6	7	4	2	7	5
Tactical situation (barricaded offender, hostage taking, high-risk entry, etc.)	Total	**53**	2	3	7	5	3	13	5	4	4	7

Source: https://ucr.fbi.gov/leoka/2015/tables/table_23_leos_fk_circumstance_at_scene_of_incident_2006-2015.xls

Table 73

Law Enforcement Officers Assaulted

Circumstance at Scene of Incident by Population Group and Percent Cleared,[1,2] 2015

Circumstance	Total	Percent cleared	Group I (cities 250,000 and over)		Group II (cities 100,000—249,999)		Group III (cities 50,000—99,999)		Group IV (cities 25,000—49,999)		Group V (cities 10,000—24,999)		Group VI (cities under 10,000)		Metropolitan counties		Nonmetropolitan counties	
			Total	Percent cleared	Total	Percent cleared	Total	Percent cleared	Total	Percent cleared	Total	Percent cleared	Total	Percent cleared	Total	Percent cleared	Total	Percent cleared
Number of victim officers	**50,212**	**89.3**	**12,799**	**91.2**	**6,496**	**88.7**	**6,100**	**89.7**	**4,122**	**87.0**	**3,784**	**89.9**	**3,865**	**84.2**	**11,102**	**89.9**	**1,944**	**88.5**
Disturbance call	16,256	91.0	3,756	93.1	2,554	90.5	2,364	92.3	1,435	89.9	1,366	90.9	1,253	83.7	2,997	91.2	531	93.4
Burglary in progress/pursuing burglary suspect	840	86.8	260	83.5	144	90.3	108	81.5	74	86.5	48	83.3	35	91.4	159	93.1	12	83.3
Robbery in progress/pursuing robbery suspect	398	87.4	110	89.1	45	91.1	57	77.2	37	83.8	23	91.3	37	91.9	85	89.4	4	75.0
Attempting other arrest	7,820	92.0	1,820	93.7	1,079	88.2	1,033	91.0	739	87.7	726	94.4	701	89.7	1,405	95.7	317	91.5
Civil disorder (mass disobedience, riot, etc.)	677	73.3	204	67.2	86	97.7	78	97.4	36	86.1	42	81.0	50	68.0	148	52.0	33	69.7
Handling, transporting, custody of prisoner	**6,143**	89.6	1,338	95.2	517	90.7	651	87.7	486	83.5	389	89.7	382	88.7	2,059	89.3	321	81.0

(Continued)

Circumstance	Total	Percent cleared	Group I (cities 250,000 and over)		Group II (cities 100,000—249,999)		Group III (cities 50,000—99,999)		Group IV (cities 25,000—49,999)		Group V (cities 10,000—24,999)		Group VI (cities under 10,000)		Metropolitan counties		Nonmetropolitan counties	
			Total	Percent cleared	Total	Percent cleared	Total	Percent cleared	Total	Percent cleared	Total	Percent cleared	Total	Percent cleared	Total	Percent cleared	Total	Percent cleared
Investigating suspicious person/circumstance	4,647	88.0	1,368	89.5	650	84.8	543	86.9	405	86.4	312	86.9	380	86.1	847	89.6	142	95.1
Ambush situation	240	75.4	119	79.0	24	75.0	11	54.5	8	62.5	9	88.9	9	66.7	41	65.9	19	89.5
Handling person with mental illness	1,710	81.3	356	87.1	192	82.3	176	74.4	139	75.5	136	80.9	212	67.0	441	86.2	58	93.1
Traffic pursuit/stop	3,972	87.5	966	87.8	519	85.0	401	89.3	301	86.4	288	89.2	371	85.4	892	89.2	234	85.0
All other	7,509	88.4	2,502	90.6	686	88.2	678	89.2	462	85.7	445	86.5	435	79.3	2,028	88.7	273	85.7

[1]Offenses reported to the national UCR Program can be cleared by arrest or exceptional means (when elements beyond law enforcement's control prevent the agency from placing formal charges against the offender).

[2]Percent cleared may include clearances for previous years' offenses.

Source: https://ucr.fbi.gov/leoka/2015/tables/table_23_leos_fk_circumstance_at_scene_of_incident_2006-2015.xls

Republished with permission of The Wall Street Journal, from The Wall Street Journal, "The Myths of Black Lives Matter," Heather MacDonald, February 12, 2016; permission conveyed through Copyright Clearance Center, Inc.

- All 44 alleged offenders were male.
- 26 of the alleged offenders were White, 16 were Black/African American, 1 was American Indian/Alaska Native, and 1 was Asian.
- 18 of the alleged offenders were under judicial supervision at the time of the incidents.
- 5 of the alleged offenders were under the influence of a controlled substance at the time of the fatal incidents.
- 1 of the alleged offenders was under the influence of alcohol or was intoxicated at the time of the fatal incident.
- 40 of the alleged offenders had prior criminal arrests.

Overview

- In 2017, the FBI collected assault data from 12,198 law enforcement agencies that employed 596,604 officers. These officers provided service to more than 269.6 million people, or 82.8 percent of the nation's population.
- Law enforcement agencies reported that 60,211 officers were assaulted while performing their duties in 2017.
- The rate of officer assaults in 2017 was 10.1 per 100 sworn officers.

Circumstances

Of all officers who were assaulted in 2017:

- 30.4 percent were responding to disturbance calls (family quarrels, bar fights, etc.).
- 15.8 percent were attempting other arrests.
- 12.4 percent were handling, transporting, or maintaining custody of prisoners.

By Heather MacDonald
    July 9, 2016 2:04 p.m. ET
    1051 COMMENTS
    Editor's Note: Originally published February 11, 2016

A television ad for Hillary Clinton's presidential campaign now airing in South Carolina shows the candidate declaring that "too many encounters with law enforcement end tragically." She later adds: "We have to face up to the hard truth of injustice and systemic racism."

Her Democratic presidential rival, Bernie Sanders, met with the Rev. Al Sharpton on Wednesday. Mr. Sanders then tweeted that "As President, let me be very clear that no one will fight harder to end racism and reform our broken criminal justice system than I will." And he appeared on the TV talk show "The View" saying, "It is not acceptable to see unarmed people being shot by police officers."

Apparently, the Black Lives Matter movement has convinced Democrats and progressives that there is an epidemic of racist white police officers killing young black men. Such rhetoric is going to heat up as Mrs. Clinton and Mr. Sanders court minority voters before February 27 South Carolina primary.

But what if the Black Lives Matter movement is based on fiction? Not just the fictional account of the 2014 police shooting of Michael Brown in Ferguson, MO., but the utter misrepresentation of police shootings generally.

To judge from Black Lives Matter protesters and their media and political allies, you would think that killer cops pose the biggest threat to young black men today. But this perception, like almost everything else that many people think they know about fatal police shootings, is wrong.

The Washington Post has been gathering data on fatal police shootings over the past year and a half to correct acknowledged deficiencies in federal tallies. The emerging data should open many eyes.

For starters, fatal police shootings make up a much larger proportion of white and Hispanic homicide deaths than black homicide deaths. According to the Post database, in 2015 officers killed 662 whites and Hispanics, and 258 blacks. (The overwhelming majority of all those police-shooting victims were attacking the officer, often with a gun.) Using the 2014, homicide numbers as an approximation of 2015s, those 662 white and Hispanic victims of police shootings would make up 12% of all white and Hispanic homicide deaths. That is three times the proportion of black deaths that result from police shootings.

The lower proportion of black deaths due to police shootings can be attributed to the lamentable black-on-black homicide rate. There were 6,095 black homicide deaths in 2014—the most recent year for which such data are available—compared with 5,397 homicide deaths for whites and Hispanics combined. Almost all of those black homicide victims had black killers.

Police officers—of all races—are also disproportionately endangered by black assailants. Over the past decade, according to Federal Bureau of Investigation (FBI) data, 40% of cop killers have been black. Officers are killed by blacks at a rate 2.5 times higher than the rate at which blacks are killed by police.

Some may find evidence of police bias in the fact that blacks make up 26% of the policeshooting victims, compared with their 13% representation in the national population. But as residents of poor black neighborhoods know too well, violent crimes are disproportionately committed by blacks. According to the Bureau of Justice Statistics, blacks were charged with 62% of all robberies, 57% of murders, and 45% of assaults in the 75 largest U.S. counties in 2009, though they made up roughly 15% of the population there.

Such a concentration of criminal violence in minority communities means that officers will be disproportionately confronting armed and often resisting suspects in those communities, raising officers' own risk of using lethal force.

The Black Lives Matter movement claims that white officers are especially prone to shooting innocent blacks due to racial bias, but this too is a myth. A March 2015, Justice Department report on the Philadelphia Police Department found that black and Hispanic officers were much more likely than white officers to shoot blacks based on "threat misperception"—that is, the mistaken belief that a civilian is armed.

A 2015 study by University of Pennsylvania criminologist Greg Ridgeway, formerly acting director of the National Institute of Justice, found that, at a crime scene where gunfire is involved, black officers in the New York City Police Department were 3.3 times more likely to discharge their weapons than other officers at the scene.

The Black Lives Matter movement has been stunningly successful in changing the subject from the realities of violent crime. The world knows the name of Michael Brown but not Tyshawn Lee, a 9-year-old black child lured into an alley and killed by gang members in Chicago last fall. Tyshawn was one of dozens of black children gunned down in America last year. The Baltimore Sun reported on January 1: "Blood was shed in Baltimore at an unprecedented pace in 2015, with mostly young, black men shot to death in a near-daily crush of violence."

Those were black lives that mattered, and it is a scandal that outrage is heaped less on the dysfunctional culture that produces so many victims than on the police officers who try to protect them.

Ms. Mac Donald is the Thomas W. Smith fellow at the Manhattan Institute and author of "The War on Cops," forthcoming in July from Encounter Books.

PERSPECTIVE ON THE KILLING OF UNARMED PERSONS

Probably no single force event raises more questions, inflames more protests, and generates more misperceptions than the police killing of an unarmed suspect.

According to "In Context: Understanding Police Killings of Unarmed Citizens" by Shelby:

The killing of unarmed individuals compelled examination because that seemed in the popular mind to be the deadly force area most likely to harbor unacceptable police conduct. Other sources assembling data on the subject, such as *The Washington Post*, Shelby writes, were good at "counting the high-level number of people killed by police" but tended to ignore important facts, "such as *why* the decedent was killed."

In short, "There was no context . . . which makes it impossible for the police to learn from mistakes and build on strengths" and for the public to better understand officers' deadly force decisions.

"[T]his lack of research and analysis," notes former Cmsr. Lawrence Murphy of the Nassau County (NY) PD in a foreword to the study, "has allowed the media to run unchecked with a narrative that claims the police are killing unarmed people of color at an alarming rate."

The task Selby and his co-authors set "was to search as far and wide as possible to get context""–from witness statements, audio and video recordings, medical examiner and coroner reports, grand jury hearings, police accounts, toxicology reports, news stories, and other publicly available information.

In the end, they documented and detailed what they believe is every so-called "unarmed" fatality at the hands of Law Enforcement Officer (LEOs) in the United States last year—153 in all.

The cases were not "cherry-picked" to support a point of view, Selby insists. The objective was "to be objective," not to "defend officers indiscriminately." Indeed, the researchers concluded that while most controversial killings were fully justified, in some cases the cops were "just plain wrong."

The 153 fatalities, one by one, month by month throughout the year are detailed. For each, the basic circumstances are reconstructed and then the three authors, each drawing on his own policing experience and other relevant expertise, offer observations on the human dynamics and other influential factors that shaped the encounter.

Among the important findings are these:

1. **The cause of these deaths is often not shooting**
   "Belying a powerful media narrative to the contrary," the authors write, "nearly half of the 153 cases involved no shooting, and the decedent died by other cause." Most often, that cause was "an abnormal reaction or complication after officers deployed tools or techniques with the intent of using nondeadly force."
   In other words, involved officers were trying to *avoid* the likelihood of an unarmed suspect's death or serious bodily harm. Even in cases where there were shootings, 27% of the time officers deployed a TASER before going to a firearm.

2. **Police are not targeting minorities for special attention**
   "Media narratives that the police are more likely to target black people in deadly encounters are, statistically speaking, demonstrably wrong," Selby writes.
   Contacts with about 70% of unarmed people who died at the hands of police were initiated by citizens complaining that the subjects were posing some danger to the community, the research shows. Even when police do select their targets, that group "does not vary significantly from the racial composition" of the group collectively identified by citizen complaints.
   But the authors state they could not determine, given the data at hand, whether the police treat white people differently once an event begins. "This is a separate question that must be answered, using a much wider array of contextual data," they note.
   The study points out: "[T]he majority of those ultimately killed by police were themselves engaging in behavior that was criminal (which brought the police to the scene) and posing direct threats to law enforcement or other civilians (which most often precipitated the use of force)." All told, 70% of the unarmed subjects killed "were in the process of violent crimes or property crimes at the time of their fatal encounter with police."

3. **Drugs and mental illness are strong factors**
   "While media, political, and activist attention has been centered on race, in our research the most significant findings by group of decedents involved illegal drug use and mental health issues," the study states. "Almost half the cases, 46%, involved suspected or proved acute narcotic intoxication and/or mental health crises–from a public health standpoint, an astonishing number."
   Unarmed mentally ill people accounted for 19% of the death toll, while 27% were under the influence of acute narcotic intoxication, meth-induced psychosis, Phencyclidine (PCP), or synthetic drugs. In almost every acute drug case, the researchers report, the "decedents fought with the police and others, and

after they were immobilized, suffered heart failure or heart attacks." In nearly 70% of these cases, officers had used tools "intended to be non-deadly."

4. **There is no systematic illegal use of force by American LEOs**

   In their case-by-case analysis, Selby and his colleagues did find more uses of force that they considered questionable than they expected; about 7% of cases "appeared to involve the unjustified use of deadly force by a police officer."

5. **Officers need to build confidence with hand-on techniques**

   Taking what they admit is a controversial position, the authors argue that officers today may be too quick to use control tools like Conductive Electronic Weapons or Oleoresin Capsicum (CEWs or OC), instead of applying hands-on tactics to subdue some unarmed subjects. The researchers say they were "struck by several incidents . . . that might have easily been addressed [successfully] by going hands-on" instead of resorting quickly to a less-lethal or deadly weapon. Sometimes unarmed "rowdy" people need to be "grabbed and secured," even though they may fight in response, Selby writes. "Officers should be expected not to treat every assault as a life-and-death situation, officers need to know how to physically control someone."

   "Over-reliance on TASER or pepper spray has its own set of dangers. Officers who do not practice fighting . . . risk being surprised by physicality, over-powered or out-maneuvered by those they confront . . . [T]hose who practice their physical skills are mentally and physically [better] prepared."

6. **Expansion of police video is urgently needed**

   In only 26% of the 153 "unarmed" cases studied were video recordings available, and often these came from bystanders or nonpolice surveillance cameras. Aggressive efforts of agencies "to expand their video coverage . . . can't be delayed any longer," the study warns.

   While video is by no means a panacea, without it officers are not protected from [false] accusations, and the agency loses community trust," the study states. Within 3 years, the researchers predict, "if video is unavailable, the police will be disbelieved on principle."

7. **Police must release more data—and soon**

   "The key finding that can drive the greatest impact from a policy perspective was informed by the very difficulty we faced finding data to support the police account of incidents," the researchers assert.

   "Law enforcement agencies simply must find better ways to release more data . . . more quickly. There is a significant public interest in this data, and the public has a legitimate right to understand how it is being policed ...."

"Police agencies failing to release information look like they're hiding something, [while] agencies that release data when they have it are invested with the trust of their communities ...."

"Release early, release often, put a face to the investigation, and don't ever appear to be hiding."

8. **A reminder, to ward off complacency . . .**

To correct media and protester implications and as a reminder for officers, Selby and his team offer this nugget of reality: "It is a mistake to equate 'unarmed' to always mean 'not dangerous.'"

Seven out of 10 unarmed people killed by police during the study period "were in the middle of committing crimes such as robbery, carjacking, assault, serious destruction of property, or burglary." More than one-quarter had already assaulted and injured civilians in violent attacks, and two had committed murders before police cut short their crimes–"this despite the fact that the decedent was not armed."

From Force Science Institute Limited. Copyright © 2016. http://www.forcescience.org. Reprinted by permission.

Gender

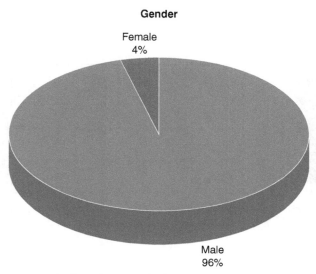

Male	948
Female	42

Courtesy of Jeffrey Schwartz/Michael Virga.

Armed or Unarmed

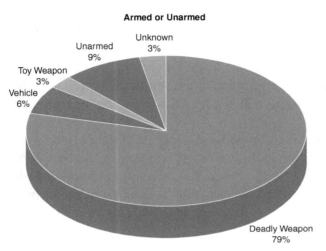

Armed or Unarmed

Deadly Weapon	782
Vehicle	54
Toy Weapon	34
Unarmed	93
Unknown	27

Courtesy of Jeffrey Schwartz/Michael Virga.

Race

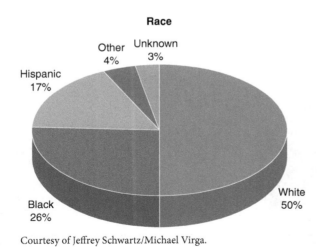

Race

White	494
Black	258
Hispanic	172
Other	38
Unknown	28

Courtesy of Jeffrey Schwartz/Michael Virga.

Signs of Mental Illness

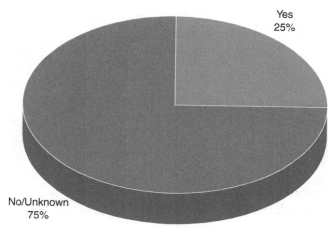

Signs of Mental Illness

Yes
25%

No/Unknown
75%

Courtesy of Jeffrey Schwartz/Michael Virga.

Yes	250
No/Unknown	740

Threat Level

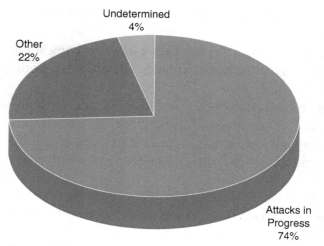

Undetermined
4%

Other
22%

Attacks in
Progress
74%

Courtesy of Jeffrey Schwartz/Michael Virga.

Attacks in Progress	730
Other	216
Undetermined	44

Seventy-seven percent of police shootings, according to *The Washington Post* in 2015, the suspect were engaging in an attack at the time of the shooting. Eighty-two percent were armed with a dangerous weapon.

494—52% white
257—27% black
The Washington Post police shooting data 2016:
963 total
466—48% white
234—24% black
99% armed (54 Unknown not counted, 51 unarmed)
The Washington Post police shooting data 2017:
987 total
458 – 46% white
223 – 23% black
99% armed (26 Unknown not counted, 68 unarmed)
The Washington Post police shooting data 2018:
756 total as of October 15, 2018
289 – 38% white
138 – 18% black
99% armed (45 Unknown not counted, 35 unarmed)
*Accuracy of data, definitions of armed or unarmed, incident type are all in question

From 2005 to 2014, 47 officers were criminally charged in fatal shootings, with 15 of those cases involving video evidence.

In 2015, 18 officers were criminally charged, with 10 of the cases involving some form of a video recording (police dash cameras, body cameras, citizen video, commercial business surveillance, etc.).

Between 2005 and April 2017, 80 officers had been arrested on murder or manslaughter charges for on-duty shootings. During that 12-year span, 35% were convicted, while the rest were pending or not convicted, according to work by Philip Stinson, an associate professor of criminal justice at Bowling Green State University in Ohio.

There is extreme debate about the use of force disparities perceived between white and black suspects. The FBI keeps statistics on OIS and other pertinent data as reported from the Uniform Crime Report (UCR). As we know, statistics take time to compile and are difficult to verify. We count on the data reported by law enforcement entities to be that of truth. However, *The Washington Post* newspaper, does not rely on the FBI statistics. In fact, the Post purports to report statistics in "real time." So, according to *The Washington Post* in 2015, 77% of suspects in an OIS were engaging in an attack at the time of the shooting. Further, *The Washington Post* stated, 82% were armed with a dangerous weapon when involved in an OIS. The race of the individual suspect was purported by the post as 52% white suspects killed and 27% black suspects killed; out of the total number killed in 2015 in OIS.

Interestingly, the Post does not list an attack in progress as a category for 2016.

If these numbers are accurate, what do we attribute the apparently high number of black suspects killed (in relation to numbers in the total U.S. population)?

But how reliable is *The Washington Post* database on OIS?

Kevin Davis, a prominent use of force trainer from Ohio, recently took a look at the Post aggregation: Officers deadly shootings of unarmed individuals.

The Post claims that 93 unarmed subjects were killed by police in the United States in 2015. Davis examined each one, using the same public information available to the Post.

His findings, published by PoliceOne.com are:

- Four individuals the Post lists as having been unarmed were, in fact, armed in the traditional sense. Most often these were reaching for or drawing a weapon when shot and killed, Davis confirmed.
- Several others were shot accidentally while in close proximity to an armed associate who was actively firing at officers. One woman, for example, was shot when her boyfriend started shooting at officers from their car and the cops returned fire.
- By Davis count, 10 subjects had some type of contact weapon other than a firearm. These included a hatchet that was thrown at officers, a large metal spoon used against an officer after a mentally ill subject tried to heave him over an apartment balcony, a tree branch, and a police radio with which two officers were savagely beaten.
- The Post describes 34 shootings as occurring during attacks in progress. Davis found 50, nearly 50% more than the post stated. These include, attempts at disarming officers and attempts to drown officers. Injuries in these cases included broken bones and head injuries, Davis reports.
- More than a dozen shootings of the unarmed were likely suicides-by-cop, Davis concluded. Often these subjects made drawing motions or pointed something at police that was mistaken to be a gun.
- In a significant number of cases, a less-lethal form of control was attempted and failed before officers resorted to deadly force.

Sample of Officers charged

- Dallas: Roy Oliver was convicted of murder Tuesday in the 2017 death of 15-year-old Jordan Edwards. Oliver, a Balch Springs police officer at the time, fired into a car packed with black teenagers who were leaving a house party in the Dallas suburb. The gunfire killed Edwards. Oliver said he thought his partner was in danger as the car drove by. But his partner told jurors he didn't fear for his life.
- East Pittsburgh, Pennsylvania: Officer Michael Rosfeld was charged in the June 19 shooting death of 17-year-old Antwon Rose Jr. after the teen fled from a traffic stop. The case will go to trial beginning on Feb. 26, 2019.
- Chicago: Jason Van Dyke is charged with first-degree murder in the 2014 fatal shooting of Laquan McDonald. The white officer shot the black teenager 16 times. The shooting made international headlines when a judge forced the city to release a dashcam video of the shooting. The video sparked massive protests, cost the Chicago police superintendent his job, and promoted federal and local investigations. He was found guilty of second-degree murder on October 5, 2018.
- North Charleston, South Carolina: After killing 50-year-old Walter Scott in 2015, Officer Michael Slager pleaded guilty to federal civil rights charges. He was sentenced to 20 years in prison in December 2017.
- Chicago: Officer Marco Proano was sentenced to five years in prison for using excessive force after shooting at a stolen car in 2013, injuring two black teenagers.
- Brooklyn: Akai Gurley was fatally shot in a New York housing project. Police officer Peter Liang, who shot Gurley in November 2014 testified that it was an accidental discharge. Liang was found guilty of second-degree manslaughter and official misconduct. The conviction was reduced Liang's to criminally negligent homicide, ruling Liang failed to perceive the risk that his actions would lead to Gurley's death.
- Cincinnati: University of Cincinnati police officer Raymond Tensing was tried twice for murder after killing Samuel DuBose, whom he pulled over for driving without a front license plate in 2015. The jury was hung both times, and the charges were dismissed. Tensing received $350,000 from the University of Cincinnati when he agreed to resign.
- Tulsa: Eric Courtney Harris was shot by Robert Bates, a volunteer reserve sheriff's deputy for the county sheriff's office in April 2015. Officers were conducting a sting operation to try to catch Harris illegally selling a gun and had pursued, then tackled him when Bates fired his pistol into Harris' back. Bates, 74, said he had meant to use his Taser, not his revolver. Bates was found guilty of second-degree manslaughter. He was sentenced in June 2016 to four years in prison.

- Milwaukee: Officer Dominique Heaggan-Brown was acquitted in June 2017 of first-degree reckless homicide after shooting 23-year-old Sylville Smith during a foot chase in August 2016.
- Falcon Heights, Minnesota: Officer Jeronimo Yanez was charged with second-degree manslaughter and other counts after shooting 32-year-old Philando Castile in 2016. He was acquitted on all charges in June 2017.
- Tulsa, Oklahoma: Officer Betty Shelby was acquitted of manslaughter after shooting a 40-year-old unarmed black man, Terence Crutcher, in September 2016. A neighboring sheriff's office then announced Shelby, who resigned from the Tulsa Police Department, would join the squad.
- Miami: Prosecutors charged Officer Jonathan Aledda with four felonies and misdemeanors, including attempted manslaughter, after he shot unarmed behavioral therapist Charles Kinsey in July 2016. Kinsey was supervising a patient with autism who was holding a silver toy truck, which a bystander mistook for a gun. Trial is pending.

Nonlethal Police Use of Force:

The Project on Policing Neighborhoods (POPN) produced a large data set (3,130 encounters) on police-citizen interactions from 1996-1997 in Indianapolis, IN and St. Petersburg, FL (Parks et al., 1997). Levels of force beyond a "firm grip," were observed in only 2.4 percent of interactions with the police (Alpert & Dunham, 2004; Mastrofski, Reisig, & McCluskey, 2002).

In 2002, Garner et al. stressed the significance in regard to how researchers measure force and the function of suspect's resistance in terms of the amount of force applied.

Our Research -

- To examine the factors driving use of force in the county
- Gender
- Race
- Intoxication/Impairment
- Type of Incident

Six (6) Departments
Years 2013-2016
482 Officers applied force in 328 Incidents
357 Subjects
Three (3) Reports for Discharge of Weapon (to euthanize deer); therefore excluded

		Subject Sex		Total
		Male	Female	
Office used a compliance hold on Subject?	No	27	9	36
	Yes	237	84	321
Total		264	93	357

		Subject Sex		Total
		Male	Female	
Office used hand/fists on Subject?	No	188	77	265
	Yes	76	16	92
Total		264	93	357

		Subject Sex		Total
		Male	Female	
Office used kicks/feet on Subject?	No	252	92	344
	Yes	12	1	13
Total		264	93	357

		Subject Sex		Total
		Male	Female	
Office used chemical/ natural agent on Subject?	No	229	86	316
	Yes	35	7	42
Total		264	93	357

Schwartz/Virga 2017 Cross Tabulations of Type of Force Used by Gender

		Subject Sex		Total
		Male	**Female**	
Office used baton/other object on Subject?	No	253	92	345
	Yes	11	1	12
Total		264	93	357

		Subject Sex		Total
		Male	**Female**	
Office used canine on Subject?	No	262	93	355
	Yes	2	0	2
Total		264	93	357

		Subject Sex		Total
		Male	**Female**	
Office used other force on Subject?	N/A	249	86	335
	Yes	15	7	22
Total		264	93	357

Schwartz/Virga 2017 Cross Tabulations of Type of Force Used by Gender

		Subject Race			Total
		White/ Caucasian	**Black/ African American**	**Hispanic**	
Office used a compliance hold on Subject?	No	16	15	5	36
	Yes	214	99	8	321
Total		230	114	13	357

		Subject Race			Total
		White/ Caucasian	**Black/ African American**	**Hispanic**	
Office used hands/fists on Subject?	No	174	81	10	265
	Yes	56	33	3	92
Total		230	114	13	357

		Subject Race			Total
		White/ Caucasian	**Black/ African American**	**Hispanic**	
Office used kicks/feet on Subject?	No	220	111	13	344
	Yes	10	3	0	13
Total		230	114	13	357

		Subject Race			Total
		White/ Caucasian	**Black/ African American**	**Hispanic**	
Office used chemical/ natural agent on Subject?	No	206	99	10	315
	Yes	24	15	3	42
Total		230	114	13	357

Schwartz/Virga 2017 Cross Tabulations of Type of Force Used by Gender

		Subject Race			Total
		White/ Caucasian	Black/ African American	Hispanic	
Office used baton/other object on Subject	No	222	111	12	345
	Yes	8	3	1	12
Total		230	114	13	357

		Subject Race			Total
		White/ Caucasian	Black/ African American	Hispanic	
Office used canine on Subject	No	229	113	13	355
	Yes	1	1	0	2
Total		230	114	13	357

		Subject Race			Total
		White/ Caucasian	Black/ African American	Hispanic	
Office used other force on Subject	No	217	107	11	335
	Yes	13	7	2	22
Total		230	114	13	357

Schwartz/Virga 2017 Cross Tabulations of Type of Force Used by Race of Subject

		Subject under the influence?		Total
		No	Yes	
Subject Injured?	No	230	188	418
	Yes	22	58	80
Total		252	246	498

		Subject under the influence?		Total
		No	Yes	
Office Injured?	No	230	236	466
	Yes	22	10	32
Total		252	246	498

Schwartz/Virga 2017 Cross Tabulations for Injuries by Subjects' Intoxication

Gloucester County New Jersey

Total population White Black Asian Hispanic Diversity Index

2000: 254,673   87%   9%   1%   2.5%   26

2010: 288,288   83%   10%   2%   4.7%   33

2060: 301,561   69.6%   10%   3%   9%   57

- A number — on a scale from 0 to 100 — that tells you the chance that any two people chosen randomly from an area will be different by race and ethnicity.

Gloucester County, NJ has a population of 291,479 people with a median age of 40.4.

Rising diversity, state by state

The USA TODAY Diversity Index shows on a scale from 0-100 the chance that two random people are different by race and ethnicity.

Diversity Index   0-25   26-40   41-55   56-93

Source USA TODAY analysis by Paul Overberg of data from Census Bureau, NHGIS at University of Minnesota and ProximityOne
Frank Pompa, USA TODAY

Between 2014 and 2015 the population of Gloucester County, NJ grew from 290,951 to 291,479, a 0.18% increase.

The population of Gloucester County, NJ is 79% White, 8.98% Black, and 5.87% Hispanic. Gloucester County, NJ is composed of 230,195 White residents (79%), 26,172 Black residents (8.98%), 17,112 Hispanic residents (5.87%), 9,334 Asian residents (3.2%), and 8,230 Two+ residents (2.82%).

Gloucester County, NJ is the 14th most populated county in New Jersey.

Took a 3-year sample (2013–2015) of use-of-force reports from of a Mid-Atlantic U.S. county, to demonstrate fundamental statistical reporting using descriptive statistics.

One of the records available to the public via an OPRA request, and commonly requested, is the *use-of-force report*, which is mandated and governed by the New Jersey State Attorney General Office.

The use-of-force report covers several details of the encounter, including but not limited to race; gender, age, time of day, type of incident, type of force, injuries or deaths, and so on. Therefore, it is important to look at the actual form to understand the strengths and weaknesses of this data-gathering tool.

Use-of-force incidents inevitably lead to injuries, sometimes even death. Through the course of the 3 years represented by this data, no deaths occurred (Officers or Subjects). When these encounters turn violent, the result can typically end with medical attention on the scene or even a trip to the hospital. In this study, of the 1,151 incidents where the police used any type of force, only 178 (15.46%) subjects were injured and 78 (6.78%) police officers.

"The key finding that can drive the greatest impact from a policy perspective was informed by the very difficulty we faced finding data to support the police account of incidents," the researchers assert.

In Summary:

The Graham decision, as previously discussed, informed the American public that people seeking relief for injury sustained during an arrest, where excessive force is alleged, is to be ruled under the "reasonableness" standard under the 4th Amendment, a departure from the previous "substantive due process" criteria (*Graham v. Conner, 490 U.S. 386 [1989]*).

The landmark Graham decision eliminates hindsight or "Monday-morning quarterbacking." The Graham decision emphasizes the need to understand the situation objectively from the perspective of a "reasonable" officer assessing the environment as it unfolds before him or her. The courts, after Graham, follow the precedent set, which maintains the situation must be viewed as whether a "reasonable" officer in the same scenario, with comparable training and experience, would have applied the same amount of force necessary to accomplish lawful objectives.

klublu/Shutterstock.com

The theme is perpetually similar. Courts, police departments, and citizens, should all be familiar with the Graham decision and the calculus of objective reasonableness. However, based on emotion; rather than point of law, often the public is judge, jury, and find guilt without due process of a police officer in use of force (particularly lethal force). There is no argument that any loss of life is tragic. We often lose sight of the human side of policing. Police are human not robots. Unless we have sociopathic persons employed as law enforcement officers, the horrible reality of taking another life is devastating. Statistics and analysis in this chapter should be used to generate discussion to bridge gaps in communities, to further policing diversity and transparency, to educate on the rule of law, to show the inherent dangers of law enforcement and the need to be mindful of such reality, to understand police should not have to place themselves in harm's way unnecessarily, to dispel myths and posit change.

> Discuss the following:
> What do we expect of the police? Do we expect law enforcement offi-
> cers to be cannon fodder? Do we expect the police to place their lives
> or well-being at risk unnecessarily? I think not. Do we abolish the police?
> Is anarchy a better answer to the inevitable use of force in policing?

As we read in *The Washington Post*'s own reporting on OIS in 2015 in the United States—82% of those killed were in possession of deadly weapons, over 77% were engaged in an active attack. The years following to date, The Washington Post reported nearly every person killed was in the possession of some type of weapon. Should police ignore those with deadly weapons? Should police ignore those attacking them or innocent persons? How can one reasonably stop a person with a deadly weapon, actively engaged in an attack, without resorting to lethal force themselves?

Therefore, what can you conclude about police use of force? Does the average police officer engage in criminal homicide on a daily basis? Are the disparities in arrests, convictions and sentencing akin to disparities in use of force by the police?

Ultimately, there is accountability. However, should a police officer who used deadly force in a justified situation be persecuted? Why are police officers, regardless of race/sex/religion or anything else, guilty until proven innocent? Action will always beat reaction. The police are always at a disadvantage in confrontations. If the public or an agency creates a culture of policy decisions based upon public or political opinion, will officers hesitate to use force when it is absolutely the correct course of action to use force?

The use of force does not need to be "right." The use of force needs to be "reasonable." According to Supreme Court of the United States (SCOTUS), an offi-cer's evil intention will not make a good use of force bad, nor will an officer's good intention make a bad use of force good.

a katz/Shutterstock.com

There is absolutely no constitutional right to resist arrest, even if the arrest is unlawful. In 99.9999% of the cases resulting in deadly force, noncompliance (aside from attacking an officer or other person/being armed) is the impetus of the encounter turning deadly. Unfortunately, individuals with mental illness present as much danger while holding a weapon/attacking someone/being noncompliant, then individuals who are not mentally ill. Although the police would like to mitigate and de-escalate a situation, it is not always possible. If time and distance can be created, enough to isolate the mentally ill person from potentially harming others, then a process needs to be in place to have professional help available. However, it is already the law; deadly force cannot be used if something else could be used.

> Discuss the following:
> Take time to find facts. Remove emotions and replace feelings with facts. Objectively review the situation with the laws and policies in mind. Do we have 700,000 psychopathic police officers in the United States? Or, do the actions of a few bad officers reflect the norms of policing?

Discussion Points

1. Do police officers have an opportunity to take time in assessing a violent confrontation and the exact response that is appropriate?
   - Is it excusable for officers to mistake a fake gun or unloaded gun in the possession of a suspect for a real or loaded gun?
   - Should officers only shoot (if justified) once or twice at a suspect?
2. When viewing video footage of a violent encounter, why can we see things that the officer did not?
   - Should officers be trained better?
   - Why do you think deadly force is used in some encounters?

Student Name _____   Date _____

Course Section _____   Chapter _____

Has your view on police use of force changed after reading the text and/or taking the course on Police Use of Force in America?

_____

_____

_____

_____

_____

_____

_____

_____

_____

_____

_____

_____

_____

_____

_____

CPSIA information can be obtained
at www.ICGtesting.com
Printed in the USA
LVHW051141180620
658146LV00001B/1